D1106179

THE TRAITS OF CHAMPIONS

The Secrets to Championship Performance in

BUSINESS,
GOLF,
AND LIFE

ANDREW WOOD
AND BRIAN TRACY

For permissions requests or for other products by Executive Excellence, contact the publisher at:

Executive Excellence Publishing
1344 East 1120 South
Provo, UT 84606
phone: 1-801-375-4060
toll-free: 1-800-304-9782
fax: 1-801-377-5960
www.eep.com

Printed in the United States

Cover design by Nichole Klein

Printed by Publishers Press

10 9 8 7 6 5 4 3 2 1

Library of Congress Cataloging-in-Publication Data
Wood, Andrew, 1962-
   The traits of champions : the secrets to championship performance in business, golf and life / by Andrew Wood & Brian Tracy.
      p. cm.
   ISBN 1-890009-86-5 (hard : alk. paper)
   1. Sucess--Psychological aspects. 2. Success in business. 3. Attitude (Psychology)
I. Tracy, Brian. II. Title.
   BF637 .S8 W666 2000
   158.1--dc21

00-008273

This book is dedicated to The Captain,
a trusted adviser, mentor, and friend.

"This book helped me to understand my own potential and to better manage my time and life to achieve positive goals."

—Linzy Clark, Jr., Legacy Golf Club

"The authors put you in the company of golf's greatest players. Associating with the 'right' people is paramount to becoming and maintaining success in all areas of life."

—Bart Patterson, G.G.P.C.

"Exceptional ideas for motivating yourself and other people."

—Thomas Eayres, Fernandina Beach Golf Club

"Right on the money! Makes being successful fall into a step-by-step process."

—Norm Haglund, Master Golf Corporation

"Inspiring, motivational and enjoyable. *The Traits of Champions* has given me insights into what I can accomplish if I put my mind to it and follow through."

—Chris Eichstaedt, Kissimmee Bay C.C.

"This book will open your eyes to things you know but never put into practice."

—John Viera, Mission Inn Resort

"This book will give you the motivation to change your direction in life and business."

—Tom Hampton, Mount Plymouth Golf Club

"I will immediately implement many of the ideas to help me attain my goals. Without hesitation I can recommend this book to anyone looking to get somewhere."

—David Tomczak, The Practice Tee

"Dynamic, life-directing, priceless—great source of leadership and motivation ideas."

—Monty King, Rockledge Country Club

"This book provides inspiration to achieve your dreams and goals. I feel rejuvenated and motivated."

—Ian Shepard, Stoney Brook C.C.

CONTENTS

Introduction 7

1	Dream Big Dreams 11
2	Fire in the Belly 23
3	Preparing a Championship Strategy 39
4	Great Shots 55
5	Perfect Practice Makes Perfect 67
6	Building a Championship Image 85
7	Champions Have Class 101
8	Championship Motivation 119
9	Conquering Fear 139
10	Confidence—the Weapon of Champions 159
11	Attitude is Everything 179
12	Creativity—Sure Sign of a Champion 195
13	Championship Problem-Solving 207
14	In the Zone 215
15	Determination—the Championship Difference 231
16	Inspiring Determination 239
17	Beating the Odds 249
18	Putting It All Together 267

INTRODUCTION

Parallels Between Golf and Life

The game of golf has a lot in common with life in general. I know that's not a unique observation. Others have recognized the fact and, in a few cases, have debated and discussed it at length. What's different about *my* point of view? First of all, you need to know that I'm a true golf addict. I love the game, the people who play it, and the places where it's played. I've been hitting the ball, finding it, and hitting it again pretty successfully for most of my life. Second, I'm also addicted to life. By that I mean I live life to its fullest and try to squeeze every ounce of potential out of each new experience. Last, and by no means least, I'm a businessman. I don't work merely to make a living, I work because I love what I do. I've managed to achieve a considerable measure of success because of something I realized quite early in life: the techniques for achieving success in golf and success in business are basically the same.

Becoming a championship golfer requires practice, hard work, and persistence. You must set goals, plan your strategy, and continually sharpen your skills. Sometimes you will find sand traps, water hazards, and other problems standing between you and your goals. On these occasions your creativity and problem-solving ability will play a major role in the outcome. If you successfully circumvent the hazards, your score won't suffer; if not, you must regroup, and you may need to adjust your game plan. Sometimes you can make up for lost ground with a birdie or an eagle. Remember, even when you have reached the green and you are just feet from the hole, you still have to make the putts! This will test not only your touch and skill, but also your courage and your nerves.

7

THE TRAITS OF CHAMPIONS

The qualities evident in great golf champions, like Jack Nicklaus, Arnold Palmer, Ben Hogan, Greg Norman, Walter Hagen, Nick Faldo, Seve Ballesteros, and Tiger Woods to name only a few, will give you insight into the characteristics from which greatness springs—not just on the golf course but in every aspect of life. You will see how the effective use of certain traits—such as dedication, creativity, courage, and many others—leads inevitably to success.

Each chapter begins with a discussion on how to follow the champions of golf to greatness. Then, at the end of each chapter, Brian Tracy, the world's foremost expert on human potential, offers a few words of "real world advice" for when you're back in the club-house discussing those big deals. These observations are designed to help corporate leaders, managers, entrepreneurs, and business owners take the knowledge they have acquired from golf's great champions and apply it to their everyday business problems.

Together, we will enjoy a very special round of golf at the Pebble Beach Golf Course on the Monterey Peninsula in California. As we travel the fairways and greens of one of the world's most beautiful and famous courses, I urge you to take notes, highlight key points that catch your attention, and answer any questions that arise during the round. You will reap higher rewards by actively involving yourself. Put yourself in our player's cleats. Feel the green grass beneath his feet. Breathe the salt air coming off the blue Pacific.

We'll have a very unusual caddie. His name is Tom. It's hard to tell from his appearance how old he is, but one thing's certain—he's spent much of his life outdoors. He's in excellent shape, although he does tend to stoop just a little, which makes him look shorter than he is. He's handsome in a well-weathered kind of way. Some people say he bears more than a passing resemblance to Sean Connery, especially around the eyes! Those eyes have seen it all. Tom can help you play the game of your life. Listen carefully to what he has to say. If you do, you'll be rewarded handsomely. In his graying head he carries not only a broad knowledge of the game, but also the secrets of the ages . . . the traits of champions.

Good morning, Sir. It's a pleasure to meet you. My name's Tom. Here, let me get your clubs . . . No problem, Sir! I'm used to carrying much bigger bags than this one . . . This is your first time at Pebble Beach? In that case you're in for a rare treat.

You were told I was a special sort of caddie? Well, in some ways I guess I am . . . Can I help you play like a champion? I've been asked that before, Sir, and I believe I've helped quite a few over the years, especially the ones who really wanted it . . . You'll do whatever it takes? If you're really serious, Sir, I can help you do better than you ever thought possible—not just in today's round, mind you, but in the future as well. I'll show you little things it took others decades to learn, and believe me, that knowledge will save you more than just strokes on your golf game.

But before we even go out on the course today, let's take a minute or two to think about what you want to shoot and how you're going to do it.

The first thing you must do before you can start playing like a champion is think like a champion. As Arnold Palmer's father, Deacon, once remarked, "Ninety percent of golf is played above the shoulders." Or as the great Bobby Jones said, "Golf is a game played mainly in the 6-inch space between the ears." That's as true in life as it is in golf. The way you think directly affects your physical actions and, therefore, determines the outcome of everything you do.

DREAM BIG DREAMS

Thinking Like a Champion

I recently overheard a group of four young pros talking about what it takes to be a champion. As it happens, the discussion was not limited to golf. They were talking in more general terms. Who are the people destined to make it to the top in golf, in business, or in life?

What is it, these young players wondered, that makes it possible for an otherwise average person to raise his performance to championship levels? What determines who will be the ones to shoot in the 60s, lead the sales figures, head up major corporations, and generally live life on their own terms?

It seemed obvious to one of them, in spite of his lack of worldly experience, that the qualities that make a champion in one area are likely to parallel those in any other field. He was in good company on this point. Shortly after Ben Hogan won the British Open in 1953 to complete a hat trick of major championships for the year, a reporter asked him to name the greatest player that ever lived. Hogan wisely replied, "I have always felt that a man who can be champion in one era could be a champion in any other era, because he has what it takes to reach the top."

As the conversation progressed, the second of the young men gave his opinion. He suggested that the only thing that separated the winners from the losers was luck. "Some people have it—other's don't," he sighed. He apparently felt he didn't have his fair share of this mythical attribute!

The third maintained he would have done much better if his father had been rich and able to support him like some of the other guys' dads. He had been forced to work at a range and sometimes as a part-time bartender in order to make ends meet while he was trying to qualify as a competitor. What chance did he have against the rich kids who could play golf all day and every day? They never had to worry about the rent, or putting food on the table.

The fourth young player declared that racial prejudice had kept him from getting a golf scholarship at a major university, and this had impeded his progress. He believed his career would have been much further along the road to success had he been able to experience the competitive challenge of college golf.

Champions Decide They Are Going to be Champions

I realized a long time ago that the people who "make it" in life are the ones who *decide* to make it. The people who become champions are those who dream big dreams, set tough goals for themselves, put some plans on the table, and "go for broke." It doesn't matter if they are rich or poor, black or white, young or old. The people who reach the pinnacle of success in this world—the men and women who become champions in whatever field they choose—are the people who accept that they and they alone are in charge of their own destiny.

I smiled as I imagined myself telling Chi Chi Rodriguez, Walt Zembriski, and Calvin Peete they wouldn't have qualified as champions if rich parents, luck, or ethnic descent hadn't given them a helping hand.

Chi Chi, Walt, and Calvin are three of my favorite golfers, and also three of my favorite people. Now, I know they aren't as glamorous as Greg or Arnie, but their stories are worth hearing because they help put a lot of things into perspective. They serve to demonstrate that many champions are regular, everyday people who produce superior performance. Their pedigree is character, and that gives hope to the average man.

I don't believe champions are born. Champions are made, or to be more accurate, they make themselves. By following the same key principles that have guided others on their way, you can become a champion in golf or, for that matter, in any other worth-while endeavor.

It's What You Make of Yourself That Counts

Juan Rodriguez, or Chi Chi, as millions now know him, tells everyone he was born lucky—he was born into poverty. Those are his words not mine. "A lot of people think poor people are disadvantaged. Not me," says Chi Chi. "I think poor people are lucky. Poor people have to work hard. They do manual labor, they exercise when they work, so they become stronger. A poor person never has anything to prove; a rich guy has to prove himself all the time. He has to prove he can make even more money. The goal of a poor person is to make something out of himself."

Chi Chi certainly wasn't born into the country club set. The son of a field worker, he was one of five children. His father worked for 30 years in the fields of Puerto Rico, never making more than $20 a week—not much to support a family of seven. Rodriguez is quick to point out, however, that the family was happy and never hungry, although dinner was almost always the same: rice, beans, corn, and bananas. Because of his poor diet, Chi Chi was afflicted with rickets when he was six years old and was not expected to live. But he survived, although the disease caused his hands to be bent. He quips, "Thanks to God, they form a perfect golf grip!"

By the time Chi Chi was eight years of age, he was working in the sugar cane fields, making a dollar a day. Later he went to the local golf course and began to work as a caddie. The pay was even less, but the work was much more to his liking, and he was soon hooked on golf. By the time he was 12, Chi Chi was already an excellent player, breaking par one day by holing out five wedge shots in a single round.

After dropping out of school in the 11th grade, Chi Chi eventually decided to escape poverty by joining the army. He found his way into Special Services, where he had the opportunity to spend some of his time working on his game. He even won an army championship. He was also a featherweight boxing champ. Chi Chi chuckles, "I didn't hit them very hard, but I hit them often." The fighter in him never died, and when he later became a golf professional, his fighting spirit would serve him well.

After his discharge from the army, Chi Chi begged Ed Dudley, the head pro at the Dorado Beach Hotel, for a job. He was employed as a caddie-master. In this exalted capacity, he picked up range balls, shined shoes, and stored clubs seven days a week for $75. After work and in the early morning, Chi Chi would work on his game, especially his wedge play.

In 1959, Peter Cooper took over as head pro of the famed resort and quickly became a mentor for the young Chi Chi. Under his tutelage, Chi Chi hit thousands of balls and honed his skills to razor sharpness. The following year, with a little backing from none other than Lawrence Rockefeller, who owned the resort, Chi Chi arrived on the PGA Tour. For over two years he toured the country in an old Pontiac, often sleeping in his car to save money. With only one top-10 finish and an average income of just $2,000 a year, this period in his career couldn't be judged a success, even by Chi Chi's ever-optimistic standards. Although he wasn't a tournament winner, however, Chi Chi's wonderful personality and amusing antics on the course did bring him some attention from the fans.

Chi Chi finally won his first tournament in 1963, the Denver Open. He promptly used his prize money to buy a new home for his mother in Puerto Rico. Generosity was to become the trademark of this great champion. He has regularly donated substantial amounts from his winner's checks to orphanages, hospitals, and other worthy charities.

Although Chi Chi never set the PGA Tour on fire, he was a regular contender and a gallery favorite for more than 20 years, winning over $1 million. As the years went by, of course, it became tougher and tougher for him to stay in contention. At only 5 feet 7 inches and 120 pounds, and playing on the heavily watered fairways of the tour, he was having to give away too much in terms of distance to the younger guys, who just seemed to get bigger and stronger every year. Fortunately for him, the Senior PGA Tour developed and exploded in coverage, interest, and prize money at precisely the right time, giving him a wonderful opportunity and a new set of goals.

Chi Chi joined the senior tour in 1985 and only had to wait a few months for his first victory in the 1986 Players Championship. It would be the first of many, and along with Lee Trevino, he has became one of the best liked and dominant players on the Senior Tour. He is adept at charming the crowd after making long putts with his trademark sword dance. At other times, he entertains his galleries when he makes a birdie by throwing his hat over the hole, then peeking underneath to make sure the ball is still there. The hat routine goes back to an occasion when, as a youngster, he and some friends were in the habit of sneaking onto the course to play for a nickel a hole. During one such match, he holed a long putt and walked forward to retrieve his ball. As he did so, the ball popped back out of the hole, closely followed by a large frog! Chi Chi's effervescent behavior and broad smile brought to the Senior Tour what the regular Tour sometimes lacked—personality.

In 1987 he won seven times and was the leading money winner, earning over $500,000 in one season. To date, Chi Chi has won over $1 million in PGA Tour events and almost $6 million and 22 tournaments on the senior circuit. Not bad for someone who used to cut sugar cane for a living! These days, however, making money is not the only thing that arouses his enthusiasm.

His pride and joy is the Chi Chi Rodriguez Foundation, founded in 1979 to help troubled youths. The foundation aids about 650 children a year and, among other things, features its own school and golf course. It is Chi Chi's goal to help as many children as possible regain their self-esteem and build better lives for themselves. He hopes that some of these young people may someday become great champions. If they pursue their dreams, it will happen. After all, look what happened to Chi Chi!

Hope for the Common Man

Being young, poor, and Puerto Rican wasn't enough to prevent Chi Chi from becoming a champion. Neither would being middle-aged and poor stand in the way of a retired steelworker with dreams bigger than the skyscrapers he helped build.

Walt Zembriski always dreamed of being a golf pro. In his early years growing up in New Jersey, he learned the game the old-fashioned way—as a caddie. He didn't enjoy a particularly distinguished amateur career, but after serving for 14 years in the armed forces, he did win the 1966 New Jersey Amateur Championship.

This victory encouraged him to try the PGA Tour Qualifying School, known to its long-suffering alumni simply as Q-school. Considering his history, it is a tribute to his determination and tenacity that he survived the ordeal, receiving his tour card on the first attempt. After qualifying, he spent two frustrating and fruitless years on tour without making a dime. His sponsor abandoned him, and his wife told him it was time to find regular employment. The best job he could find was as a steelworker, earning $13 an hour, where the early starting schedule afforded him plenty of free time in the afternoon. While his buddies went for a few beers, Zembriski headed for the driving range to hit golf balls.

For the next eight years he worked hundreds of feet above the ground, moving steel beams into position and changing New York's skyline. During this period, several of his friends and co-workers fell to their deaths. Although he escaped this fate, he suffered a crushed thumb that required major surgery to save it. Fortunately for him, it did not affect his golf game permanently. His career as a steelworker ended when he was knocked from a steel beam by a load of lumber being moved by a crane. Zembriski grabbed the wood and held on for his life.

That may have been the very moment he decided it was time to return to the profession he loved. In any event, he packed up his clubs and headed for Florida. For a few years, he eked out a bare living on the mini tours, playing against such future stars as Paul Azinger, Mark Calcavecchia, and Bob Tway. Averaging $800 a week in prize money, he wasn't close to breaking even. In order to cover his travel expenses and tournament entry fees, he had to take part-time jobs cleaning swimming pools and working on golf course maintenance crews. It was a tough life, but he kept on grinding week after week, knowing that his only alternative was to go back into construction work. And he'd already had enough of that to last a lifetime!

By the time Zembriski turned 50 in 1985, the Senior Tour was in full swing and he was ready to take a shot at it. Finishing third in Senior Tour Q-School, Walt Zembriski, a card-carrying union member and retired steel worker, was ready for his second chance at the big time.

His first year was solid, although he didn't record a victory. Nevertheless, the $103,000 he won to finish 19th on the money list was the most money he had ever earned in his life. The following year he doubled his earnings, still failing to break into the winner's circle. His breakthrough finally came in 1988, when he won the Newport Cup and, a few months later, followed with a victory in the Vantage Classic. That year Zembriski earned $348,000.

In the years that followed, some of Zembriski's other cherished dreams become reality, as he played side by side with his lifelong idols: Nicklaus, Trevino, and Player. Stars he had been limited to watching on television, sat next to him to put on their golf shoes and walked the fairways with him as playing partners. To date, his senior tour earnings are just a little less than $2 million—a major difference in lifestyle for someone who lived on the basis of financial survival for much of his life. As he approaches his 60th birthday, he talks about playing in the Super Senior division. "After all," he points out, "what else would I do?"

A Diamond in the Rough

As we have seen, champions aren't invariably the product of elite country clubs, as was Nicklaus. They don't always appear from behind the caddie shack, as Zembriski did. They aren't all schooled in the pressure of gambling at a fast-paced municipal course, like Trevino, and they don't all start at the age of three, like Sandy Lyle, or even two, like the latest phenomenon Tiger Woods. Sometimes champions have their origins in places you would least expect, but the traits and qualities that enable them to convert their talents from raw coal to fine diamonds remain the same.

Calvin Peete was born in Pahokee, Florida, one of the poorest, least attractive, beat up little towns on the planet. Surrounded by swampland, Pahokee is the reason that the state bird of Florida is the mosquito. There were no less than, count them, 19 children in the Peete household. With very few options, Calvin dropped out of school in the 8th grade to pick fruit and bring in a little more money to help the family survive. At 18 he bought an old station wagon and went into business for himself. He drove up and down the rural areas of the East Coast, selling clothes and a variety of other goods to migrant farm workers. In an effort to express his individuality, Peete had diamonds inserted into his front teeth. The people with whom he traded knew him simply as "the diamond man."

At the age of 23, never having played or caddied in his life and with no desire to learn, a couple of friends coerced Peete into playing a round of golf with them. He was instantly hooked on the game, and although he seemed initially to have no real aptitude, he decided he was going to become a golf pro. For the next five years he practiced every spare minute he could find, continuing to hit practice shots each night after dark on floodlit baseball fields.

It took Peete less than two years to become a scratch golfer, and he turned pro three years later. Not content with teaching others or looking for a club job, he decided he wanted to play on the PGA Tour. It took him three attempts to make it, but eventually, at 32 years of age, he graduated from Q-school and received his player's card. For three more difficult and discouraging years, Peete didn't win enough money to meet his travel expenses. His wife, a teacher, supported both of them and their family of four children. Finally in 1979, he entered the ranks of tournament champions by winning the Milwaukee Open. He followed with three straight years of earnings in excess of $100,000. Although he was never renowned for his power, he led the PGA Tour in driving accuracy, and in 1984, won the Vardon Trophy, awarded to the player with the lowest stroke average for the season. Before long he had joined the elite group of players with over $2 million in career earnings and at least 10 tour victories—12 to be exact.

This notable level of success was achieved by a man born into abject poverty, who broke his left elbow in a fall as a boy and was partially crippled as a result of poor corrective surgery, which caused his left elbow to be permanently locked in one position.

Can you imagine the remarks he had to listen to?

"You want to be a what, son? A golf pro? I see."

"Say, have you been smoking some of that funny stuff?"

"You say you've learned the secret? Well don't keep us all in suspense. Let us in on it!"

"Is that a fact? All you have to do is start with a big dream, then add mental discipline and countless hours of practice until you can do it every time, automatically. Just keep it simple, you say."

"OK; if you say so, Calvin."

Follow your dreams; they may come true!

First There Must be Dreams

"To win you must have talent and desire—but desire is first."
Sam Snead

The journey for many, if not all, champions starts at night as they drift into sleep. While others summon up visions of mansions and sports cars, *they* dream of green jackets and claret goblets (the trophy awarded to the winner of the British Open). They fantasize about playing in a foursome with Palmer, Nicklaus, and Woods. In their dreams they outdrive their heroes, strike confident iron shots that spin to a stop a few feet from the pin, and roll fearless putts on the perfect, slick greens that disappear into the center of the cup. They break course records at Pebble Beach, Baltusrol, and Augusta, and as the necessity arises, they hit amazing recovery shots that are described with awe in the sports pages of every newspaper in the country.

Indeed, *the first trait of champions is to dream big dreams*, for it is only big dreams that can produce the level of motivation, dedication, and desire needed to become a champion.

Swing Thoughts

- Champions are made, not born.

- Victory is oblivious to creed, color, bank account, age, injury, or hardship. It judges its champions strictly on the basis of performance.

- People who become champions are people who believe they can become champions.

- Champions have big dreams, for big dreams are the only kind that produce the motivation, determination, and persistence to succeed.

- Champions have the courage to follow their dreams, regardless of how others rate their chances of success.

Back in the Clubhouse

If a skinny caddie, a retired steelworker, and a migrant farm worker can all become golfing millionaires, what on earth are *you* worrying about? Shortage of money and apparent lack of opportunity, common to Chi Chi, Walt, and Calvin in their early lives, could have been overwhelming barriers if they had allowed them to be so. Yet all three, and many others like them in every walk of life, have hung in there and done what it takes to taste the sweetest fruit life has to offer, the fruit of victory. The key to their success—the common thread that connects them—was dreaming big dreams.

In your career and professional life, the starting point of great success and achievement has and always will be the same—dream big dreams. Nothing is more important, and nothing works faster in casting off your own limitations, than dreaming and fantasizing about the wonderful things that you can become, have, and do.

As a wise man once said, "You must dream big dreams, for only big dreams have the power to move the minds of men." When you begin to dream big dreams, your levels of self-esteem and self-confidence will go up immediately. You will feel more confident about yourself and about your ability to deal with what happens to you. The reason why so many people accomplish so little is because they never allow themselves to imagine the kind of life that is possible for them.

A friend of mine is one of the most highly paid commission professionals in the United States. One of his big dreams was to double his income in three to five years. He applied the Pareto Principle, or 80/20 rule, to his client base. He found that 20 percent of his clients contributed 80 percent of his profits, and that the amount of time spent on a high-profit client was pretty much the same amount of time spent on a low-profit client.

So he called other professionals in his industry and very carefully, politely, and strategically handed them the 80 percent of his clients who represented only 20 percent of his business. He then put together a profile of his top clients and began looking in the marketplace exclusively for the type of client who fit the profile—in other words, one who could become a major profit contributor to his organization and whom he could serve in the excellent manner to which his clients were accustomed. And instead of doubling in three to five years, his income doubled in the first year!

What is holding you back? Is it your level of education or skill? Is it your current career or job? Is it your current location or environment or level of health? What is standing in the way of your achieving your dream?

What are your limits?

Three keys to living without limits are clarity, competence, and concentration. *Clarity* means that you are absolutely clear about who you are, what you want, and where you're going. You write down your goal, and you make plans to accomplish it. You very carefully set priorities, and you do something every day to move toward your goals. And the more progress you make toward accomplishing what is important to you, the greater self-confidence and self-belief you have, and the more convinced you become that there are no limits on what you can achieve.

Competence means that you are very good in the key result areas of your chosen field. You apply the 80/20 rule to everything you do, and you focus on becoming outstanding in the 20 percent of tasks that contribute to 80 percent of your results. You dedicate yourself to continuous learning. You never stop growing. And you commit yourself to doing something every day that enables you to become better in your field. You realize that excellence is a moving target.

Concentration is the self-discipline to force yourself to focus single-mindedly on one thing, the most important thing, and stay with it until it's complete. Concentration is perseverance, without diversion or distraction, in a straight line, to accomplish the things that can make a real difference in your life.

When you allow yourself to dream big dreams, and when you creatively abandon the activities that take up too much of your time and focus your energies on alleviating your main constraints, you start to feel an incredible sense of power and confidence. As you focus on doing what you love to do and becoming excellent in those few areas that can make a real difference in your life, you begin to think in terms of possibilities rather than impossibilities, and you move ever closer toward the realization of your full potential.

Questions to Ponder

- How big are your dreams?

- Where could your business and career go with no restraints?

- What would you do differently in your life if you knew there was absolutely no possibility of failure?

We have just time for you to warm up before your round . . . Quite right, Sir. No hurry at all. We have nothing to worry about except having a fine day's golf . . . You say you'd like to know a little more about those dreams champions have? Certainly, Sir!

FIRE IN THE BELLY

"Jack Nicklaus was totally attentive, he asked intelligent questions, he had an infinite capacity for hard work, and his desire knew no bounds. He was certain to be a star"
Jack Grout, golf instructor

Dreams

Dreams are the start of the journey. They're like the flag at the end of a long, uphill par five that guides us to our objective. Dreams allow champions to see themselves accepting the recognition of the crowd and the other players as they hold up the U.S. Open trophy. Dreams convey what it might feel like to be on the inside of a green jacket. But in the morning, when the last few seconds of sleep glide away and the dreams are gently fading from memory, we must turn our attention to more concrete things— things like a sense of determination and a consuming passion to make those dreams come back and come true. You need fire in the belly—a burning desire to succeed that is so strong you can see, taste, touch, feel, and smell the sweetness of victory.

Burning Desire

The great Scottish pro, Tommy Armour, was a machinegunner in the British army during World War I, prior to emigrating to the United States. The war ended for him when he was wounded in combat and lost the sight of one eye, but before that happened, he was involved in an encounter where he single-handedly captured an enemy tank. When the commander of the tank refused to surrender, a fearful fight ensued, and Armour emerged as the winner only after strangling his adversary with his bare hands.

Take a moment and try to imagine yourself in that situation. You are in a desperate struggle for your life in a very small, confined space with no possibility of escape. Your enemy's hands are closing around your throat, even as you clutch at his. You feel his fingers gripping your neck with vise-like power, and your air supply has been all but shut off. There is no one in the world to help you; you are alone. Somehow you must get beyond your lack of oxygen, beyond the stifling heat, beyond the terror. You are fighting for your very life. If you can visualize this situation, you will understand the sort of grim determination and fire in the belly that made Armour a champion.

It's the same kind of burning desire that enabled Hogan to come back from a near-fatal car crash and win tournament after tournament as he hobbled around the fairways on badly damaged legs. It's the level of desire that enabled Nicklaus to dominate the game for three decades. It's the same burning intensity that drove Gary Player to pump weights, run marathons, and hit balls until his hands bled. All great champions have that kind of desire. Without it there is only mediocrity.

How Badly Do You Want It?

How badly do you want a better golf game, or the financial freedom to control your own life? You can achieve almost anything if you want it enough. It's not so much a matter of whether or not you can do it, it's much more a question of whether you are willing to pay the price. I have met golfers who could play to scratch at the age of 13, and on the other end of the spectrum, I have played with scratch golfers who never even touched a golf club until they retired at 65. Anyone with average coordination and in reasonable physical shape is capable of playing scratch golf, just as anyone who is really determined can become a millionaire, too.

The question is, what are you willing to give up to achieve success at a championship level? Make no mistake about it, champions in all walks of life pay a price. It could be years of your life spent on the practice ground. It could be years of low income from part-time jobs, to give you the time to acquire the knowledge and skills that will allow you to live your dreams. It might mean leaving your family and friends and moving to an area, perhaps halfway around the world, where your talents are in demand. It might entail a limited social life, a special diet, or constant study. Whatever the price, at some point you must decide if you are willing to pay the freight. Most are not!

I Could Have Been a Contender

Naturally, there are other, safer options that can be followed; dreams and goals can be tailored to fit your determination quotient. A player can tell himself it's not worth all that extra effort; after all, you need to live a little. Any good professional golfer can make a decent living on the all-exempt tour without winning championships. The money from product endorsements, pro-ams, affiliation with an expensive resort, etc., will allow him to lead a comfortable life. Indeed, the majority of people in every field are conditioned from an early age to look for the easy ticket, the safe route, which is part of the reason there are so few champions.

The sad fact remains that for every hundred players who take that route, four or five will regret their decision for the rest of their lives, reduced to murmuring to themselves, or anybody else who will listen, Marlon Brando's famous line from *On the Waterfront*: "I could have been a contender." If only they had possessed the desire to make it happen.

> *"99 percent of all the putts I leave short don't go in."*
> *Hubert Green*

Creating a Vision

Once the dream's in place, the next step in the champion's journey is to **develop the dream into a vision**. This vision is a more focused concept of how the dream will become reality. All great champions have a clear vision of just how far their talents can take them.

At a very early age, Jack Nicklaus made a basic and monumental decision that was to shape his entire career and influence the golfing world for the second half of the 20th century. If he had avoided that decision or failed to plan his entire life to accommodate it, Jack Nicklaus might well have become just another good player. Nicklaus made the decision because he is a true champion. He decided to focus himself entirely, in thought and action, on winning major tournaments. He decided he was going to be the best player in the world. He planned his tournament schedule, travel arrangements, and life around the Masters, the British Open, the U.S. Open, and the PGA Championship. While other top players may have made a conscious, extra effort at these four events, Nicklaus made them his life. All other tournaments became, in effect, a build-up or tune-up, diminished in importance because of his primary agenda of winning major championships and being universally regarded as the world's greatest golfer.

For four decades, beginning with the 1959 U.S. Amateur Championship, Nicklaus was the man to beat in the majors. Time and time again during this long period of supremacy, the fans wrote him off, thinking that even he must finally be through with top-class competition. Time and time again, he came back in the majors. After a few winless years in the late '70s when the four big ones eluded him, he won both the U.S. Open and PGA Championships in 1980. Then in 1986, with some members of the media referring to him as "Olden Bear" instead of "Golden Bear," Jack came through with his historic sixth victory in the Masters.

Not only did Nicklaus win more major tournaments than any other player in history, but his overall record in these events is phenomenal. Before the Nicklaus era, the record of 13 majors amassed by Bobby Jones was thought by most informed observers to be beyond the reach of mere mortals. They were wrong. Between 1959, when he won the U.S. Amateur, and 1986, when he took his incredible sixth green jacket at Augusta, Jack Nicklaus won an unbelievable 20 major championships, finishing second and third 40 times or more. By focusing his goals and efforts on the majors, Nicklaus was able to live his lofty dreams.

Like Nicklaus, and sharing his single-minded focus, Tiger Woods also managed to achieve great things at a very early age. When Tiger's father, Earl, initially introduced his talented son to golf, he set goals of 8 or 7 as par on each hole. As Tiger grew and improved, Earl would lower the goal, giving him a new target to shoot at. Although Tiger was not too happy about this, because he wanted to shoot under par, the constant re-evaluation of goals played a very important part in preparing him for the future.

As a teenager, Woods was well on his way to becoming the best player in the world. He achieved an important intermediate goal, winning the USGA junior title not once, but three times in a row in

'91, '92, and '93. He followed this with a record three victories in the U.S. Amateur Championship in '94, '95, and '96. Having met or surpassed all his amateur goals, he took the next step and joined the professional ranks.

If he had waited until the following year, he would have received a full year's worth of sponsors' exemptions. He could have used this time to win enough money to be one of the top 125 players on the money list, thereby avoiding the arduous Tour qualifying process. Instead, he gave himself just three months to achieve his declared goal of making the top 125 and earning his Tour card. With typical self-confidence, Woods added that he also wanted to win a tournament. In his third tournament, the Quad Cities Open, he placed 5th. The following week he finished 3rd at the rain-shortened B.C. Open. Then, playing in just his fifth tournament as a professional, he shot 64 in the final round to win the Las Vegas Open. Mission accomplished! Then, to make sure we were paying attention, he won the Disney Classic in Orlando, and Tigermania was in full swing!

At 24 he already had seven majors to his name, and in his first Masters, U.S. Open, and British Open victories dominated play as no player before. He has already achieved his goal of becoming the best golfer in the world. He is the youngest player in history to complete the career Grand Slam of winning all four majors. Now he has his sights set on becoming the best player ever! He will accept nothing less. He knows that he will be judged against just one man—Jack Nicklaus. To be regarded as the best he must win more than 20 majors. All his thoughts and actions are concentrated on this mission.

Goals are the Fuel of Desire

With the overall vision in place, the next step a champion must take is to **break that vision down into manageable goals** that will create and maintain maximum desire. The first step in creating burning desire is to decide exactly what you want. Do you want to be a scratch player, the club champion, a touring pro, or just reduce your handicap from 18 to 9? Your target must be absolutely specific. It must also have a time frame and a series of benchmarks along the way, so you can measure progress.

Sounds simple enough, doesn't it? Well, do it, because 95 percent of the people reading these words will not, thereby virtually eliminating themselves from championship contention before they have even reached the first tee. Champions need goals to create desire, and goals are nothing more than dreams with a deadline.

It is one of the those remarkable twists of fate that two of the greatest golfers of all time grew up in the same place at the same time. Both Ben Hogan and Byron Nelson learned to play golf while caddying at the Glen Garden Country Club. Their dreams, however, could hardly have been more different. While Hogan played largely for the glory of winning, Nelson had a much more practical reason for playing golf. His sole declared purpose was to earn enough prize money to buy a cattle ranch. Nelson had dreamed for a long time of being a rancher, but his wife, Louise, was less enthusiastic. She was concerned with the practical fact that neither of them knew a thing about ranching! Since they both had grown up in the depression years of the 1930s, and watched as many of their neighbors had lost their jobs and businesses, Louise was especially afraid of getting involved in any venture that involved carrying debt. So it was decided that Byron could have his ranch with Louise's full support, just as long as he paid cash for it.

In 1944, Nelson had won enough money to convince himself that, with a final concentrated effort, his dream could come true. If his plan proved to be successful, he wanted to make sure he left his mark on the game, since he knew his PGA Tour career would be over once he became a rancher. To do this, he set secondary goals to establish scoring and winning records for the year, en route to making the money he needed to reach his goal.

It was quite possibly these lofty goals that led to one of the greatest golfing feats of all time. In 1945, armed with his dream and a swing as smooth and consistent as anyone had ever seen, the man known as "Lord Byron" totally destroyed his competition. Winning a total of 18 tournaments and placing second in seven more, he enjoyed a phenomenal stretch during which he recorded 11 victories in a row. Starting with the Miami Four Ball in March of 1945 and ending in June with the Canadian PGA Championship, Nelson won all 11 tournaments he played in before finishing a dismal 6th at the Memphis Open. With a scoring average of 68.3 and more than 100 sub-par rounds, it was a truly remarkable year. Nelson had rewritten the record book: most wins in a single year, most consecutive wins, lowest winning score, and lowest scoring average. Several of these records still stand and will probably never be surpassed. The main reason he was able to achieve this feat was because of the goals he had set before the season began.

"Each drive, each shot, each chip, and each putt was aimed at getting that ranch. Each win meant another cow, another acre, another part of the down payment."
Byron Nelson

After the 1945 season, Nelson had saved enough money to live his dream, and he played just one more year of serious golf before fading into semi-retirement. From that point on, he limited his competitive participation to the Masters, a couple of local events, and some exhibition matches to maintain his cash flow while he got his ranch up and running. Even in semi-retirement the ranch remained his motivating goal. When his book, *Winning Golf*, was published, it quickly sold well over 150,000 copies. Nelson characteristically remarked to his wife that the 25 cents per book he received from the publisher would buy 500 head of cattle.

While Nelson played golf as a means to an end, Ben Hogan, like Bobby Jones before him and Nicklaus after him, was motivated by the thrill of victory. To players like these, the glory of winning major championships and the right to lay claim to being the best of their era was all they needed to fuel their fires.

"The one strongest, most important idea in my game is that I want to be the best. I wouldn't accept anything less than that. My ability to concentrate and work toward that goal has been my greatest asset."
Jack Nicklaus

Smart and Simple Goal Setting

Let's look at how Jack Nicklaus took his vision of being the best golfer in the world and broke it down into manageable steps by setting SMART goals. SMART goals, unlike dreams, follow a very specific set of rules. SMART goals must be

Specific,
Motivational,
Attainable,
Relevant, and
Trackable

Specific

Nicklaus' primary goal was to be the greatest player of all time. That in itself is not a SMART goal since it is not specific. He made it specific by deciding that he would keep score by counting the major tournaments he won during his career. He broke this goal down into long-range, intermediate, and short-range goals.

His long-term goal was to win more than 13 majors, the amount amassed by his hero Bobby Jones, who was the leader in major victories at the time. His intermediate goal, which he renewed annually, focused on winning the four majors: the Masters, U.S. Open, British Open, and PGA Championships. His short-term goal was, naturally, to win whichever tournament he was playing in. This served to boost his confidence and experience, and in the case of the majors, added to his victory total on the way to his long-term goal.

Motivational

The goals you set must have the emotional power to excite you enough so you will invest the time and effort necessary to realize those goals. That is why champions set big goals, for only big goals have the power to make them work harder and pay the price in time and sweat to bring them to fruition. One has only to check Nicklaus' record in the majors to see that the goals he set himself certainly proved to be adequately motivational.

Attainable

Although his goal was lofty, given his talent, dedication, and willingness to work, it remained attainable for the young Nicklaus. Goals can be lofty, but they must stay within the realms of possibility. If you are 56 years old and carry a 17 handicap, winning the Masters is unlikely to be within your ability! Don't be disheartened for a single moment. There are many other goals you *can* reach, so lofty goals are still perfectly acceptable.

Relevant

Nicklaus' goal of winning major golf championships was precisely relevant to his overall goal of being accepted as the best player in the world. The majors are the standard by which the golf world as a whole measures greatness. Make sure *your* short-term and intermediate goals are relevant to your overall goals.

Trackable

The Golden Bear's goal was easily trackable, not only by him but also by every golfer in the world, based on his performance in the four major tournaments each year. There were few years in which he did not capture at least one major title, moving ever closer to the record held by Bobby Jones.

If goals are not trackable, they are not very effective as a motivational tool, since you have no way of knowing if you are moving closer to your long-term goal.

Goal Setting is Essential for Championship Performance

The power of goalsetting should never be taken lightly in the making of champions. Setting goals allows you to focus all your conscious and subconscious energy on a distant flag and keeps you motivated along the way.

By fulfilling all the requirements of SMART goal setting, Nicklaus was able to plan his career and motivate himself as no other player has ever done, before or since. He focused all of his talent, energy, and time on making those goals a reality. In the late '70s, his business empire grew so large that Chi Chi Rodriguez quipped, "Jack Nicklaus is the only player I know who became a legend in his spare time!" In spite of this, he did not allow himself to be distracted by his business ventures when he felt they might conflict with his objective of winning major championships. He was able to stay fully focused on his goals when it counted.

Sir, if it's OK with you, let's go right ahead and write down a goal for our round today. What do you think? . . .72? Now that's a lofty goal, Sir, this being your first time at Pebble Beach and all, but I believe you have it in you. With me on the bag, I think you can do it. Let's set a goal for what you are going to shoot on each nine. Then we'll work out our game plan for making it all happen. You know, Sir, I think today is going to be a special round. I can feel it in my bones, and old Tom's bones are never wrong!

Swing Thoughts

- Champions have the fire of desire in their hearts.

- Champions are prepared to pay the price.

- Champions set goals because they are the fuel of desire.

- The goals champions set are SMART goals:

  Specific,
  Motivational,
  Attainable,
  Relevant,
  Trackable.

- By setting SMART goals, champions are more motivated, more organized, and more focused than the competition.

Back in the Clubhouse

Back at work, the ability to set goals and make plans for their accomplishment is the master skill of success. It is the single most important skill you can learn and perfect. Becoming an expert at goal setting is something that you absolutely must do if you wish to fulfill your potential as a human being. Goals enable you to do the work you want to do, to live where you want to live, to be with the people you enjoy, and to become the kind of person you want to become. And there is no limit to the financial rewards you can obtain. All you have to do is to set a goal for financial success, make a plan, and then work the plan until you succeed in that area.

The payoff for setting goals and making plans is being able to choose the kind of life you want to live. So why do so few people set goals? According to the best research, less than 3 percent of

Americans have written goals, and less than 1 percent review and rewrite their goals on a daily basis. So the reasons why people don't set goals have been of considerable interest to me. I think there are five basic reasons why people don't set goals.

The first reason is that they are simply not serious. Whenever I speak with a man or woman who has achieved something remarkable, I learn that the achievement occurred after that person decided to "get serious." Until you become completely serious and totally determined about your goals, nothing really happens.

The second reason why people don't set goals is that they don't understand the importance of goals. We find that young men and women who begin setting goals very early in life invariably come from families in which the importance of goals is emphasized. The discussion that takes place around your family dinner table is one of the most powerful formative influences in your life. If your parents didn't have goals, didn't talk about goals, didn't encourage you to set goals, and didn't talk about people outside the family circle who had goals and who were moving toward a higher level of achievement, then you very likely grew up with the idea that goals are not even a part of normal existence. This is the case for most people. And for many years, it was the case for me.

The third reason why people don't set goals is because they don't know how to do it. One of the greatest tragedies of our educational system is that you can receive 12 to 16 years of education in our schools and never once receive a single hour of instruction on how to set goals. Yet we find that in certain schools where goal-setting programs have been introduced since first grade, young people become excited about goal setting—even if the goal is only to increase grades by 5 or 10 percent over the course of the semester or to be on time every day for a month. Children become so excited about achieving goals that by the third or fourth grade, they love to go to school. They get the best grades. They are seldom absent. They are excited about themselves and about their lives. So encourage your children to set worthwhile and realistic goals from an early age.

The fourth reason why people don't set goals is fear of rejection. The fear of rejection is caused by destructive criticism in early childhood, and it is manifested in adulthood in the fear of criticism from others. Many people hold back from setting worthwhile goals because they have found that every time they do set a goal, somebody steps up and tells them they can't achieve it, or that they will lose their money or waste their time.

Because each of us is strongly influenced by the opinions of those around us, one of the first things you must learn when you begin setting goals is to keep them confidential. Don't tell anyone about them. Often, it's the fear of criticism that, more than any other factor, stops you from goal setting in the first place. So keep your goals to yourself, with one exception. Share your goals only with others who are committed to achieving goals of their own and who really want you to be successful and achieve your goals as well. Other than that, don't tell anybody about your goals, so no one is in a position to criticize you or to discourage you from setting them.

The fifth reason why people don't set goals—and perhaps the most important reason of all—is the fear of failure. People don't set goals because they are afraid they might fail. In fact, the fear of failure is probably the greatest single obstacle to success in adult life. It can hold you back more than any other psychological problem.

The primary reason why you may fear failure is that you probably do not understand the role failure plays in achievement. The fact is, it is impossible to succeed without failing. Failure is an indispensable prerequisite for success. All great success is preceded by great failure. If you wish to fulfill your potential, you have to be willing to risk failure over and over; there is no way you can ever accomplish worthwhile goals until you have fallen on your face so many times that you have eventually learned the lessons you need for great achievement.

So an important key to succeeding through goal setting is expecting temporary setbacks and obstacles as inevitable parts of the goal-achieving process.

In order to be successful, you need to focus your mental and physical energy in a single direction toward a predetermined objective. People who are especially energetic or talented have a hard time with this. They are the ones who try to do several things at once and end up doing nothing well.

Setting well-defined goals enables you to channel your efforts and focus your energy toward something that's important to you. Goal setting gives you a target to aim at, and enables you to develop the self-discipline to continue working toward your target rather than becoming distracted and going off in other directions.

Let me share with you five keys that will help you to reach your goals more effectively. Each of these keys starts with one of the letters in the word *goals*. Whenever you find yourself getting off the track, simply repeat the word *goals*, and think about how each letter stands for a key that just might apply to your current situation.

The first letter is G, and it stands for "Get to it!" Sometimes, the only difference between a successful person and a failure is that the successful person has the courage to get started, to do something, to begin moving toward accomplishing a specific goal.

For example, when I was younger, I realized I was stuck in a low-paying job because of my limited education. I began reading the want ads and decided that I wanted to work in advertising, especially as a copywriter. I went to an advertising agency and applied for the job of writing advertisements. The head of the agency was very polite, but he told me I was unskilled and totally unsuited for the position. He thanked me for coming in and wished me luck.

Now I was back on the street, but I had a goal. I wanted to be an advertising copywriter. I immediately took the first step, which was to learn more about how to write copy, so that I would not be turned down in the future because of a lack of ability. I went to the local library and checked out books on the subject of advertising and copy-writing. Over the next 12 months, I read every single book in the library on the subject. Meanwhile, I read magazines and newspapers and thought about how I could improve their advertising. I wrote sample advertisements and began taking them to advertising agencies.

To make a long story short, at the end of the 12 months, two of the largest advertising agencies in the country offered me a job as a copywriter, and I accepted one of those offers. My income doubled. I had worked at other jobs in the meantime. But I had never lost sight of my goal, and I had kept on doing the things I needed to do to put myself in a position to eventually achieve my goal.

You, too, may have a long-range goal. In order to achieve it, you need to sit down and make a list of all the steps you will have to take to get from where you are to where you want to be. Then take action on the first and most obvious step on that list. Complete it, and then start on number two. Don't worry about the long term. Just concentrate on the obvious first step you can take. Surprisingly enough, everything else will take care of itself. The Confucian saying, "A journey of a thousand leagues begins with a single step," is popular in many languages because it is so true.

The second letter, O, stands for "Opportunity." Successful people do not wait for opportunities to turn their goals into reality;

rather, they make their opportunities, because they are perfectly clear about the kind of life they wish to create. Once you have taken the time to decide exactly what you want, you will experience an endless flow of opportunities to help move you in that direction.

For example, a young woman worked for me as an executive secretary. At the same time, she had a goal to be a successful real estate agent and investor. So while she worked for me, she regularly took night courses to get her real estate license and to learn how to buy and sell real estate profitably. Over the course of a year, she and her husband bought, fixed up, and sold three houses. They made more money from their real estate transactions than they did from their jobs. At the end of the year, she passed the test and received her real estate license.

Within a few days of getting her license, she and her husband were sitting in a small restaurant, and they got into a conversation with a woman at the next table. It turned out that this woman was a very successful real estate agent who needed an executive assistant to work with her and learn the real estate profession. They got along so well that my executive secretary was offered the job, where she would be earning double what she could earn as a secretary and would have an unlimited upside potential.

My secretary did not wait for an opportunity to come to her. She set a goal, made a plan, and went to work to prepare herself for the opportunity when it arose.

The letter A stands for "Ability." Many people hesitate to set high, challenging goals because they lack the ability necessary to turn those goals into reality. But remember, we all lacked knowledge and experience when we started out in our careers or fields of expertise.

Do you remember when you started your first job? You probably felt a little clumsy, inadequate, and unsure about how to do it well. As you progressed and got more experience, you became more and more confident, and in many cases, you did an excellent job without even thinking much about it.

Since you gain the ability necessary for high achievement through knowledge and experience, if you increase the speed at which you acquire both of those qualities, you increase the speed at which you move ahead.

The letter L stands for "Leadership." Leadership is simply the ability to get results. And you begin to get results when you accept ͡ˑll responsibility for yourself, for your job, and for the outputs ed in your position.

You demonstrate leadership when you refuse to make excuses or blame anyone or anything for the problems you are having. The acceptance of the responsibility of leadership enables you to move ahead and take action.

When you are not satisfied with your job or income, and you sit down and make a written plan to change it, and then take action on that plan without waiting for anyone's approval or permission, you are behaving like a leader.

The final letter, S, stands for "Stay with it"—the resolution to persist in the face of adversity until you succeed. Between you and every goal you wish to achieve, there is a series of obstacles, and the bigger the goal, the greater the obstacles. Your decision to be, have, and do something out of the ordinary entails facing difficulties and challenges that are out of the ordinary as well. Sometimes your greatest asset is your ability to stay with it longer than anyone else.

When you look around, you will see that all achievement is the triumph of persistence. You will see men and women everywhere who are struggling with and overcoming adversities in order to accomplish something that is important to them. And so can you.

So remember the five keys to setting and achieving goals. The first is "Get to it!" Get started; take the first action at hand. The second is "Opportunity." Begin to prepare yourself now so you will be ready for the opportunities that will inevitably arise. The third is "Ability." Resolve to learn what you need to know to live the kind of life you want to live. The fourth key is "Leadership." Take charge of your time and your life, and accept responsibility for your results. And finally, "Stay with it." If you stay with it long enough, nothing can stop you from finally winning.

Questions to Ponder

- Does your mission statement reflect a burning desire to be the finest in your industry? Are you willing to pay the price?

- What extra effort are you expending now, and what more could you do to speed up your progress?

- Do you have a clear set of written, SMART goals for yourself and your company? Does your staff have the same set of SMART goals?

How do champions plan their strategy for the course, Sir? Well, there's a lot more to it than there used to be. When I first caddied, golf was a much simpler game. It was played with hickory-shafted clubs, hand-forged irons, and balls that often felt like putty. Tournaments were run much less efficiently, but in my opinion, except for the Masters, most of them were more fun than they are today. It's all so deadly serious now, with yardage books and distances marked right on the sprinkler heads. Still, that's the price you pay for progress. I can't argue with the facts; over the last 40 years the players have learned how to prepare themselves better, and it shows in their scores. Good planning really lays the foundation for a good score . . . Do we really need such a detailed plan before we tee off, Sir? You bet we do!

Preparing a Championship Strategy

Planning Your Attack

Even if he is armed with all the traits of champions, a player endangers his chances of becoming a champion if he doesn't have a specific strategy for putting his talents to work. It's essential to know your strengths and weaknesses and to have a game plan in place long before venturing out on the course. You must carefully analyze yourself, the conditions, and the course if you are to achieve your goal at the end of the day.

A Businesslike Approach

Ben Hogan was probably the first great player to employ statistics and carefully prepared data in his approach to the game. This is illustrated by a story about him that was widely circulated during his days as a regular PGA Tour competitor. Facing a crucial approach shot to a par four, he turned to his caddie and asked for a yardage. After consulting his notes, the caddie replied, "It's 157 yards, maybe 158." Hogan turned his famous, steely gaze on the caddie. Then, after a few moments of uncomfortable silence, he barked, "Well? Which is it?"

Planning a Strategy

Golf holes designed by the great course architects, like Donald Ross, Alister Mackenzie, and Robert Trent Jones, Sr., offer golfers a number of options on how they approach the playing of the hole. For example, the 18th at Pebble Beach is a relatively easy par five when the wind doesn't blow. The conservative player drives his tee shot to the right side of the fairway, hits a mid-iron for his second, and leaves himself something like a 9-iron to the flag. The bolder golfer prefers to drive his ball close to the Pacific Ocean, which hugs the left side of the hole during its entire length. This more daring approach effectively shortens the hole, allowing him the opportunity to reach the green in two, provided of course that he is daring enough to play chicken once again with the ocean. Being rewarded for your courage with an eagle on this superb hole is a splendid prospect. The penalty for failure, however, can be severe. Nicklaus himself, with millions watching on television, once made an embarrassing eight, the dreaded snowman, on the hole.

Another fine risk/reward hole is the 13th at Augusta National, which is a short and relatively easy par five, if one elects to use three shots to reach the green. Yet the lure of getting home in two for an easy birdie or perhaps an eagle leads many of the world's finest players to give up their ball to the devilish clutches of Rae's Creek, which guards the front of the green.

Every goal in life can be achieved in more than one way. For each action he takes, the champion must weigh the reward that may accrue against the risk and ensuing penalty he may sustain. Life gives every player similar options. We may select a steady but pedestrian march toward retirement. We may occasionally opt to be a little more aggressive without taking any major chances. Or we can take the bull by the horns and "go for broke" like Arnie.

The Calculated Approach

When Jack Nicklaus joined the tour, he quickly adopted Dean Beman's statistical approach to pre-game preparation and moved it to new heights. While it is now common practice among tour players, Nicklaus was one of the first to measure yardages on each course before he played it. Like a general studying the battlefield, he planned his strategy in minute detail. He drew diagrams of each hole, marked distances from specific and recognizable features to the front of the greens, and made notes about which way and how much the putts broke on different parts of the green. I believe this precise planning and meticulous attention to detail contributed greatly to making Nicklaus a dominant player from the earliest stages of his career.

The "Backward" Approach

"Adequate preparation and knowledge of the course are essential."
Ben Hogan

The champion who went to the greatest lengths to plan his campaign in advance was Ben Hogan, and he had a different technique for preparing himself. Hogan studied each hole he would play backward, from green to tee. He would stand on the 18th green and look back up the fairway to determine the best position from which to attack the green. From the spot he selected, he would look at the tee and determine whether a driver, a 3-wood, or a long iron might be the best club to reach that exact position. On a downhill par five, he might play a 1-iron off the tee to keep the ball on level ground, rather than leaving himself a more difficult shot from an awkward downhill lie, albeit closer to the green. When making an approach shot, he was always conscious of whether the best putt at the hole would be from a position short of or beyond the hole. Just like a championship pool or billiards player, every shot he played was always struck with the next shot in mind. It was said of Hogan that his biggest problem was having to play out of the divots he had made the day before.

Prior to a tournament, Hogan would spend considerable time putting in extra practice with certain selected clubs. These would be the clubs he expected to use most frequently in that particular competition on that specific golf course. In one event, a fellow player noticed that Hogan had played the first two rounds of the tournament without a 7-iron in his bag. On the third day, seeing that Hogan was once again without a 7-iron, he couldn't resist asking Hogan to explain why he had left such an important club out of the bag. Hogan replied unsmilingly that he was not carrying a 7-iron because there was no shot on that particular course that demanded such a club.

Once Hogan had formulated his game plan, he always stayed with it unless something unusual was called for at a critical stage. After a round at the Masters, a young player with whom he had been paired asked him why he had chosen to lay up short of the water hazard on the par five, 13th hole, when he easily could have reached the green with his second shot and been in position to make a three. Hogan looked at the youngster for a moment and then stated firmly, "I didn't need a three."

This brings us to the first key to planning a solid strategy. It is necessary to gather an adequate supply of up-to-date, specific, and relevant information about the task that lies ahead and the particular challenges you are likely to encounter along the way.

Don't Kid Yourself; Be Honest with Yourself

The second key in selecting a strategy for your round is complete honesty with yourself regarding your personal skills. We all know a golfer who has recorded a score of 81 once in his life, yet insists to anyone who can be persuaded to listen that the 98s and 99s he posts week after week are due to a putting slump or some minor flaw that has crept into his swing. In his mind he believes himself to be a much stronger player who has suffered a temporary loss of form. Even though the slump continues for years, he still insists he is a "low 80s" shooter.

Many pros complain about playing in pro-ams year after year with partners who aim down the middle and slice 18 shots a round into the woods and the rough on the right side of the fairway. Each time they tee up, these partners manage to persuade themselves that they "have the answer now and this one will go down the middle."

Champions don't lie to themselves. They make an honest and sometimes even brutally accurate assessment of their strengths and weaknesses. To quote Clint Eastwood, a fine actor and an enthusiastic golfer, "A man's gotta know his limitations." Champions either find a way to play within those limitations or take decisive remedial action to prevent their inadequacies from rearing their ugly heads at precisely the wrong moment.

Ego Shots

We all know players who try to kill an 8-iron when a 6-iron was the appropriate stick. Then, having come up short, they insist disgustedly that they caught the shot a little heavy or a sudden gust of wind prevented the ball from carrying to the green. Other self-deluding players continually endeavor to hit their driver off the tee with no success, when a 3-wood shot would have placed them in the fairway within easy reach of the putting surface. Why do so many average players do this? It is purely and simply a question of ego. You won't see a champion make this kind of mistake as he wins the Masters or the U.S. Open. When it comes to decision making, ego has no place in golf, in business, or in life.

A realistic appraisal of your personal strengths and weaknesses is an admirable way to begin any endeavor to move forward. Seve Ballesteros, for instance, accepted right from the start that he was wild off the tee. In order to become a champion, he knew he had to develop a broader range of tee shots, frequently using the 3-wood or the 1-iron in order to keep his ball in play and, therefore, remain in a position to win.

Jack Nicklaus realized early in his golfing career that he was weak in bunker play and chipping, and he practiced even harder on that aspect of his game to overcome the flaw. He also realized he had to work not just on his score, but on his image if he wanted to win the hearts of the fans and the media. This may have been his greatest personal challenge, but he was able to meet it successfully because he acknowledged its existence.

The Courage to Admit and Address Your Weaknesses

If you really intend to become a champion, you must not only practice your strengths, but know and control your weaknesses as well. It has been said that scoring well in golf is not so much a matter of how good your *good* shots are, but of how good your *bad* shots are. Practicing your best shots is easy—it's fun to do things we're good at. Practicing shots you tend to execute poorly, in order to improve, is not nearly as much fun. The world's top golfers hit their strongest shots on the range before they play in order to build their confidence. After they have completed their rounds, and on days when they aren't involved in tournament play, they spend long hours working to correct their bad shots, not stroking their egos by practicing their good ones. Next time you attend a PGA event, be sure to visit the range in the late afternoon. There you will find the greatest players on tour struggling with their own personal devils.

When we discover we have a weakness that is holding us back, we must have the courage and desire to confront it and overcome it. Admitting we perform poorly in any area does not come easily to anyone. Unfortunately, many people go to great lengths to deny or conceal their weaknesses, fearing the criticism or even scorn of their peers. This results in preservation and enlargement of the area of weakness. For example, you may be able to live with your slice by constantly aiming left, but you are likely to develop an even bigger slice by doing so. Then, when you find yourself on a beautiful course among the pines in North Carolina, you can't aim as far left as you need to because of the trees, and your entire game rapidly falls apart. Weaknesses ultimately come to the surface, and usually at the most inopportune time. Have the courage to confront your weakness, and spend more than 50 percent of your practice time on it until it is no longer a weakness.

Identifying Your Limiting Factor

Once you have a clear picture of the various strengths and weaknesses in your game, you should work on what you have identified as your limiting factor. If you drive the ball only 180 yards off the tee because of a vicious slice, it is almost impossible to shoot par on a championship course. Your limiting factor in this case is distance. No matter how well you putt, chip, or hit your irons, par will remain beyond your reach because you will not be able to reach most of the greens in regulation. The first order of business is to eliminate your slice, build up the strength in your arms, and find a way to add 60 yards to your tee shot. Conversely, no amount of huge drives and accurate iron shots will ever help you shoot par if you take 40 putts per round. Most players, indeed most people generally, won't work on their limiting factors because, as has been previously stated, we all prefer to do those things at which we excel.

Beating the Dreaded "Yips"

Bernard Langer became one of the world's best players and a two-time Masters champion by identifying his limiting factor and overcoming a problem few players in history have ever conquered. At a very early age, he developed the putting "yips." In a nutshell, that means he lost control of the muscles in his hands and arms when facing short putts. From three feet he might leave a putt short by 18 inches; then, on the very next green, he would be forced to watch in anguish as his unruly putter fired the ball 10 feet past the hole. Recognizing that this problem would permanently prevent him from reaching his goals, no matter how good his iron play, he spent hour upon hour, week after week, working to overcome his limitation. He took Gary Player as his model, and through determination and will power, he finally found a stroke that would work for him.

For several years he was among the top players in European golf. Then, without warning, the dreaded yips returned.

Once again, he was compelled to go back to the practice putting green in search of a cure. Eventually he discovered a unique and creative grip that entails placing his left hand about 10 inches down the shaft and letting the shaft rest against the inside of his left forearm. He then locks the grip of the club in place by gripping both the shaft and his left wrist with his right hand. While it may be one of the most unorthodox grips in history, it has enabled him to play competitive golf at the highest level once again.

Many other fine players have had to leave the game when they became afflicted with an identical problem. Langer, through personal honesty, courage, and dogged determination, overcame his limiting factor and showed himself for what he is, a true champion.

Strangling the Hook

The great Ben Hogan was plagued with a vicious hook, even after he became the PGA Tour's No. 1 player. In the mid-1940s he went back to the driving range and started to rebuild his swing. His fellow pros thought he was crazy to fool around with his swing; how, they wondered, could the best get better? As was Hogan's invariable habit, he confounded his critics and all the other naysayers. When he returned to the tour, he announced he had discovered the "secret." Discussion and speculation continued for years about what changes he had made. He declined to unlock the mystery. The bottom line was that he had traded his hook for a much more controllable fade, and he went on to play the best golf of his remarkable career.

By clearly identifying the one key area that will hold them back, champions make a quantum leap toward success and progress even further the moment they start focusing their efforts on solving that problem. If more than one area creates difficulty for them, they prioritize their efforts based on what must be done first. For example, changing your swing plane is unlikely to cure your hook if your grip is showing four knuckles of the left hand and your right hand is completely under the shaft. The grip must be corrected first in order to make real progress.

The Good, the Bad and the Ugly

On this occasion, we aren't talking about the famous "spaghetti western" of that name. We are going to make an honest appraisal of your game. It is time to ask yourself:

- What is the best part of your golf game?
- In which area are you weakest?
- How much better would you score if you were able to improve in this area until it is as good as the strongest part of your game?

The tendency of most players is to focus their attention on the areas of the game in which they do well, since this gives them the most pleasure. The tendency is also to focus on the driver and other "ego" clubs at the expense of the wedge and putter, which are really the scoring clubs. Well over half the shots in a round of golf are hit with these two weapons, yet the majority of players spend a minimal amount of time practicing with them. Champions realize the importance of the scoring clubs and concentrate their efforts on becoming expert in their use.

Through careful analysis of the course, detailed plans for playing it, and an honest acceptance of their own strengths and weaknesses, champions waste little effort proceeding in the wrong direction. They identify the steps that need to be taken first and follow a careful plan that leads them to victory. Champions know they only have a certain amount of time and energy with which to pursue their dreams. That's why they plan!

Well, you're really in luck, Sir! If your limiting factor is a hook, you won't have to worry much here at Pebble; they say it's a hooker's layout, except for number 18 of course. Besides, there's hardly any rough to speak of; they just cut it short so it'll grow back strong in time for the Open. So, if you do hit an occasional wild shot, it won't hurt you too badly, at least on most holes. Your strength is your chipping and putting, which will be a real plus on these greens. They're like glass this time of year. The basic strategy you shared with me for playing each hole sounds good; if we have to, we can make minor adjustments as we go along.

I know you've heard enough locker room chit chat. Let's go up to the range. That'll give you a chance to stretch your muscles and sharpen your game. We both know the practice ground is the place where championships are won and lost. Oh, they may be contested in other places, but as sure as the sprinklers come on at dusk, the range is where champions get ready to win the battle.

Swing Thoughts

- Champions prepare detailed strategies for accomplishing their goals on a day-by-day, course-by-course, and shot-by-shot basis.

- Champions arm themselves with an adequate supply of specific information about the course and the conditions they will face during the tournament.

- Champions know their strengths and their weaknesses.

- Champions identify their limiting factors and work to remove or control them.

Back in the Clubhouse

Earl Nightingale once said that if a person does not prepare for his success, when his opportunity comes, it will only make him look foolish. You've probably heard it said repeatedly that luck is what happens when preparedness meets opportunity. Only when you've paid the price to be ready for your success are you in a position to take advantage of your opportunities when they arise. And the most remarkable thing is this: the very act of preparation attracts to you, like iron filings to a magnet, opportunities to use that preparation to advance in your life. You'll seldom learn anything of value without soon having a chance to use your new knowledge and your new skills to move ahead more rapidly.

There is a series of things you can do to become ready for success. All of these activities require self-discipline and a good deal of faith. They require self-discipline because the most normal and natural thing for people to do is to try to get by without preparation. Instead of taking the time and making the effort to be ready for their chance when it comes, they fool around, listen to the radio, watch television, and then they try to wing it and dupe others into thinking they are more prepared than they really are. And since just about everyone can see through just about everyone else, the unprepared person simply looks incompetent and foolish.

Preparation also requires a lot of faith because you have no guarantee in advance to demonstrate that the preparation will pay off. You simply have to believe deep within yourself that everything you do of a constructive nature will come back to you in some way. You have to know that no good effort is ever wasted. You have to be willing to sow for a long time before you reap, knowing that if you do sow in quality and quantity, the reaping will come about naturally and inevitably.

Look at your work. Be honest and objective about your strengths and weaknesses. What are you good at? What are you poor at? What is your major area of weakness? What must you absolutely, positively be excellent at in order to move to the top of your field? What one skill do you have that, because of its weakness, may be holding you back from using all your other skills?

Norman Augustine, who was president of Martin Marietta Corporation, once said that the most important thing he learned in the last 10 years of business was that a person's weakest important skill determines the extent to which he can use all of his other talents and abilities. In looking at the hundreds of people who worked below him in his corporation, he had found that people's careers were largely determined not only by their strengths, but also by their weaknesses. The very act of overcoming a particular weakness, through preparation and practice, was enough to propel a person into the front ranks in his career.

In preparing for success, one of the very best questions you can continually ask yourself is, "What can I—and only I—do that, if done well, will make a real difference in my career?" Usually, there is only one or perhaps two answers to that question. Your ability to honestly appraise yourself and to identify the particular skill area that may be holding you back is critical.

Remember that preparation requires self-discipline, because your natural tendency is to do more of those things that come most easily to you and to avoid those areas you don't enjoy because you're not particularly good at them yet. It requires character for you to admit your weaknesses in a particular area and then resolve to go to work to develop yourself so those weaknesses don't hold you back.

The greatest change that has taken place in our society in the last 20 years is that it has become an information-based society. More than 50 percent of the working population is in the business of processing information in some way. This means that we now have a knowledge-based society as well, and that you're a knowledge worker. You work with your mind, your brain, your mental talents and abilities. You no longer "tote that barge, lift that bale." You work by thinking, and the more effectively you think and the more positive you are mentally, the more productive you'll be.

One thing that has helped me enormously over the years is the habit of getting up early in the morning and spending the first 30 to 60 minutes reading something uplifting. Many people read material that is motivational or even inspirational or spiritual. Henry Ward Beecher once said, "The first hour is the rudder of the day." This is often called the "golden hour." It's the hour during which you program your mind and set your emotional tone for the rest of the day. If you get up in the morning at least two hours before you have to be at work or before your first appointment and spend the first hour investing in your mind—taking in "mental protein" rather than "mental candy," reading good books rather than the newspaper or magazines—your whole day will flow more smoothly. You'll be more positive and optimistic. You'll be calmer, more confident, and more relaxed. You'll gain a greater sense of control and well-being by the very act of reading healthy material for the first hour of each day.

After just three days of reading for 30 to 60 minutes in the morning, you'll notice a profound difference. You'll begin to develop what Dr. William Glasser called a "positive addiction." As a result of your early-morning reading, you'll feel so good about yourself and your life that you'll develop a desire and motivation to get up earlier, even though your tendency in the past was to sleep later. Try it and see. It's a wonderful experience, and it can have a profound impact on the rest of your life.

In the period of time before work, another thing that highly successful people do is plan and prepare for their entire day. They review all of the tasks and responsibilities they have for the coming hours. They carefully make a list of all their activities, and they set clear priorities on the activities. They decide which things are most important to do, which are secondary in importance, and which things should not be done at all unless all the other things are finished. They then discipline themselves to start working on their most important tasks and to stay with them during the day until they're complete.

Again, the natural tendency of the low performer is to do what is fun and easy before he or she does what is hard and necessary. Underachievers always like to do the little things first. They are drawn to the tasks that contribute little to their careers or future possibilities. But high achievers are not like that—they discipline themselves to start at the top of their list and to work on the activities in order of importance, without diversion or distraction.

By the way, whenever you have money problems of any kind, you should look upon them as a signal telling you that you need to reorder your priorities and to prepare more thoroughly to accomplish more of the things that contribute the greatest value to your life. For example, if you're in sales, you should spend fully 80 percent of your time prospecting until you're so busy with presentations and proposals that you have no time left to prospect at all.

Another way to prepare for success is to eat right. Energy and dynamism are essential to your success, and they're possible only when you're sharp and alert. There are highly nutritious foods that give you high energy and vitality through the day. Also, there are foods that you usually eat by habit that are hard for your system to digest and that tire you out and make you slow and drowsy in the morning and the afternoon.

The chief culprits in diets are foods with a high fat content. More and more nutritional research suggests that fatty foods, which require the greatest effort on the part of the body to break down and digest, are the real enemies of human performance. Fats are becoming closely linked to many illnesses and ailments. One reason people drink so much coffee in the morning is to counteract the drowsiness that occurs naturally because their stomachs are so loaded down with fatty foods.

You see, the process of digestion is the activity of your body that consumes the most energy. When you eat foods that are hard to digest, your body rushes blood from everywhere to the digestive system to break them down. In this process, the digestive system draws blood away from the brain and the muscles. The reason you feel drowsy after a large meal is because the blood has gone from your brain to your stomach. The reason you get cramps when you engage in vigorous physical exercise immediately after eating is because a substantial amount of blood has been drawn from your muscles to aid in the process of digestion.

In preparing for success throughout the day, you should also talk to yourself in a positive way. The work by Dr. Martin Seligman has demonstrated that the way you talk to yourself largely determines your emotions, how you feel about yourself on a minute-to-minute basis. If you don't deliberately and consciously think about what you want and talk to yourself in a positive way, your mind will tend to drift toward and dwell on your worries and concerns. And negative thinking takes the edge off your enthusiasm, which is so important to your success with people.

I've learned that a key to keeping yourself positive and optimistic is preparation in advance for the ups and downs you'll experience each day. For example, if you're in sales, you can change the way you talk to yourself by viewing yourself as a "rejection specialist" rather than a "sales specialist." If you define yourself as a sales specialist, you'll be setting yourself up for failure, disappointment, and lowered self-esteem with every rejection you get. But on the other hand, if you look upon yourself as a rejection specialist, you'll be setting yourself up to feel like a winner every time someone turns you down for any reason. Also, you can look upon every rejection as a percentage of a sale. If it takes you 20 calls to make a sale, you can look upon a rejection as 5 percent of the commission you receive for making that sale. In this way, every person you speak to actually pays you money. You simply collect it by making the sale that is inevitable when you speak to enough people. Every time someone turns you down, you're a winner. You're just that much farther ahead. You're just a little bit closer to the sale that must come if you keep on keeping on.

A few years ago, Dr. Abraham Zaleznik of Harvard University did an interesting study on disappointment. He found that successful people bounce back from disappointments far faster than unsuccessful people do.

Use every setback or disappointment as a spur to greater effort. Decide that nothing will ever get you down. Decide that you will bounce back instead of break. Develop a resilient or hardy personality. Become the kind of person who is always cheerful, no matter what happens on the outside. Develop an attitude of gratitude, and give thanks for everything that happens to you, knowing that every step forward is a step toward achieving something bigger and better than your current situation. In this way, you become a far more resourceful and effective person. And prepared mentally, you become almost unstoppable.

For example, if you're making sales calls, resist the "parking-lot mentality" of the average salesperson. The average salesperson doesn't think about the client until he or she drives onto the parking lot, and stops thinking about the client when he or she drives off. Instead, prepare thoroughly for each call. Review your file of notes on the customer, and establish a clear set of call objectives before you go in. Know what you're doing and why. Be very clear on what you want to accomplish with a call. If a person were to ask you how you would judge whether or not your upcoming call was successful, you should be able to tell that person exactly what you want to accomplish, and after the call, you should be able to tell that person exactly what you achieved. Most salespeople never do this. When you ask them if a call was successful, they don't know how to answer you because they have no basis for evaluation.

In everything you do, preparation is the key. If you want to be ready for success, you have to plant the seeds well in advance of the harvest you expect. Do what the winners do: think on paper. Memorize the winner's creed: "Everything counts." Everything you do is either moving you toward your goals or away from them. Everything is either helping you or hurting you. Nothing is neutral. Everything counts.

A young man once asked a successful businessman how he could be more successful faster. The businessman told him that the key to his own success had been to "get good" at his job.

The young man said, "I'm already good at what I do."

The businessman then said, "Well, get better!"

The young man, somewhat self-satisfied, said, "Well, I'm already better than most people."

To that, the businessman replied, "Then be the best."

Those are three of the best pieces of advice I've ever heard: Get good. Get better. Be the best!

Remember, we live in a knowledge-based society, and knowledge in every field is doubling approximately every seven years. This means that you must double your knowledge in your field every seven years just to stay even. You're already "maxed out" at your current level of knowledge and skill. You've reached the ceiling in your career with your current talents and abilities. If you want to go faster and farther, you must get back to work and begin to prepare yourself for greater heights. You must put aside the newspaper, turn off the television, politely excuse yourself from aimless socializing, and get back to working on yourself.

A quotation by Abraham Lincoln had a great influence on my life when I was 15. It was a statement he made when he was a young lawyer in Springfield, Illinois. He said, "I will study and prepare myself, and someday my chance will come."

If you study and prepare yourself, your chance will come as well. There is nothing that you cannot accomplish if you'll invest the effort to get yourself ready for the success that you desire. And there is nothing that can stop you but your own lack of preparation.

Think about the message in this beautiful poem by Henry Wadsworth Longfellow: "Those heights by great men won and kept/ Were not achieved by sudden flight; / But they, while their companions slept, / Were toiling upward in the night."

Questions to Ponder

• Do you have a detailed strategy for accomplishing your goals?

• What will you do *today* to move closer to your goals?

• What about tomorrow? Next week? Next month?

• Do you perform an analysis at least once a year to determine your strengths and weaknesses and the opportunities and threats that lie ahead?

• Have you clearly identified any limiting factors in your plan?

They'll finish mowing the range in a couple of minutes; then you'll be able to hit a few warm-up shots. While we wait, why don't we use the time to warm up mentally? . . . How do we do that? Well, tell me, Sir, what's the best shot you ever remember making? You know what I mean—the one that means the most to you, personally—a hole-in-one, a fine long-iron shot, or a shot from out of the sand to snatch victory from the jaws of defeat. Whatever it was, I bet it brings back happy memories . . . You say you can think of several? Well, good for you! We all have great shots we love to remember. Most of us also like to talk about them for years after they happened. My favorite was the 80-foot putt I made for birdie on the 15th hole of the golf club where I learned to play. That putt helped me win the Caddies Club Championship when I was 15 years old . . . You're right, Sir—that was a few years ago. But I get just as much pleasure thinking about some of the shots I've seen made by great champions as I do from my own. Let me tell you about a few of them and you'll see what I mean.

GREAT SHOTS

The Shot Heard 'Round the World

It was during the second Masters tournament, in 1935, that the story of a single, remarkable shot was heard around the world. It not only immortalized the man who made it, but also established the Masters as a major tournament when the shot was described in the pages of every widely read newspaper in every country where golf was played. Strange as it may seem to us, in these days of global television coverage and huge crowds, this fabled moment in golf's history was observed by only a handful of specta-tors. One famous and highly respected writer said he had talked to hundreds of people during his lifetime who claimed to have witnessed the historic shot. He found this strange, not to say amusing, since he, together with Bobby Jones, was one of only 20 or so people who were actually present at the time! Most of the spectators were following tournament leaders Wood and Picard at that moment of the tournament.

It was a little before 5:30 when Gene Sarazen, partnered with Walter Hagen, came to Augusta's par five, 15th hole. Sarazen hit a beautiful drive, with just enough draw to keep the ball bounding down the fairway like a scared rabbit until it came to rest just 220 yards from the green. As he strode down the fairway toward his ball, a massive roar erupted from the 18th green. Within minutes the word had filtered back to the spot where Sarazen was approaching his second shot. Craig Wood had made a magnificent birdie three at the 18th, giving him a total of 282. When he heard this, Sarazen turned to Stovepipe, his lanky old caddie, and asked, "What do I need to win?" Hagen, who was no longer in contention, stifled a chuckle, but Stovepipe replied, "You need four straight threes Mr. Gene; that will do it." Four straight threes meant an eagle, a par and two birdies, but Sarazen felt up to the challenge.

His confidence must have wilted as he drew level with his ball and found it laying on bare ground in the back of a small divot. Although the yardage called for a 3-wood, Sarazen decided, because of the lie, he would have to hit a 4-wood. At this point Sarazen remembered the lucky ring that had been given to him in his hotel lobby the night before. He pulled it from his pocket and rubbed it over Stovepipe's head to arouse its powers. Sarazen would later comment that it wasn't a matter of invoking magical powers, but of breaking the tension of the situation and helping him to relax before taking up his stance beside the ball.

The combination of the lie, the distance he had to cover, and the club he had to use required Sarazen to hood the face of the club a few degrees and put into his swing every ounce of strength his body could muster. He struck it dead center, and the ball shot toward the pin, never rising more than 30 feet above the ground. It carried the water hazard by several feet and hopped toward the cup. The small gallery at greenside exploded, jumping in the air and cheering wildly, as the ball disappeared into the cup. Sarazen had achieved that rarest of golfing feats, a double-eagle, a two on a par five, and he had done so under the greatest possible pressure. History had been made, and the Masters at Augusta National was to become one of golf's four major championships.

When Sarazen reached the green, he could hear a young man arguing on the scorer's telephone about what had happened. The boy was insisting that Sarazen had made a two on the 15th, a par five, and not on the 16th, a par three. Craig Wood could only wait in the clubhouse as Sarazen played the last three holes in par to tie him at 282. In a playoff the next day, Sarazen emerged the winner and donned the coveted green jacket.

The Drive that Started a Legend

Now let's "fast forward" 25 years to 1960 and another great shot—one that served as a launching pad for golf's most legendary player. Although Arnold Palmer had already won two Masters championships and several tournaments by the time play began in the 1960 U.S. Open, he had not yet become famous for his patented "charge." "Arnie's Army" was recruited as a result of one monumental shot played in Denver, Colorado, at the Cherry Hills Country Club, during the final round of the U.S. Open Championship.

At that time, U.S. Open contestants were required to play 36 holes on the final day. Mike Souchak held the lead after the morning round with a score of 208, but concluding his third round play with a double bogey at 18 had brought him back to the field. Fifteen players were now within seven shots, with Palmer being one of nine at 215, which most observers believed to be too far back. At lunch, Arnie was not his usual cheerful self—hardly surprising when one considers his position with just 18 holes to go. He was pensive and even angry with himself. He was eating a hamburger in the company of his old friend Bob Drum, a sports writer from Pittsburgh.

"What would happen if I shot 65?" Palmer asked Drum, aggressively.

"Nothing," shot back Drum quickly. "You're out of it!"

"The hell I am," Palmer snapped back. "65 would give me 280, and 280 wins the Open."

"Well, of course, if you drive the first green and make a hole-in-one, that would give you a head start," said Drum.

"That would give me a heckuva start; I'm going to do it," said Palmer as he got up from the table, his lunch only half consumed.

Palmer's angry mood persisted as he prepared to tee off just before noon, but he intended to use his anger in a positive way. The first hole at Cherry Hills is a 346-yard par four, played from an elevated tee to a small green with heavy rough in front of it. Palmer had tried to drive the green in the previous rounds and had carded a six, a five, and a four, but this time would be different. Most of the other players were hitting 3-woods or long irons into position for an easy wedge shot to the green, but Palmer needed a 65, and you don't shoot low numbers by laying up. With the characteristic hitch of his pants (for which he would become famous) and a glare that could crumble mountains, Palmer stepped up to the ball and crushed his drive. The ball streaked through the thin Denver air, dead on target. It bounced, as he had planned, in the rough just short of the putting surface and rolled to the heart of the green, finishing just 20 feet from the pin. The eagle attempt was unsuccessful, but he two-putted for the first of four consecutive birdies. By the time he reached the turn, he had recorded six birdies and an army of fans had arrived. A couple of hours later, he would roll in his final putt for a round of 65, a tournament score of 280, and victory in the U.S. Open Championship, two shots ahead of a young amateur named Jack Nicklaus. It was his drive on the 1st hole, reinforcing his already positive attitude, that led to the string of birdies that created the Arnold Palmer legend. From this point on, he would be famous for his "charge," and the loyal fans who would follow him for 40 years would proudly proclaim themselves to be "Arnie's Army."

Who Owns This Hole?

Our third great shot was played by (who else?) Jack Nicklaus. It wasn't the shot that launched his career or created his reputation; that had been earned years before. This timely masterstroke was just one in a career replete with such memorable shots, but it could be the one that established Nicklaus as the greatest player in the history of the sport. Although there were many great moments before and after this one, it is hard to recall one that was equally dramatic.

Imagine we are making a movie about the golf tournament to end all tournaments, starring three of the greatest players of the era. The scene is the 1975 Masters Tournament, to be enacted in brilliant April sunshine at the Augusta National Golf Course.

Let's set the stage. On the par five, 15th green we have the final twosome. It consists of the hottest player currently playing the game, Johnny Miller, along with another heir apparent to the golfing throne, Tom Weiskopf. Just a few yards away, waiting to play his tee-shot on the 16th is Jack Nicklaus. Weiskopf and Nicklaus currently share the lead at 11 under par for the tournament. Miller trails by one shot. Are you ready on camera? OK . . . Lights! Action!

Weiskopf lies over the green in two shots at the par five. He chips weakly, and is now faced with a slippery birdie putt across 20 feet of lightning fast Augusta green. Nicklaus knows the situation as he glances over toward the 15th green, then steps up to his ball and hits his tee shot to the par three, 16th hole.

For the final round, the flag on 16 is usually located in the back left part of the green, allowing players to play down the right side. The putting surface slopes towards the water hazard to the left of the hole, and shots landing on the right half of the green feed down to the cup. This will not be the case today. The flag is back right, and any shot that is not absolutely perfect will roll back down toward the water, resulting in a putt of at least 30 feet. Nicklaus' attempt is weak. In fact, by the exacting standards of Jack Nicklaus at this point in a major championship, it is downright terrible! Barely on the front left part of the green, he leaves himself 45 feet away from the difficult hole placement.

As Jack reaches his ball, he glances at the 15th green again. His view is obscured by spectators and trees, but he doesn't need to see what's going on because he soon hears a tremendous roar from the crowd that bounces around the tall pines. Some even claim it was heard all the way back at the clubhouse. Weiskopf has made his birdie putt—dead center—and now has a one-shot lead over Nicklaus with three holes to play. Moments later, the tall, slim figure of Weiskopf appears on the 16th tee, where he will be able to watch his destiny unfolding. As he stands there, he must surely be considering the possibility that his lead might soon be two shots, judging by the difficulty of the putt Nicklaus now faces.

Nicklaus methodically performs his customary pre-shot routine, picking a spot a few feet in front of the ball over which he intends it to travel. He hunches over the ball in his familiar putting stance. The silence is absolute. He strikes the putt. Weiskopf and Miller watch as the ball curves up the slope. No—it couldn't, could it? It disappears into the hole as Nicklaus leaps into the air, with putter raised high, and his caddie does the same with the flag stick. If the cheer for Weiskopf's putt at 15 could be heard in the clubhouse, the roar for Nicklaus can be heard in downtown Atlanta! He is tied for the lead again.

On the 16th tee it's hard to guess what's going through Tom Weiskopf's mind as he stands there looking on in silence. His face is a mask, but being human, he is no doubt affected to some degree by the pressure, and he leaves his tee shot short of the putting surface, more than 100 feet from the hole. His first putt catches the wrong side of the slope and drifts left, 25 feet away from the flag. He can do no better than a bogey. Nicklaus is now one ahead of Weiskopf and two shots ahead of Miller with just two holes left to play. The atmosphere is electric. Who will win? Will there be a playoff?

As it happens, Miller will birdie the 17th hole to join Weiskopf at just one shot off the pace, and both of them will have makeable birdie putts at 18 to tie for the lead. It isn't to be. Neither of them is able to hole his putt. There is a sense of inevitability about the Golden Bear's victory. Nicklaus has rarely lost an important tournament when he has been in a position to win. He has always had an unmatched, almost uncanny ability to make the shots and hole the putts that really count.

End of scene. Cut! Print! It's a wrap!

More than a decade later in 1986, in the commentator's booth covering the same hole, Jim Nantz asks Weiskopf to speculate on what is going through Jack's mind, as he is about to hit another immortal shot. Weiskopf laughs and replies, "If I knew that, I would have won the tournament." This time, Nicklaus puts his 5-iron shot two feet from the cup. He records birdies at 16 and 17, and goes on to win his 6th green jacket, shooting 30 on the back nine in the final round. Jim Nantz remarks in open admiration, "Jack owns this hole." Weiskopf offers no disagreement.

> *"Even if I take time off, I am out there beating golf balls.*
> *You've got to hit balls until your hands bleed."*
> *Lee Trevino*

Three great players, three different eras, one common thread. Each of these three shots has gone down in history. Two of them were instrumental in determining greatness in a player. Although these crowning moments or pivotal points lasted mere seconds, none of the three could have been achieved without tremendous preparation and practice over many years. Days and nights at the driving range, hitting balls until your hands are torn and blistered, so that one day, faced with your opportunity for glory, your mind and body become one and perform in flawless harmony to produce the desired result. Yes, perfect practice does indeed make perfect. It worked 60 years ago, 35 years ago, and 20 years ago; it still works today, and it will continue to work in the future.

Swing Thoughts

· Champions remember great shots and stellar victories. Then, when the occasion arises, they recall them in order to motivate themselves to greater heights.

Back in the Clubhouse

After studying the research done in cognitive psychology over the last 25 years, I've come to a simple conclusion: the degree to which you feel in control of your life will largely determine your level of mental well-being, your peace of mind, your happiness, and the quality of your interactions with people. Cognitive psychologists call this a "sense of control." It is the foundation of happiness and high achievement. And the only thing in the world over which you have complete control is the content of your conscious mind. If you decide to exert that control and keep your mind on what you want, even when you are surrounded by difficult circumstances, your potential will be unlimited.

Your aim should be to work on yourself and your thinking until you reach the point where you absolutely, positively believe yourself to be a total winner in anything you sincerely want to accomplish. When you reach the point where you feel unshakable confidence in yourself and your abilities, nothing will be able to stop you. And this state of self-confidence comes from, first, understanding the functioning of your remarkable mind and, second, practicing the techniques of mental fitness over and over until you become a completely optimistic, cheerful, and positive person.

Italian psychiatrist Dr. Roberto Assagioli left us two remarkable pieces of writing, *Psychosynthesis* and *The Act of Will*. In those books, Assagioli brought his remarkable intelligence to bear on the subject of human potential and human happiness. He studied the mind and personality for his entire lifetime, and he came up with several ideas that are profoundly simple and powerfully effective in helping us to lead happier, more satisfying lives.

In *The Act of Will*, he laid out a series of psychological principles, or laws, that can be very helpful to you in understanding the way your mind works and how you can take control of it.

Assagioli's first law explains that your thoughts, whatever they are, trigger mental pictures and emotions that then lead to your saying and doing certain things that are consistent with those thoughts.

For example, when you think about a person you care about, that thought will trigger a mental picture of that person plus the emotion of affection or love that you have for that person. When you think this way, you will speak positively about that person to others and to yourself, and you will have an urge to do something nice for him or her—to call the person or to buy him or her a card or a gift. Your initial thought will trigger the entire flow of events.

With regard to success, when you think of what success means to you or think about being a great success in your career, you'll think about the things you want to achieve and feel the pleasure of achieving them. You'll talk like a success and begin to take actions that will lead you to the success you desire. The starting point is always to think like a winner.

The second law Assagioli described is a paraphrase of his first law. He said that your feelings will tend to trigger thoughts and mental pictures that will then lead to your doing certain things.

For example, when you feel positive and optimistic, you will smile and be cheerful. You will be more animated and energetic. You will tend to be more enthusiastic and more efficient and effective in the things you do. Your positive feelings will trigger positive responses at all levels, and your world will be a more positive place. You will even attract into your life positive people and positive circumstances that are consistent with your feelings.

In fact, many success psychologists and researchers say that to achieve your goals, the most important thing to do is to "get the feeling" that you would have if the goal were already achieved. This is another way of saying that if you can create the state of emotion consistent with the goal or lifestyle you wish to attain, you will create a force field of energy that attracts what you want to you. That is a remarkable power, and many people are not aware they have it.

The third of Assagioli's laws is that images or pictures, either from within or from the outside, will trigger thoughts and feelings consistent with them. In turn, those thoughts and feelings will trigger behaviors that lead to the realization of the pictures.

For example, when you become absolutely convinced you are a total winner and you are meant to be a complete success in anything you really want to do, every picture or image you see that represents winning to you will trigger thoughts of what you could do to achieve that same state. The picture will also trigger the feeling of excitement that will motivate you to take action.

A friend of mine who was a sales manager had a simple technique to make new salespeople successful, and it worked in more than 90 percent of the cases. When he hired a salesperson, he would take that person to a nearby Cadillac dealership and force the person to trade in his current car on a new Cadillac. The payments on the Cadillac would be substantially more than the new salesperson had ever imagined paying, and he would strongly resist getting into the commitment. However, the sales manager would insist until, finally, the salesperson bought the new Cadillac and drove it home.

No matter how unsure or insecure the salesperson felt, when his spouse and friends saw the new Cadillac and he experienced the pleasure of driving it down the street, he began to think about himself and to see himself as a big success selling his product. And in almost all cases, it turned out to be true. Those salespeople went on to become great successes in their field.

Take every opportunity you can to surround yourself with images of what success means to you: get brochures on new cars; get magazines containing pictures of beautiful homes, beautiful clothes, and other things you could obtain as a result of achieving the success you are aiming for. Each time you see or visualize those images, you trigger the thoughts, feelings, and actions that make them materialize in your life.

Assagioli's fourth law is that thoughts, feelings, and images trigger the words and actions consistent with them. This is another way of saying that your inner impressions will motivate you to pursue the outer activities that will move you toward achieving your goals.

Assagioli's fifth law is that your actions will trigger thoughts, emotions, and images consistent with them. It is one of the most important success principles ever discovered.

Simply, the law says that you are more likely to act yourself into feeling than you are to feel yourself into acting. On many days, you wake up feeling less positive and optimistic than you would like. However, if you act as if you already have the feeling you desire, the action itself will trigger the feelings, thoughts, and mental pictures consistent with them.

In her book *Wake Up & Live*, Dorothea Brande said that the most important success secret she ever discovered was this: "Act as if it were impossible to fail, and it shall be."

In the book, she went on to explain that you need to be very clear about the success you desire, and then simply act as if you already had it. Act as if your success were inevitable. Act as if your achievement were guaranteed. Act as if there were no possibility of failure. And you will be right.

There is a principle called the Law of Expression that says that whatever is *ex*pressed is *im*pressed. This means that whatever you say, whatever you express to another in your conversation, is impressed into your subconscious mind.

The reverse of this law is that whatever is impressed will, in turn, be expressed. It will come out. Your conversation reveals an enormous amount about you, the kind of person you are, and the things that you believe about yourself and others.

One of the most important facts for you to realize is that your brain is a multisensory, multistimulated, extremely complex, interactive organ. Everything that you think, imagine, say, do, or feel triggers everything else, like a chain reaction, or like a series of electrical impulses going out in all directions and turning on lights everywhere.

Let's say you are driving down the street, listening to the radio and thinking about a variety of things. Suddenly, you hear a song that you associate with an old romance you had many years before. Instantaneously, your brain reacts and recreates all the sensations that were present when you were with that person a long time ago. You instantly get a mental picture of the person. You see and remember where you were and what you were doing when the song was playing back then. You feel the emotion you experienced at that time. You recall what was going on around you—the sounds, the activities, the people, and the season. You temporarily forget whatever you were thinking about and are transported, in a split second, back across the years. Sometimes, the emotion you recall is so intense that it brings you close to tears or fills you with happiness.

That is the way your mind works. By understanding that process, you can make your mind work for you as a powerful engine of growth and development. You can consciously surround yourself with a series of sensory inputs that bombard you with messages and cause you to think and feel like a total winner.

Thinking like a winner is the first step to living like a winner. You do become what you think about most of the time. You are not what you think you are; but what you think, you are. In fact, you are what you most intensely believe. And if you think like a winner and do the things winners do to keep their minds positive and optimistic, you will be a winner.

Questions to Ponder

- Do you maintain a detailed account of your victories and the reasons for them?

- What do you impress upon your mind, knowing that you will inevitably express what you impress?

- Are your thoughts positive and optimistic, thereby helping you to act and feel like a winner?

Look! They've finished mowing the tee. I'll get you some balls. It's time to loosen up your swing and get you ready for your round.

That's the way, Sir. A couple of moments stretching will loosen up those muscles. Here's your wedge . . . Quite right; it is best to start off nice and easy . . . You think some of those great shots we just talked about were a bit lucky? Well, I can tell you a thing or two about luck, Sir!

PERFECT PRACTICE MAKES PERFECT

"If you hit erratic shots, you get erratic breaks. If you hit perfect shots you don't have to worry about the breaks."
Johnny Miller

Getting Lucky

When Gary Player arrived in the United States in the late 1950s, he was already becoming known as a "world traveler." His schedule was at first limited; nevertheless, he quickly made an impression on many of the home-grown pros and soon developed a reputation among them as a "lucky" golfer. As is common when faced with someone who is more successful, many of the regular tour players decided Player was winning because he was luckier than they. Incidentally, this epithet would also be hung around the neck of Seve Ballesteros when he burst upon the tournament golf scene.

Rumors of Player's lucky play were circulating in the clubhouse after he had won a PGA tournament, and a less than tactful reporter asked him to comment on the matter. Throughout his career, Player has always seemed to be at his best when the odds were against him, and he summed up his feelings about luck by paraphrasing Thomas Jefferson.

"Sure I'm lucky," he told the journalist, "and the more I practice the luckier I get."

Make no mistake about it. The key to dramatically improving your "luck" is practice. Other pro golfers were reluctant to admit, even to themselves, that Gary Player practiced harder than they, hitting thousands more balls as he grooved and fine tuned his swing. Or that he showed up before dawn and stayed after dusk, then went to bed early, avoiding parties and hangovers. They also ignored the fact that he compensated for his small stature with a rigorous program of exercises and muscle building, long before it became fashionable to do so. Player was almost fanatical about his diet, his body and his physical conditioning, all with the objective of playing better golf. Other pros dismissed his fine performance as "lucky" because is was more comfortable than facing the cold, hard truth. He was better than most of them because he worked harder and tried harder.

One in a Million?

In 1982, when Tom Watson chipped in on the 17th at Pebble Beach, then birdied the final hole to win the U.S. Open, some called it a lucky shot—a one-in-a-million shot. Well, maybe it was and maybe it wasn't. Bear in mind that Watson, in practice before the tournament, had dropped balls in the rough fringe and practiced chipping from that exact spot. Remember, too, that Watson had played literally thousands of shots in similar situations, even if the results were less crucial and less was at stake.

The following year, at Sawgrass in Florida, the USGA wanted Watson to recreate the shot for a television promotion. Watson stepped to the edge of the green and threw down a ball in the heavy rough. Then he looked into the camera and smilingly spoke his line, "They say practice makes perfect." Without further delay, Watson took his wedge and hit the ball, bingo, straight in the hole. The only problem was that the camera wasn't running because the operator thought Watson was just warming up. It appeared they could all be in for a long afternoon of retakes, but undeterred, Watson threw down another ball and duplicated the result with his second attempt. There really *must* be something to this practice thing!

Practice Is the Path to Greatness

"The clubs are fine. The rules are fine. The problem with golf
is there isn't enough daylight in a day to practice."
Ben Hogan

68

According to the National Golf Foundation, 89 percent of people surveyed about their golfing habits said they would play more golf, spend more money on the game, and enjoy it more if they played better. Would it surprise you to learn that only 13 percent of the same survey group had taken a golf lesson in the previous 12 months. Like most people, they seek more pleasure and success, but are apparently unwilling to work harder in order to reap the rewards. Well, if they don't, they won't!

Whether you are golfing, selling, supervising, managing, or leading, your ultimate level of success depends on the quality and quantity of your preparation. That includes academic preparedness, but even more important, it means your knowledge of your business and your continued commitment to increasing your level of service to your customers, your company, and yourself. How do you become a better salesperson? Practice. How do you become a better manager? Practice. How do you serve your customers better? Practice.

Tony Lema, a great golfer who died tragically in the crash of a private plane in 1966, liked to tell people he didn't learn to play on a golf course. He maintained the shots that won tournaments for him were all forged on the range. He proved his point when, in 1964, he traveled to Britain to play in the Open Championship. Other commitments prevented him from arriving until two days before the tournament. The weather was appalling, with heavy rain and strong winds. Practice rounds were abbreviated and served little to prepare him for the championship. In spite of this, Lema was able to card a 75 on the first day in a torrential downpour; then, when the weather improved, he went on to victory. He didn't expect to find his game on the golf course—he brought it with him. Lema considered practice to be a lonely and often discouraging exercise, as did many other great players. All of them, however, also knew it to be the only way to acquire mastery of their art.

"About 50 percent of the population are sold on the idea that only horses work. The other 50 percent are inclined to go along with this proposition, only they never saw a horse."
Tony Lema

Perfect Practice

Given a fair degree of natural ability and reasonable physical fitness, there is almost no player who cannot become a low handicap golfer, or even a scratch player, if he is prepared to devote enough time and effort to the game. Does it matter how you practice as long as you do enough of it? Absolutely! Practice needs to be regulated and intelligent. Practicing faults until they are grooved and ingrained produces a poorer player, not a better one.

How Not to Practice

"A golf ball should never be hit without thought."
Gary Player

Not all types of practice are equal. For players at all levels, there is definitely a wrong way to practice. Let's let Tom describe an example:

See that gentleman driving up to the range? That's Mr. Healy. He plays nearly every day, and he always does exactly the same thing before he tees off. Watch this. He parks his cart by the very first spot, even though that patch is always a little soft and wet from the sprinklers. This area here is the best part of the range. The turf is firmer and gives you a better angle at the targets. Now he carries his huge tour bag over to a bag stand and pulls out—yes, of course, his driver. He tees the ball up—not much shoulder turn there—lunges at the first shot and tops it 50 yards. He grimaces and rolls his neck around. Could it be he's a bit stiff? Maybe he should have loosened up for a few moments. Now he tees up another one. That's a little better. It starts off dead straight but veers 50 yards to the right. Five more swings, all different.

Now he throws down his driver in disgust and reaches for the 5-iron. He hits another five or six shots without even looking up to see where the ball is going. (He must be working on feel.) His swing is flowing more freely, so he changes to the 3-iron and starts beating balls down the range. This reminds me of the last scene in an old Star Trek episode. When the helmsman asks Captain Kirk, "Where to, Captain?" Kirk points vaguely to the thousands of stars on the viewer and says, "Out there!" It's a great line if you're Captain Kirk, but not much good if you're trying to improve your game. Mr. Healy has his rhythm now, though. He's firing 3-iron shots off into the distance like an AK47; whoosh, whoosh, whoosh. Look, he has two in the air at the same time!

His supply of balls is almost exhausted. A couple of token wedge shots and he's nearly ready. He's trying a few putts, starting with three 40-footers. Well, the closest finishes some 10 feet away. He misses all three. (That'll do wonders for his confidence.) That's enough! Time to rush to the 1st tee. The memory of his poor drives on the range is fresh in his mind as he stares down the first fairway. Oh dear; he tops it and drives off miserably to a spot just a few yards from where he started. Another topped shot with his 3-wood and it looks like he's destined to make his customary seven on the first. Mr. Healy probably wonders why he bothers to hit all those practice shots. It never seems to work for him the way it should.

How Champions Practice

"I always practice as I intend to play."
Jack Nicklaus

Champions agree you must have a specific purpose in mind when you practice. Watch the great players on the range at any PGA Tournament, and you'll notice the difference between what they do and what you'll see the typical amateur doing at your local country club.

Hear Tom describe the right kind of practice—the practice of a champion:

There's one of the all-time greats walking casually toward the range with his caddie. He's here to practice for the Open. He pulls off his green sweater with the personal logo and goes through a short stretching routine.

Now he takes his sand wedge, picks a brown spot about 50 yards down range, and hits a couple of short pitches. Wait a moment; what's this? He thinned one! Well, it just goes to show you—it happens to the best of us! During the next 40 minutes he'll hit a few with each club in the bag. He won't hit one shot without aiming

71

and taking the same painstaking care with his set up and swing that he does in a tournament. He'll end the session by making a variety of special shots. First a hook, then a fade, then maybe a couple of real low ones and a couple even higher than normal. When he's satisfied that everything's in order, he'll head for the putting green, where he'll practice that famous stroke for about five minutes before teeing off. How do I know? I've seen him going through that same routine for decades, and it works.

Always Set a Specific Objective

"It you don't take it with you, you won't find it out there!"
Anonymous

Never begin a practice session without a clear idea of what you want to achieve before you leave. Never hit a shot without aiming at a specific target. That way you can gauge the degree of success of each shot. Stand far enough away from your range balls so you have a moment or two to stop and think between swings, and try to hit each practice shot exactly as you would in a major tournament.

Five Effective Ways to Improve the Quality of Your Practice

Playing round after round, without intervening practice sessions, does little to improve your game. You may have a few real life experiences that prove you should have taken a penalty shot and dropped out of trouble, instead of hitting it deeper into the woods, but that's learning the hard way. Here are five keys to quickly and dramatically improve your performance in your game, your business, and your personal life.

1. Record, Shoot Video, or Take Notes

Keep a record of your actions and the results they produce for you. By recording your performance, on videotape if you are golfing, or by using audio tape or notes if you are at work, you can start to look for helpful or harmful patterns.

How many putts a round do you average? Do you hit all your drives in the right rough or are most of your bad shots pulled? What percentage of prospects do you close?

This type of self-evaluation will indicate clearly to you the areas most urgently in need of improvement. As you collect this valuable information, continue to take notes, writing down both the problem and solution. Chart your progress and monitor your results frequently, even daily.

In the heat of battle, it is amazing how even the most proficient among us tends to forget the simplest of fundamentals, like keeping our heads still, taking the club head away slowly, or remembering to ask for a sale. Brief notes in a diary, on scraps of paper, or even on table napkins have provided a written reminder of a key fundamental and resulted in victory in many a tournament. For some champions, the secret is contained in a single word or phrase taped inside their locker door.

When Britain's Tony Jacklin arrived at his locker on the final day of the 1970 U.S. Open Championship, he found his good friend Tom Weiskopf had taped a message to the door. The message was short and sweet. There were only two words: "Tempo, Jacko."

Now who would have thought the reigning British Open Champion, a man going into the final round with one of the biggest leads in U.S. Open history, would need such basic advice? As it happened, Jacklin gave much of the credit for his victory to those two little words. The difficult Hazeltine National course made some of the big name players of the day pay a severe toll. Dave Hill, who finished second, said, "All this course lacks is 80 acres of corn and some cows." Well, in spite of Hill's lack of affection for the venue, Jacklin maintained a smooth tempo and became the first Briton to win the U.S. Open since Ted Ray in 1920, and by seven shots, the second largest margin in history. Weiskopf's little reminder helped him achieve his victory.

As you know, we may not always need to be told, but we do need to be reminded from time to time.

2. Take Lessons, Read Books, Attend Clinics

Self-monitoring is just fine if you can do it, but most of us need some outside help in order to achieve faster and more lasting results with our games. The first and most obvious road to golfing success is to find the best teaching pro in town and book a series of personal lessons. Whatever it costs, pay it! All those years of teaching experience and firsthand knowledge are available to help you unleash your own potential ability.

If time or money does not permit this form of personal enlightenment, try group lessons or a few days at a golf school, where you can get a comprehensive amount of instruction in a short time. Jimmy Ballard's school at the Palm Beach Polo Club is one of the finest in the East, while the Golf University in San Diego is one of the best on the West Coast.

The most convenient way to improve your game is by reading. Although this method does not provide the real life feedback you enjoy when you actually perform, the information you find in books can often make a big difference in your game. After reading several hundred golf books, I still pick up new tips, ideas, and drills, and even refresh fundamental ideas, each and every time I bury my nose in a good instructional volume. How many of today's golfers picked up *Golf My Way* by Jack Nicklaus and were inspired and affected as they read it? I know I was. It is said that Nick Faldo took up golf after watching the Masters on television and picking up a copy of Jack's book. How many senior golfers grew up within easy reach of Tommy Armour's *How to Play Your Best Golf All the Time* or Ben Hogan's *The Five Modern Fundamentals of Golf*?

Never underestimate the power of the written word to improve your putting, your swing, or your life. Although it isn't a good idea to be constantly tinkering and fiddling with your basic game, don't be afraid of looking for valuable knowledge in the pages of a book.

3. Find a Mentor

> "We all continue to learn; if we didn't we would be in trouble. I've learned an awful lot from playing with great golfers, with the exposure to them and talking with them."
> Jack Nicklaus

Since it is perfect practice that makes perfect, and not just practice, we must decide by whose standards we are going to define perfection. Seek out a coach and mentor, and accept his advice on the steps needed to achieve perfection. A gaggle of pros follow coaches like Jimmy Ballard and David Leadbetter. This group includes players like Nick Faldo, Nick Price, Sandy Lyle, and Johnny Miller. Arnie had in his father, Deacon Palmer, a person whose knowledge of his swing he could trust and on whose help he could rely to improve, repair, and revamp his game as necessary.

Nicklaus' mentor and coach was Jack Grout, the local professional at the country club in Ohio, near Nicklaus' home. At the beginning of each new golf season, Jack would go to Grout and say,

"I'd like to take up golf. Show me how to hold the club, address the ball, and swing the club." This not only demonstrates the value of having a sound instructor, but also the value of going back to the basics of your craft, whatever it may be. I can't overstress the importance of a yearly review of your techniques and strategies with someone who both knows and cares about the desired outcome. Regardless of your profession, it is easy to slip into bad habits that inhibit your progress. By allowing someone knowledgeable to critique your performance, you can often uncover basic flaws that are costing you strokes, sales, time, money, and customers.

4. Mirroring

Alternatively, we can find another golfer whose swing or method we can attempt to emulate in the hope of achieving similar results. Greg Norman is an excellent example of this technique. He modeled his swing and many of his mannerisms after Jack Nicklaus, and it has paid off handsomely for him.

Ben Hogan, who dropped out of school prior to graduation, made up for his lack of education by being a voracious reader and a keen observer. He studied the golf swing as no one had done before. He viewed newsreel films of the best players to modify his hip action. He picked up his club head waggle from U.S. Open winner Johnny Revolta, and worked with his swing plane night after night in the bathroom mirrors of his hotel room. Other players hated to room next to him because of the incessant thump of golf balls hitting the baseboard as he practiced his putting stroke at all hours of the day and night.

When mirroring a golfer, it pays to find a player of similar age, height and build, making it easier to copy his swing.

5. Practice Role-playing

"When I was a little kid, I would pretend I had a shot to win
the Masters or the Open, to make me try my best."
Hale Irwin

The practice range is the only place you can find your faults and work at correcting them without it costing you strokes or money. The same is basically true of public speaking, selling, or almost anything you can think of. Practice allows you to record, film, examine, and critique your own performance in a positive way to bring about change for the better. That's why role-playing is such an important part of learning. A delightful TV ad depicts a teenager golfing alone among the evening sprinklers. He addresses his ball, takes a last glance at the green, and says something like, "He needs a birdie on this one to beat Freddie." Then he hits a shot that comes to rest a few feet from the flag. Picking up his bag, he adds, "It looks like we have a new PGA champion!"

I'm sure you've played similar mind games, especially if you've been playing golf since childhood. Perhaps you've played two balls in practice rounds—one for you and one for Nicklaus. You may even have played tournament rounds in your head. Tom Watson said, after winning the 1977 British Open at Turnberry in an historic battle with Jack Nicklaus, that he played well because he had done it many times before. When reporters questioned this, he went on to explain that he had, on many occasions during practice rounds, role-played a one-on-one confrontation with Nicklaus. As a result, he was not intimidated by the situation when it finally arose in real life.

A Champion's Secret

> *"I think anyone can do anything he wants to, if he's willing to*
> *study or work hard enough."*
> Ben Hogan

No matter which field of endeavor we contemplate, it is clear that great champions reach the pinnacle of success largely as the result of practice. It is equally apparent that true champions have no time for complacency once they have risen to the highest level. If they want to stay on top, they know the time will never come when they can cut back the quantity, quality, and intensity of their training.

At the peak of his career, after shooting a blistering 64 in pouring rain, Hogan signed his card and headed for the range. Drenched to the skin, he returned to the clubhouse an hour later. Fellow Texan Jimmy Demaret asked Hogan why he felt the need to practice after such a perfect round. Hogan replied, in typical fashion, "I practiced because I want to keep this form up tomorrow if I can."

Hogan definitely believed that the knowledge of the golf swing he acquired over the years allowed him to remain successful longer. While other players would have hot streaks that lasted a couple of years until the "wheels fell off," Hogan knew his streak would continue because he had a clear understanding of every minute detail of his own swing. Because of this, he could quickly pinpoint mistakes and avoid going into a slump. Others with less insight found when their games went bad that their desperate attempts to fix the problems often wound up doing irreparable damage to their swings or their confidence.

Instant Replay

"I always achieve my most productive practice right after a round. Then, the mistakes are fresh in my mind, and I can go to the practice tee and work specifically on those mistakes."
Jack Nicklaus

It is a trait of champions to employ the "instant reply mode" after every round. What shots were executed well, and what shots were executed badly? What were the physical errors and the mental errors? How and where could improvements be made?

Spend five minutes each and every day reflecting on your performance. Pat yourself on the back for your accomplishments, but don't fail to clearly analyze your mistakes and mentally rectify them before you start the next day. Decide what strategies you can use tomorrow that will be more effective. Commit to more preparation.

Winning Demands Self-discipline

"The only way one can become proficient at anything is self-discipline and dedication."
Byron Nelson

Becoming a champion in any field demands a great deal of self-discipline and sacrifice. Are you willing to pay the price? If you are, your chances of success are extremely high. If you want to hit better trap shots, stay in the practice bunker and hit sand shots until you hole one; then you can go get something to eat. That's what Gary Player did as a youngster, and it was often dark when he finally holed one. If you want to hit better iron shots, practice till you hands bleed. That's what Lee Trevino did. There is no substitute for the repetition of good, solid fundamentals to ensure success in any endeavor. Don't waste too much of your valuable time looking for short cuts. You may lose your way.

Setting a Practice Schedule

"I believe the one factor that has helped me most in achieving success has been self-discipline. Believe me, without self-discipline it is hard to get yourself up at 6 a.m., practice many long, hard hours, and work until 11 at night. The main motivation for keeping such a schedule was my long-range goal: to become the best golfer in the world."

Lee Trevino

Humans are great creatures of habit. It may take us a long time to acquire habits, but it is hard to break them once we do! A key trait of champions is developing the habit of practice.

The problem may be actually finding the time to do what you know must be done in order to improve. This, once again, is a question of self-discipline. You and you alone decide how you will spend your time each day. Top pros have massive demands on their time, from business interests to writers, fans, sponsors, and charity organizations. You can be sure, however, that Greg Norman still sets aside adequate time to practice. He does this by deciding that, at a specific time, nothing is going to prevent him from working. Yes, he has phone calls to return, people to see, and things to do, but they must wait for an hour while he practices his craft.

Set up a training schedule for yourself that will allow you to put in enough practice to reach the goals you have set. Have the self-discipline to stick to that schedule. Cheating on your training is cheating on yourself. The first time you find a reason not to practice makes the second time a whole lot easier. Make training and improvement a daily part of your routine. Make self-improvement a habit you can't break, no matter how young, old, or successful you already are. Get the edge on others whose self-discipline and determination don't match yours!

——T hat was a fine practice session, Sir. You hit a few with every club in the bag, and your chipping and putting were excellent. You're looking really smooth. We'd better head for the 1st tee now. It's almost time.

Swing Thoughts

- Great shots and great victories are the result of great preparation and practice.

- Practice makes you lucky.

- Practice must always have a specific objective.

- Practice can be enhanced in five ways:

    1. Through videotapes, audio tapes and notes.
    2. By lessons, clinics, seminars, and reading.
    3. By mentors.
    4. By mirroring.
    5. By role-playing.

- Champions never stop practicing, even when they reach the top.

- Champions evaluate their performance daily and resolve to improve in specific areas immediately.

- Practice demands self-discipline and time management. Champions master both.

Back in the Clubhouse

We have moved from an era of manpower to an era of mind power. Today, the chief sources of value in our society are knowledge and the ability to apply that knowledge in a timely fashion. In the Information

Age, knowledge is king, and those people who develop the ability to continuously acquire new and better forms of knowledge will be the movers and shakers in our society for the indefinite future.

When you practice the techniques for continuous learning, when you join the learning revolution; you will unlock the incredible powers of your mind. You will become a master of your fate rather than a victim of circumstance. You will take complete control of your present and future destiny so that you can accomplish and achieve anything you want in life.

Knowledge is doubling every two to three years in almost every occupation and profession, including yours. This means that your knowledge must double every two to three years for you to just stay even. People who are not aggressively and continuously upgrading their knowledge and skills are not staying in the same place. They are falling behind. You see this manifested all over the place by massive layoffs, declining wages, and growing insecurity in the workforce. You see it in the increasing bewilderment and despair on the part of people who are being displaced from low-skill jobs that have either moved overseas or disappeared altogether. We are in the midst of a societal revolution, where unionized industrial workers are becoming a smaller percentage of our workforce each year.

Today, with workforce requirements changing so rapidly, you must continually ask yourself, "What is my next job going to be?" You must also ask yourself on a regular basis, "What is my next career going to be?"

Imagine for a moment that your entire company or industry vanished overnight and you had to start all over in an entirely new business doing an entirely different job. What would it be? And don't think this question is speculative or that it applies to someone else. It is a question you will probably have to deal with, perhaps far sooner than you expect. In thinking about your new job and your new career, here is the most important question of all: "What do I have to be absolutely, positively excellent at doing in order to earn an excellent living in my new job and my new career?"

The answer to almost every question and the solution to almost every problem in the world of work is to learn and practice something new. When you learn how to use the incredible power of your brain to absorb and apply new ideas and information, you will be able to lead the field and rise to the top of any profession.

Here's another question for you: What is your most valuable asset? In terms of cash flow, what is the most valuable thing you have? Well, unless you are very rich or have a family trust account, your most valuable asset is your earning ability. It is your ability to earn money. It is your ability to apply your knowledge and skill in a timely fashion to get results for which others will pay.

All your education, knowledge, experience, reading, training, and work has contributed to building up your earning ability. According to research, the so-called "rich" in America and other countries are almost invariably people who started from common beginnings, often with great disadvantages, and then overcame those circumstances by investing an enormous amount of time and effort in developing their earning ability. And you can do the same thing.

Management consultant Peter Drucker says that the truly educated person today is a person who has learned how to learn continuously throughout life. Tom Peters says that continuous learning may be the only real source of sustainable competitive advantage for individuals and corporations. And Peter Senge, who wrote *Fifth Discipline*, says that only learning organizations, those organizations that are capable of taking in new information, adapting it, and using it faster than their competitors, will survive in the fast-changing, competitive world of tomorrow.

The more you know, the better you will be at solving problems and getting results for which people will pay you. The more you know, the more freedom and opportunity you have. And the more and faster you learn, the more rapidly you move upward and onward in your career and in every other area of your life.

Between where you are and where you want to go, there is almost always a gap, and in almost every case, you will find that you can bridge this gap with knowledge and skills. In order to get from where you are to your goals, you have to learn and practice something new and different. You have to learn new skills and abilities. You have to learn new attitudes and methods. You have to learn new techniques and practices. If you want to be a better parent, you must learn and practice better parenting skills.

If you want to be a better spouse, you must study and practice relationship skills. If you want to earn more money, you have to determine what people will pay more money for, and then get busy learning and practicing those behaviors.

Specific knowledge and specific skills will become obsolete with the passing of time, but continuous learning is a practice that will keep you on the cutting edge all the days of your life. The people who join the learning revolution, like those people who first learned how to operate computers, will be able to earn more in one or two years of work than the average person earns in perhaps five or 10 years.

By joining the learning revolution, you will enhance every area of your life. You will be able to help your spouse and your children unlock and realize more of their individual potential. You will be a better friend in helping your friends use more of their abilities. And you will be a better manager, developing the skills that will enable you to get far more out of yourself and other people than ever before.

Questions to Ponder

- Do you read more than one book each month in an area that will increase your business effectiveness?

- Do you attend three or more seminars each year related to your field?

- Do you constantly seek quality, concentrated information from recognized experts about what's going on in your industry?

- Do you encourage your staff to continue the learning process at all times?

This 1st hole's a slight dogleg right, par four, playing right at 382 yards today, Sir. This one's not as famous as some of the other holes, but it's a good, fair starting hole—not too long, not too much trouble, except on the right. Keep your drive down the left side of the fairway and you'll have a much better angle to the flag. A solid drive will leave you with only a 7- or 8-iron, and you'll have a good chance for a birdie. Now, Sir, just relax and show me a nice, smooth swing . . . That one's a little right of perfect, but it's a good drive anyway. You'll have about 140 yards from there.

Yes, the other guys do look sharp, don't they, Sir? But you don't have to play second fiddle to anyone in that respect; you look pretty good yourself . . . Do champions work hard to build a good image? They sure do!

BUILDING A CHAMPIONSHIP IMAGE

The Importance of Perception

"I think golfers who look like they got dressed in the dark should be penalized two strokes each for offending the public."
Doug Sanders

Right or wrong, we are a society that tends to judge a book by its cover far more readily than by its contents. Being a true champion involves more than just playing great golf, winning tournaments, and amassing wealth. Champions have a responsibility to present and maintain a good image and to be a positive role model for others. It is necessary for them to be friendly and gracious to the fans, caddies, marshals, workers, and their peers who have all contributed to their success. In addition to playing like champions, they must look like champions and act like champions, both on and off the course, if they expect to be considered *true* champions.

Sir Walter

Walter Hagen clearly understood the importance of image. He began his career as a professional golfer in the days when pros were not even allowed to set foot in the clubhouse. Unimpressed by the dismal accommodations made available to the pros and tired of being treated like a

85

second-class citizen, he decided to demonstrate his dissatisfaction publicly. He started showing up for tournaments in a huge, chauffeur-driven limousine. He had his lunch served, complete with appropriate fine wines, in his car, which was conspicuously parked were everyone could see him. After lunch, he would change from his formal clothes into impeccable golfing attire and go to work. He waltzed around every course he played as if he owned the club, and the galleries loved him for it. Many people credit Hagen with raising the golf pro from the rank of common laborer to that of the professional, on equal terms with doctors, attorneys, and businessmen. It was shortly after he achieved the status of a champion that country clubs gradually opened their doors to professional golfers, allowing them to use the locker facilities and other areas of the clubhouse previously reserved exclusively for members.

By the mid-1920s, Hagen was making more money than home-run king Babe Ruth, most of it in payment for the 100 or so exhibition matches he played each year. He liked to say, "I don't want to be a millionaire, just live like one," and he was as good as his word. After winning a tournament in Canada and receiving the unheard of amount of $3,000, Hagen threw an all-night party at his hotel, running up a tab up of $3,400. A notorious partygoer and playboy, it was not unusual for him to appear on the tee dressed in the tuxedo he had presumably worn at the previous night's festivities and change into his golfing attire as he prepared to play the first hole. Sometimes his ruffled tux suggested he had come straight from a wild party, when he had actually slept soundly in his room all night. While it is certainly true that he enjoyed life, many of his antics were pure showmanship. Hagen often poured his drink into a nearby plant, maintaining his public persona as a party animal without actually having much to drink. It was all part of his image.

Hagen's wonderful showmanship was not confined to his off-course activities. On the final hole of the 1919 U.S. Open, played at the Brae Burn Club in Newton, Massachusetts, Hagen needed to hole an 8-foot putt to force an 18-hole playoff the next day with Mike Brady. Upon reaching the green, Hagen held up play while he sent a marshal into the clubhouse to fetch Brady, so he could watch the putt go in. He made it, of course!

That night, Hagen held a huge, and somewhat premature, victory party at his hotel. As the party continued past midnight and into the early hours, one of Hagen's guests sensibly pointed out that his opponent for the next day's playoff had been in bed for several hours. "Yes," said Hagen, "but you can bet he isn't sleeping." The next day Hagen won the head-to-head contest by one shot.

Hagen counted among his friends many sporting giants of the era like Babe Ruth, with whom he had much in common. He was just as comfortable in the company of presidents and kings as he was among the fans and his fellow players. He developed a huge circle of friends in high places, including the Prince of Wales and President Warren G. Harding. Habitually late for appointments, Hagen complained to President Harding that he was always getting speeding tickets trying to make up for lost time on the road. Harding solved Sir Walter's problem by appointing him as a secret service agent, complete with official badge, in case anyone ever asked to see it.

By being part showman, part actor, and part athlete, and by living life on his own terms and treating everyone he met with the same warmth, Hagen was the original colorful player on tour. He blazed a trail for others, like Jimmy Demaret, Tony Lema, Doug Sanders, and Payne Stewart, to assume the mantle in their turn.

The winner of 11 "majors" in his career, Hagen was surpassed in this respect only by Nicklaus and Bobby Jones.

Remaking the Golden Bear

Although Jack Nicklaus wasted no time proving himself to be the world's best golfer, he was not immediately accepted by the golfing public. In spite of always being pleasant and polite with fans and fellow competitors, his image was killing him. When he joined the tour as a youngster, he was overweight, talked in a squeaky voice, and had a haircut like a marine corps recruit. On the other hand, the idol of the fans, Arnold Palmer, was articulate in a folksy way, handsome, well-dressed, and very charismatic.

Nicklaus, publicly gracious but privately distressed by the attitude of the fans, did what any champion would do. Rather than crying about being misunderstood, he set out to change his image. Today he is the consummate champion, both on and off the course. What effect did this image adjustment have on his career? It quickly won him favor with golf fans and, in the long term, helped him become one of the richest athletes in the world.

As he moves gracefully into his 70s, and occasionally scores lower than his age, Arnold Palmer is also among the highest paid athletes. Although he hasn't won on the PGA Tour since 1973, his residual income is larger than that of Nicklaus. On the one hand, we have the most naturally charismatic of players, with an image 10 times larger than life; on the other hand is someone with the intelligence and determination to build and redefine his image. Both great champions demonstrate the importance of image, whether you start out with it or find it along the way.

You *can* improve your image. Nicklaus smoked in the early '60s, but stopped after seeing himself on film, playing Palmer in the play-off for the 1962 U.S. Open. As he watched himself lining up a putt with a cigarette dangling from the corner of his mouth, he decided that it was about the ugliest thing he had ever seen. He never smoked on the course again. Another change occurred toward the end of the '60s, when he decided to shed almost 50 pounds from his bulky 230-pound frame. Having made the decision, before the diet had even begun, he ordered new clothes to fit his target waistline. Sure enough, after a few months his new clothes were a perfect fit for a brand new, 180-pound Nicklaus.

Even allowing his blonde hair to grow longer helped win the crowds over to him. To them he was Fat Jack, a spoiled kid from Columbus with a squeaky, soprano voice, who was crashing King Arnie's party. Now he was trim and fit, his hair and clothes were in style, and he displayed a total respect for the game and all who played it. In this way, he demonstrated not only his commitment to being a better role model, but also his excellent self-discipline. The adjustments to his image helped Jack became the undisputed top dog of the links, a position he would maintain for two more decades.

The Norman Image

In the late '70s, at a British golf club where a major tournament was scheduled to take place later in the week, rising star Greg Norman's Jaguar XJ6 pulled into the slot next to mine. He opened the trunk to reveal a set of clubs and a two-level shoe rack. The shoes were in color combinations ranging from plain black to white with lime green trim. Norman put his right foot on the rear bumper and hitched up his pants to coordinate his shoes with his slacks and socks. He selected a white pair with canary yellow trim that were exactly right. If you think that may be carrying style to the extreme, bear in mind that this incident occurred long before Norman became the No. 1 player in the world. When he did so, his well-chosen, eye-catching outfits were a perfect match for his masculine good looks and bold playing style.

Norman also had the good fortune to acquire a memorable nickname early in his career. After a fine performance in the second round of the Masters, he was being interviewed in the press tent and mentioned that he loved to fish for sharks in his native Australia. The press corps just loved it. The next day the *Augusta Chronicle* ran a banner headline reading, "Great white shark near Masters lead." Norman loved it, too, and the name stuck, adding to his image as a strong, aggressive man's man.

Some great players, like Tom Kite, one of the all-time leaders on the money list, don't make nearly as much income off the course as others because of perception and image. Although Kite is one of the nicest men in the world, he has failed to make the most of his talents. Others, like Scott Simpson and two-time Open champion Andy North, never reached their full potential as marketable properties.

On the other hand, Tony Jacklin, winner of one British Open and one U.S. Open, parlayed his two major victories into something approaching godlike status in Europe, and is still well known in the United States. After his success as a player had begun to wane, this popular personality led the European Ryder Cup team to its first victory against the American team in almost 40 years, and his star began to rise all over again.

Laura Baugh turned a U.S. Women's Amateur title, won at age 16, into a very lucrative, multi-million dollar golfing career. She did this by capitalizing on her pert good looks and an effervescent, college cheerleader personality, and in spite of *never* winning an LPGA tournament in her 20 years on tour. Now that's the value of developing a positive image at its most powerful!

Standing Out from the Crowd

Cleveland attorney Mark McCormack did a fabulous job of building his clients, Palmer, Player, and Nicklaus, into the "Big Three." Although many other great players were still playing on the tour, including Hogan and Snead, McCormack helped each of his clients develop a unique and powerful superstar image, en route to building his own global sports empire. Nicklaus became the Golden Bear, Palmer the working man's hero, and Player the Black Knight. Player originally wore white outfits to reflect the sun and keep cooler. When he changed to all black, he told reporters he did it to absorb the sun's energy, but the truth of the matter was that it made him easily identifiable, even at a distance. It became his trademark.

Hats

Hogan always wore a flat, white hat pulled down low over his hawk-like eyes, and it suited him perfectly. Gardner Dickinson modeled himself on Hogan, even to the extent of affecting the same style of headwear. At a casual glance, he could be mistaken for his idol. Perhaps he wore similar headgear just in case some of Hogan's magic rubbed off on them! Snead was recognizable in his later years for his straw fishing hat, and Norman started a new trend on tour by wearing a low-crowned, cowboy-style hat. For each of them, the hat became an integral part of their persona.

The Knickers

Before his tragic death in a plane crash, Payne Stewart was one of the most colorful players on tour. His 1920s-style cap and knickers made him stand out among an army of PGA clones. He adopted the style in the early '80s, after walking onto the practice tee one morning and finding six other players beating balls, all dressed exactly as he was, in white shoes, red golf slacks, and white shirts. Stewart's father, a furniture salesman, gave him this advice: "Always stand out from the crowd. That way people will remember you." With that in mind, Stewart switched to cap and knickers, sometimes called plus-twos. He was quickly rewarded with a lucrative contract from the National Football League, which required him to wear the colors of the NFL team most popular in the area currently being visited by the tour. More lucrative opportunities came his way because he stood out from the other players. Stewart ignored jibes from his fellow pros and maintained the outfits were cooler and more comfortable to wear than regular golf slacks. They were certainly "cool" for him and for the legion of fans that will always remember him as much for the way he dressed as for his outstanding play, humor, and competitive personality.

What's in a Name?

Long before Earl Woods nicknamed his son "Tiger" after an army buddy in Southeast Asia (replacing his more cumbersome given name of Eldrick), there was another fine young amateur golfer on the West Coast named Miller. When the handsome, blonde California kid turned pro, he was instantly an agent's dream, but manager Ed Barner had Miller change his name from John to the more "apple pie" sounding Johnny. Although this was undoubtedly a good move in a promotional sense, Miller went along with it grudgingly. If you come across an early autograph, you will see he used to sign himself John "ny" Miller.

Gene Sarazen also changed his name, albeit a little more dramatically. He was born Eugene Saraceni, but when he saw his name in the paper after winning a local tournament, he decided it was a great name for a musician, but a lousy name for a golfer. After picking the name Gene Sarazen from the list he had made for himself, he went directly to the phone book. He wanted to make sure he would be the only one in it with that name. He was determined to be an "original."

The Right Stuff

Winning a golf tournament or prevailing over your competitor to nail down a business contract is not, by itself, enough to ensure long-term success. You must also build and preserve your image. In our culture, perception becomes reality, and we expect positive facial expressions, gestures, comments, and attitude from our heroes. Without these attributes, the champion will never enjoy 100 percent support from spectators, sponsors, and his peers *on* the course and, therefore, cannot make the most of his talents *off* the course. The intangible extra energy this positive support generates at golf tournaments is a significant factor in the lives of champions and should not be minimized. If you never sensed the positive energy flowing from Arnie's Army into their hero as he mounted one of his famous charges, you never had the good fortune to see him play.

Y ou played a fine iron shot to be closest to the hole, but be careful, Sir. These greens are very slick, and your putt's just a little downhill . . . Good try! This group holes out everything, so tap it in . . . That's a solid par. The next tee's over this way. These gents want to hit a few practice putts; they'll catch up with us.

The 2nd's a straightaway par five, just 527 yards. Although it's out of bounds all down the right side, it's a great birdie chance. If you catch a good tee shot, you can carry that huge trap that crosses the fairway 30 yards short of the green and get home in two. Give it a good rip, Sir. Your natural draw will keep you away from those fairway bunkers and the out of bounds . . . Good shot! You can't hit it any better than that. You can get home easily from there . . . What's that, Sir? You wonder why champions become such heroes. Well, it's all a question of "people relations."

People Relations

Image can make a substantial difference, and as they say, you only get one chance to make a good first impression. However, fancy clothes and little name tricks aren't worth a hill of beans unless you have the personality to back them up.

Champions always respect the people that provide them with their livelihood. Pro golfers realize that without the fans there would be no tour. Although Ben Hogan was never much of a talker, he had an abiding love for the fans, especially after the pouring out of public support for him after his accident. At the U.S. Open one year, he commented, "I think these are the greatest fans in the world. They come out here, park a long way away, and walk for hours in the hot sun, being pushed and shoved by marshals, just for a glimpse of the players. What other fans would do that?" These words, coming as they did from a champion who said very little, endeared him to everyone who heard them.

When it comes to building rapport with the audience, there's no one like Arnie. While it took Hogan quite a while to become cherished by the fans, Palmer was the object of their affection almost as soon as he appeared in the public eye. Early in his career, he learned the value of getting the gallery on his side. It was fun to watch him working the crowd. People he stopped to chat with wouldn't trade a few words from Arnie for $1,000, and that was a great deal of money back in the early '60s. If he hit his ball into the gallery, he would always seek out the bruised spectator and reward him with a smile and an apology. When he holed a birdie putt or chipped in from the fringe, he would throw the ball to someone in the crowd, not just after the 18th hole, but all the way around the golf course. I can't remember him ever losing a ball in the rough. There were always dozens of fans eager to find it and lead him to it. When he hit it off line, the ball had an alarming tendency to find its way back into play. Arnie never approved or encouraged such "crowd participation," but the crowd loved him so much it happened anyway. He gave them excitement and pleasure, and they just wanted to help in any way they could. He was, after all, one of them.

What Happened?

In the late 1960s, Palmer was playing in the Byron Nelson Classic at the Preston Trail Country Club outside Dallas. At one of the par three holes, Arnie played a wonderful shot. The ball landed no more than a foot short of the hole and hopped over the left edge, missing the flagstick by a fraction. The second bounce was about three feet beyond the hole, after which the ball spun back, rolling over the other lip of the cup and almost going in again. It finally came to rest less than two feet away. The roar from his Army was prolonged and ecstatic. This was what they had come to see, the stuff of which dreams are made. Palmer, of course, saw the shot pretty well from the tee, but as he strode toward the green between the packed fans, he stopped and asked a delighted spectator what had happened. The spectator babbled with joy as he described to Arnie how he had almost made a hole-in-one twice with the same shot. Palmer grinned hugely, thanked the man and moved on. Before reaching the green and receiving yet another deafening ovation, he stopped two more times, asking the same question and rehearing the same account each time. They loved it, and he clearly enjoyed it just as much as they.

A Cry for Help

At the 1962 Colonial National Invitational in Fort Worth, Texas, Arnie was involved in a tough 18-hole playoff. On the 9th hole, Arnie was just off the green and faced a tough chip to get up and down, save par, and protect his one-stroke lead. Just as he was ready to play, a small boy in the gallery broke the total silence by speaking to his mother. Palmer backed off, looked around toward the boy, and broke into a smile. The rest of the gallery stared coldly at the woman and made loud "shushing" sounds. As Arnie addressed the ball again, the embarrassed mother started to scold her son. Just as he was about to play, the child started to cry as a result of the scolding. Arnie backed off once more, looked around, and started to chuckle. This time, adjusting to their hero's mood, the crowd laughed with him.

The child calmed down and Arnie returned to business. Before he could complete his shot, however, he heard choking sounds behind him and a muffled cry as if for help. He turned to see the young boy's face becoming bright red. The desperate mother had her hand clamped viselike over his nose and mouth! Arnie broke into his famous smile yet again, then walked over and patted the boy on the head, saying to his mother, "Hey, don't choke him. This isn't really all that important." The entire gallery laughed aloud. The boy was so happy at being able to breathe again that he remained quiet as Arnie marched back to his ball for the fourth time, chipped to within a few feet, made his par, and went on to win the playoff.

These incidents, just two of many, are perfect examples that demonstrate what a people's champion Arnold Palmer was and still is. I never saw him decline to sign an autograph or talk to a fan. He did it for me recently on the practice putting green at the Silverado Country Club in the Napa Valley, where he was preparing to play in the Transamerica Championship.

Who will ever forget the image of him standing on the stone bridge on the 18th at St. Andrews during the 1995 Open Championship? As he waved goodbye to us that day, on his so-called "farewell tour," what memories must have crowded through his mind, and what glorious memories we retain of him. He has always given back double to the people who have revered him and made him what he is, and they love him for that even more than for the entertainment he has given them for decades. Young or old, big shot or bag boy, Arnie knew instinctively that there are no *little* people. We all have hopes and dreams and deserve to be treated with equal respect and dignity.

I think you can get home with a 5-wood from here, Sir. Just a touch of draw will keep it away from the road. The wind's blowing right to left, so don't overdo it! . . . That's fine. It's just short, but you'll have an easy chip from there! . . . Ooh-ee! I thought for a moment that was going in. Still, that's an excellent birdie. The 3rd tee is just across the road—over that way, Sir.

Swing Thoughts

- Champions work hard to cultivate their images, and this pays great rewards.

- Champions look good, dress well, and play the part.

- Champions usually have a trademark they develop and cultivate that causes them to stand out from others.

- Champions are attentive to the "little things" that can make a more positive impression.

- Champions make those around them feel good about themselves.

Back in the Clubhouse

Have you noticed that some people receive more promotions and greater pay than their colleagues do, even though they are apparently not as competent or as capable as their colleagues are? This doesn't seem fair. Why should some people get ahead when others who seem to be working far harder, for even longer hours, get passed over for promotion and the additional rewards that go with it?

The fact is, to be a great success, it is important not only to be good at what you do, but also to be perceived as being good at what you do. Human beings are creatures of perception. It is not what we see, but what we think we see that determines how we think and act.

If your coworker is perceived as being more promotable than you are, for whatever reason, then it is very likely your coworker will get additional responsibilities and more money, even though you know you could do a better job if given the chance.

Fortunately, however, there are several things you can do to increase your visibility and accelerate the speed at which you move ahead in your career.

The starting point in attaining high visibility is to develop competence. Determine which parts of your job are most important to your boss and to your company, and then make the decision to become very good in those areas. Becoming good at what you do should be the foundation of your strategy for gaining higher visibility and rapid advancement in your career.

Employers everywhere are looking for men and women of action, people who will get in there and get the job done right as soon as possible. When you develop a reputation for competence and capability, you become more visible to the key people in your working environment.

Excellence at what you do is essential, but it's not enough. There are additional elements that go into the perception others have of you. And one of the most important elements is your overall image, from head to toe. How you appear to others makes a real difference.

A recent survey of personnel executives found that the decision to hire or not to hire is made in the first 30 seconds. Many people believe that the decision to accept or reject a job candidate is actually made in the first four seconds. Many capable people are disqualified from job opportunities because they do not look the part.

There are many elements of your life over which you have no control and which you cannot choose. But your dress and grooming are totally a matter of personal preference. Through your choice of clothes, your grooming, and your overall appearance, you deliberately make a statement about the kind of person you are. The way you look on the outside is a representation of the way you see yourself on the inside. If you have a positive, professional self-image, you will take pains to make your external appearance consistent with it.

It's a good idea to dress the way the senior people in your company dress. Dress for the position two jobs above your own. Since people judge you largely by the way you look on the outside, be sure to look thoroughly professional. Consequently, the perception of the people who can help you in your career will be positive. They will open doors for you in ways you cannot now imagine.

Another powerful way to increase your visibility is to join professional associations related to your business or field. Begin by attending meetings as a guest to carefully assess whether or not a professional association can be of value to you. Determine if the members are the kind of people you would like to know and if they are well-established in their careers. Then, if you have decided that becoming known to the key people in this association can advance your career, take out a membership and get involved.

Most people who join a club or an association do little more than attend the regular meetings. For some reason, they are too busy to assist with the various things that need to get done. This is not for you. Your job is to pick a key committee and volunteer for service. Find out which committee seems to be the most active and the most influential in that organization, and then step up to the plate. Volunteer your time, expertise, and energy—and get busy. Attend every meeting. Take careful notes. Ask for assignments, and complete them on time and in an excellent fashion.

In so doing, you have an opportunity to perform for key people in your profession in a non-threatening environment. You give them a chance to see what you can do and what kind of a person you are. You expand your sphere of valuable contacts in one of the most effective ways possible in America today. The people you get to know on these committees can be extremely helpful to you in your career.

Also, join a well-known charitable organization in your community, such as the United Way, and become active by donating your services to its annual fund-raising programs. You may not have a fortune to give away now, but you do have time, and your willingness to give of yourself will soon be noticed by the community leaders.

Many men and women with limited contacts and limited resources have risen to positions of great prominence as the result of getting to know the key leaders in their community's charitable organizations and in their professional associations.

Some years ago, I joined a statewide chamber of commerce and volunteered to work on its Economic Education Committee. As usual, very few of the other members contributed any time to the committee, so there was always lots of work for those people who were willing to put in the effort. Within one year, I was speaking at the annual convention for this organization. The audience was comprised of some of the most influential business executives in the state. The following year, I was invited to give a key briefing to the governor at the state capitol. I became so well-known in the business community that six months later I was offered a position to run a new company at triple my former salary—all from joining the chamber of commerce and becoming known to the other members!

About three years later, I volunteered to work with the United Way and had a very similar experience. In fact, my whole business life was changed because of my involvement in helping that charitable organization in its annual fund-raising drive.

It's amazing how far and how fast you will go when you begin to give your time and energy to others on a volunteer basis. It's one of the fastest ways up the ladder of success in America.

There are many other things you can do to increase your visibility—things that don't occur to most people. As I mentioned earlier, managers place very high value on a person who can set priorities and move quickly to get the job finished. Dependability in job completion is one of the most valued traits in the workforce. When your employer can hand you a job and then walk away and not worry about it, you have moved yourself onto the fast track, and your subsequent promotion and pay are virtually guaranteed.

Another way to increase your visibility is to continually upgrade your work-related skills and to make sure your superiors know about it. Look for courses you can take to improve at your job, and discuss them with your boss. Ask him or her if your company will pay for the courses, but make it clear you're going to take them regardless.

A young woman who worked for me was able to double her salary in less than six months by aggressively learning the computer, bookkeeping, and accounting skills she needed as our company grew. And she was worth every penny.

Ask your boss for book and audio program recommendations. Then follow up by studying them and asking for further recommendations. Bosses are very impressed with people who are constantly striving to learn more to increase their value to their company.

Finally, you'll be more visible if you develop a positive mental attitude. People like to be around and promote people they like. A consistent, persistent attitude of cheerfulness and optimism is quickly noticed by everybody. When you make an effort to cultivate an attitude of friendliness toward people, they, in return, will go to extraordinary efforts to open doors for you.

In summary, here are five keys to increasing your visibility so you can be more successful faster in your career:

1. Become excellent at the important things you have been hired to do. Excellence in your job is the first stepping-stone to a higher position and better pay.

2. Look, act, and dress the part. Become knowledgeable about styles, colors, and fabrics. Dress the way senior people in your company dress.

3. Develop your contacts, both inside and outside the company. Always be looking for ways to give of your time and effort, as an investment, so others will be willing to give of their time and effort to help you sometime in the future. The most successful men and women in any community are those who are known by the greatest number of other successful people. Join a professional association or club, and volunteer for a local charity that you care about and that also has a prestigious board of directors.

4. Take courses to upgrade your skills, and make sure everyone knows about it. Ask your boss for book and audio program recommendations. Then read and listen, and go back to your boss with your comments on what you've learned and to ask for further recommendations. When your boss feels you are eager to learn and grow, he or she will often become a mentor to you and will help you up the ladder of success. This process of being mentored or guided has been instrumental to the careers of many successful executives in America.

5. Be positive, cheerful, and helpful. Be the kind of person others want to see get ahead. Treat people with friendliness and patience, and always have a good word to say to the people you work with.

Questions to Ponder

• Does your company have a special image that distinguishes it from others?

• Is your company a "people" company?

• Do your employees, suppliers, and customers feel the same way? Try asking them!

• Do you take the time to make everyone feel special?

The 3rd is a relatively easy dogleg left. It's just 368 yards and downhill. The fairway is wide, and there's no advantage to trying to cut the corner and getting blocked out by those big pines on the left, so aim for the right center of the fairway. Fire away, Sir! . . . Good one! You shouldn't have more than a 7-iron. You'll have a good chance to make birdie from there.

You really shouldn't be surprised the other gentlemen here are so friendly. That's just the way folks are in these parts. All the great champions are like that, too, you know. It's a special trait known as class, and no one had more class than Mr. Jones . . . Right, Sir! Bobby Jones.

CHAMPIONS HAVE CLASS

"It's great to win, but it's also great fun just to be in the thick of any truly well and hard fought contest against opponents you respect, whatever the outcome."
Jack Nicklaus

Grace in Victory

Class is a key trait that goes much deeper than developing image, or the superficial trappings of fine clothes or a catchy nickname. This intangible quality is, without doubt, absolutely essential if you are ever going to be universally recognized as a champion by friends, peers, and enemies alike. All champions have class.

Robert Tyre Jones was the epitome of the true Southern gentleman. He was known the world over as the complete sportsman, and this resulted in large part because he never had anything but praise for his opponents. In 1930, Jones won the Gram Slam by winning both the British and U.S. Amateur Championship, as well as the British and U.S. Open titles, a feat that has never been, and almost certainly never will be, equaled.

The first of his four historic victories, in the British Amateur, occurred on the windswept links of St. Andrews in Scotland, the birthplace of golf. In an early round, Jones found himself engaged in a tense and strenuous duel with British Walker Cup player Cyril Tolley—a match Jones likened to a sword fight to the death.

At the famous 17th, the "road hole," the match was even. You've probably seen the road hole on TV. It's named for a road running parallel to the 17th green that has spelled disaster for many a would-be champion. Following a good drive and playing first, Jones took a 4-iron and hit the ball long and a little left of the green. In this way he avoided both the road on the right and the cavernous road bunker on the left. Tolley, seeing Jones in position for an easy chip and a putt to make four, went for the green. It is entirely possible that feelings of doubt may have crept into his mind, for he rolled his hands on the shot and pulled it short and left. Jones chipped up to eight feet. Now Tolley was faced with a devilish short pitch, downwind to a raised green, with the menacing road bunker between him and the putting surface and the road directly beyond the green. Bobby Jones himself describes Tolley's shot.

"It cannot be stated as fact, but it is nevertheless my conviction that Tolley's third shot on this hole has never been surpassed for exquisitely beautiful execution. I shall carry to my grave the impression of the lovely little stroke with which he dropped the ball so softly in exactly the right spot, so that in the only possible way it finished dead to the hole."

Jones made his putt and eventually defeated Tolley at the 19th hole. He went on to win the Championship and the Grand Slam, hitting many superb shots along the way. Thirty years later, however, Jones still maintained that the finest golf shot he ever saw was made by Tolley on the 17th at St. Andrews.

Talk of the Town

Another incident that took place several years later gives us added insight into Jones the man and the power of his image in the minds of the golfing public, especially the knowledgeable fans of St. Andrews. When Jones first visited the Old Course as a young man, he had torn up his score card and left the sacred turf in a fit of anger, without completing his round. Over the years, however, he came to love this cradle of the game, and the city of St. Andrews returned the affection and adopted him as one of their own.

In 1936, some six years after his retirement from competitive golf, Jones and some friends were staying at Gleneagles, a fabulous 54-hole golf resort a few hours by road from St. Andrews. On their last day, the group decided they would play the Old Course. Jones and his party arrived unannounced, but were, not surprisingly, quickly accommodated with a tee time. By the time he and his group had reached the first green, word had spread through the town like wildfire. Young and old alike, townspeople stopped one another in the street to pass the word, "Bobby's back!" On the second hole, the crowd already numbered some 2,000 people, and soon thereafter the entire town, for all intents and purposes, had shut down for the day.

Bobby Jones later wrote that it was during the festival atmosphere of this enjoyable round that he was paid the greatest and most sincere compliment of his life. Who complimented him in such a memorable fashion? A famous opponent? A beautiful woman? Could it have been the Lord Mayor of St. Andrews himself? None of these. It was a 12-year-old boy. Faced with a difficult recovery shot on the 12th hole, Jones played a majestic 4-iron shot into the heart of the green. His young caddie looked at him with awe and said in his strong Scottish accent, "Mister but ye're a wonder!"

Jones' golfing ability made him famous. His graciousness, style, and charm, apparent to all he met, made him the most popular athlete of his era, especially in the hearts and minds of the people who lived in the "auld gray toon," golf's Mecca.

Grace Under Pressure

Considering the fierce competition of recent Ryder Cup matches, it is easy to forget that the biennial event was, until quite recently, a one-sided romp won by the American team time after time. You had to go back to 1957 to find a defeated U.S. team. Between that occasion and the European victory in 1985, the closest the United States came to losing was a historic battle played in September of 1969, on the seaside links at Royal Birkdale in Lancashire, England. That year, an Englishman had won the British Open Championship for the first time in almost 20 years, and the British had high hopes for victory. More than 10,000 people crammed every sand dune and vantage point they could find around Birkdale's 18th hole. The evening was gray and damp, and the light was fading as the final twosome reached the tee. The result of the Ryder Cup was in the balance and rested squarely on the shoulders of these two men. One of them was the world's greatest player, playing in his first Ryder Cup. The other was the reigning British Open champion and his team's leader. The entire competition had reached its dramatic focal point. The winner of this final hole would secure victory for his country.

With the destination of the Ryder Cup in question for the first time in many years, Tony Jacklin drove first. He had just holed a birdie putt on the 17th that he later described as "one of the most important putts of my life." It had enabled him to pull even with the great Jack Nicklaus. Both hit good tee shots down the short, par five hole and strode down the red stone path toward the fairway. Jacklin was walking several yards ahead when Nicklaus called to him. Jacklin paused and allowed Nicklaus to catch up with him.

"How do you feel, Tony?" asked Nicklaus.

"Bloody awful!" replied Jacklin.

"I thought you might," said Nicklaus, "but if it's any consolation to you, so do I!"

Their eyes met briefly in mutual understanding of the pressure of the moment and the expectations of their respective countrymen. Then they walked to their balls. Nicklaus played first, his ball coming to rest in the heart of the green, some 30 feet from the flag. Jacklin responded with a bold shot over the left sand trap, but his ball bounded to the back of the green, some 40 feet away from the hole. After delivering standing ovations for both men as they approached their balls, the crowd fell deathly silent. Supporters of both sides rubbed their eyes, gnawed on their knuckles, and held their collective breath.

Jacklin's putt for eagle was on line, but came to rest some two feet short of the hole on the damp turf. Now Nicklaus putted boldly for the win, barely missing the hole but running some three or four feet by. The pressure was intense, but Nicklaus, taking his time as usual, hunched over the ball in his familiar way and stroked it dead center into the cup. Jacklin was now faced with the longest two-foot putt of his life. If he made it, the Ryder cup was tied. If he missed it, he would be the scapegoat for the loss and would no doubt be crucified by the British sporting press, ever ready to turn on yesterday's hero. Jacklin stepped toward his ball marker, but before he could replace his ball, Nicklaus bent down and picked up Jacklin's marker, conceding the tying putt. As he extended his hand he said, "Tony, I'm sure you would have made it, but I wasn't prepared to see you miss it."

Their match was halved, the Ryder Cup was tied, and the United States would retain the trophy. This fine gesture was typical of Nicklaus, demonstrating the highest qualities of sportsmanship and class we expect of all great champions.

Grace in Defeat

Picture yourself as the winner of your Club Championship or President's Cup. You have played the finest golf of your life. Everyone is congratulating you, shaking your hand, and slapping you on the back. You are basking in the glory of your accomplishment. Suddenly the pro appears and, as politely as he can, tells you that you have not won because you entered an incorrect score on your card. Your playing partner wrote down 5 when it should have been 3, and you signed the card, making it official. Under Rule 38, the committee has, regrettably, no option but to adjust your card by adding two shots to your total score. With this slip of a pencil, someone else is the champ and you are a chump! How do you feel? Angry, depressed, embarrassed, or all of the above?

Now let's look at the same situation, only instead of your Club Championship, the tournament becomes the Masters. At the conclusion of play, our apparent hero is the dashing and popular Argentinean player and current British Open champion, Roberto De Vicenzo. De Vicenzo, a former caddie from Buenos Aries, was the first of professional golf's world travelers. During a remarkable career, he amassed some 150 victories worldwide, but the 1968 Masters was not destined to go down in the record books as one of his greatest.

De Vicenzo started the final round two behind the leader, Gary Player. This lead did not last long. A thunderous drive on the 400-yard 1st hole left De Vicenzo a 9-iron shot, which he promptly holed for a 2. De Vicenzo followed with a birdie at the 2nd, then hit the flag stick again at the 3rd to go four under for the first three holes. He birdied another hole before the turn and was out in a blistering 31. It was the best of birthday presents for a man who was celebrating his 45th birthday that very afternoon.

De Vicenzo finished with a 65, one of the lowest final round scores in Master's history. Playing immediately behind him, a charging Bob Goalby shot 66. Everything seemed set for a playoff the following day. That is, until the official scorekeepers discovered the mistake. On the 17th hole, Tommy Aaron, his playing partner, had inadvertently recorded a 4, instead of a 3, on De Vicenzo's scorecard. De Vicenzo, perhaps noticing only the total score of 65, had failed to detect the error and had signed his card. As I pointed out before, a score on any hole marked higher than the score taken must stand.

That gave De Vicenzo a final round 66 instead of a 65, and it gave Bob Goalby the Masters Tournament.

When he received the devastating news, De Vicenzo made his now famous remark, "What a stupid I am." Only minutes later at the presentation ceremony, he spoke with great dignity despite his broken English. He took full responsibility for the costly error he had made and even suggested it may have been due to the relentless pressure Goalby had exerted on him coming down the stretch. Throughout the rest of his career, this classy champion never felt the need to blame anyone but himself for this major misfortune.

Y ou have about 162 to the flag, Sir. It's downhill, and the ocean breeze comes into play, so club selection can be difficult. It's best to be short rather than long, so let's go with a 7-iron . . . Go, ball, go! Yes! What a shot! That's a tap in!

This is the closest you've ever been to the Pacific Ocean? Well, you'll see quite a bit of it today. Framing the entire right side of this 4th hole as it does, it has the effect of making players pull the ball to the left. If you put your tee shot in the rough or the trap, hitting that tiny green on the edge of the cliff, surrounded by sand, is none too easy. It's only 325 yards, so you can go with an iron if you like, Sir; position is more important that length on this hole . . . Yes, a 3-iron just right of the trap sounds perfect . . . Good swing; that'll leave you a 9-iron in, and you might have another chance at birdie . . .

How else can you tell a champion has class? Well, another way is to watch how he gives back. Believe me, they all do, and the great ones often give the most.

Champions Give Back

The stop at the Harbor Town Golf Course in South Carolina is one of the most popular on tour, always attracting a top-quality field, and 1988 was no exception. Greg Norman was warming up on the range just before the start of Friday's round, when a tournament official brought a small freckle-faced boy inside the ropes and introduced him to Greg. The boy, although he was 17, looked much younger, due to his small frame. Greg talked with him for a while, then set off for the first tee with the teenager a few steps behind him.

He would shoot a solid 70 to add to Thursday's 66 and a share of the lead at eight under par.

After a brief appearance in the press tent, answering the customary less-than-probing questions, Norman headed for the putting green. The boy was still in tow, and reporters were starting to wonder who he was. Word quickly passed from mouth to mouth that his name was Jamie Hutton and that he was seriously ill, a victim of leukemia. He and his mother were attending the tournament as Greg's guests, thanks to an organization set up to grant wishes to seriously ill children. Jamie had originally planned to stay only for Friday's round, but Norman arranged for him to stay the rest of the week and fly home on a specially chartered plane.

On Sunday, Norman started the final round four shots back, but everyone could see that special fire in his eyes on the first tee. By the 15th hole he held a one shot lead, and he maintained it until reaching the 18th tee. Now he hit an excellent tee shot down the famous 18th hole, right at the trademark red and white lighthouse, but his second fell short of the green. After he hit his chip to two feet, everyone's eyes turned toward young Jamie Hutton, sitting just off the edge of the green with his fingers crossed under his chin. Norman made his par, then went over to shake Jamie's hand, and the two of them sat together, waiting to see if he would win over closest pursuers Fred Couples and David Frost. A few minutes later, Frost arrived at the final green needing to hole a 25-foot birdie putt to tie Norman. The crowd was silent and Jamie was nervously biting his nails. Frost rolled his putt across the green and . . . missed. Jamie smiled with relief, and a tournament official gave him a red tartan blazer like the one awarded annually to the winner of the tournament. As Norman, with his arm around Jamie, walked across the green for the presentation ceremony, he was interviewed by TV commentator Steve Melnyk, who asked him if this was a special win for him. "Most definitely, Steve," said Norman, addressing the huge TV audience. "I'd just like to thank little Jamie here. He shows inspiration and courage that everybody out there should see."

After he had received the Heritage trophy, Norman held it up, then gave it to his young fan saying, "Jamie, I'd like you to take this and put it in your room. This is *your* trophy."

Greg's well-publicized generosity is by no means unusual in the cutthroat world of championship golf. Gary Player donated his first place check at the 1965 U.S. Open to charity. Arnold Plamer built a children's hospital in Orlando, Florida, and Chi Chi Rodriguez has given away large sums to the needy, especially the young ones, in his native Puerto Rico. Champions are never reluctant to give back!

What Is Class?

Class is an intangible attribute, but there's no doubt that all *great* champions have it. Can I define it? To me, class is a combination of qualities, all of them essential in a well-rounded champion. Champions are admired not only because of their triumphs and the way they look, but for the way they carry themselves and behave. That includes the way they react to others and the respect they have for themselves, their profession, and the people who admire them. It's about the way they perform in the heat of battle and the ability, at the end of the day, to see their accomplishments in the proper perspective. Champions accept their victories with pride and acknowledge with praise the opponents they have defeated. Class is accepting defeat gracefully and without rancor.

The class of the champion makes it much harder to beat him. Opponents know when they are facing a classy opponent. They know the galleries will be pulling for him, and whatever the outcome, the fans will continue to hold their champion in high regard. It is not uncommon for much of the interest of the fans to be focused not solely on the winner, but also on how well great perennial champions have placed. That is the power of a championship image and the perception of class that is an integral part of it. When you have class, you frequently succeed because so many people want you to succeed, and anyone who *can* help you *will* help you.

—That's not bad, Sir, but it's fading a little. Don't go any further right, ball! Oh, nice kick off the back of the trap. It looks like it rolled up to about three feet from the cup . . . Now, right edge and firm; remember it's straight uphill . . . That's three birdies in a row . . . It's the best you've ever played, Sir? Well, I'm glad to hear it.

Swing Thoughts

- Champions give credit to others.

- Champions are good winners.

- Champions are strong under pressure.

- Champions are graceful losers.

- Champions give back to their profession, the game, and their fans.

- Champions have class.

Back in the Clubhouse

Back on the job, image and charisma are vital to your success. *Webster's Dictionary* defines *charisma* as "a personal magic of leadership arousing special popular loyalty or enthusiasm for a public figure."

Charisma is also that special quality of magnetism that each person has and uses to a certain degree. You have a special charisma to the people who look up to you, who respect and admire you—the members of your family, your friends, and coworkers. Whenever and wherever a person feels a positive emotion toward another, he or she imbues that person with charisma.

In trying to explain charisma, some people speak of an "aura." This aura radiates out from a person and affects the people around him or her in a positive or negative way. The halo around the heads of saints and mystics in many religious paintings was the artist's attempt to depict the light people reported seeing around the heads of these men and women when they were speaking, praying, or in an intense emotional state.

You also have an aura around you that most people cannot see but that is nevertheless there. This aura affects the way people react and respond to you, either positively or negatively. There is a lot you can do—and a lot of good reasons for you to do it—to control this aura and make it work in your best interest.

If you're in sales, this aura, reflecting your charisma, can have a major impact on the way your prospects and customers treat you and deal with you. Top salespeople seem to be far more successful than average salespeople in getting along with their customers. They're always more welcome, more positively received, and more trusted than the others. They sell more, and they sell more easily. They make a better living, and they build better lives. Salespeople with charisma get far more pleasure out of their work and suffer far less from stress and rejection. The charismatic salesperson is almost invariably a top performer in his or her field and enjoys all the rewards that go with superior sales.

If you're in business, developing greater charisma can help you tremendously in working with your staff, your suppliers, your customers, your bankers, and everyone else upon whom you depend for your success. People seem naturally drawn to those who possess charisma. They want to help them and support them. When you have charisma, people will open doors for you and bring you opportunities that otherwise would not have been available to you.

In your personal relationships, the quality of charisma can make your life more joyous. People will naturally want to be around you. Members of your family and your friends will be far happier in your company, and you will have a greater influence on them.

There is a close association between personal charisma and success in life. Probably 85 percent of your success and happiness will come from your relationships and interactions with others. The more positively others respond to you, the easier it will be for you to get the things you want.

In essence, when we discuss charisma, we are talking about the Law of Attraction. This law has been stated in many different ways through the years, but it basically says that you inevitably attract into your life the people and circumstances that harmonize with your dominant thoughts.

In a sense, you are a living magnet, and you are constantly radiating thought waves, like a radio station sends out radio waves, that are picked up by other people. Your thoughts, intensified by your emotions, as radio waves are intensified by electric impulses, emanate from you and are picked up by anyone who is tuned in to a similar wavelength. You then attract into your life people, ideas, opportunities, resources, circumstances, and anything else that is consistent with your dominant frame of mind.

The Law of Attraction also explains how you can enhance your charisma so you can have a greater and more positive impact on the people whose cooperation, support, and affection you desire.

The critical thing to remember about charisma is that it is largely based on perception. It is based on what people think about you. It is not so much reality as it is what people perceive you to be. For example, one person can create charisma in another person by speaking in glowing terms about that person to a third party. If you believe that you are about to meet an outstanding and important person, that person will tend to have charisma in your eyes.

If someone told you he was going to introduce you to a brilliant, self-made millionaire who was very quiet and unassuming about his success, you would almost naturally imbue that person with charisma, and in his or her presence, you would not act the same as you would if you had been told nothing at all. Charisma begins largely in the mind of the beholder.

Ten Powers of Personality

Lasting charisma depends more upon the person you really are than upon the things you do. Nevertheless, you can increase the perception of charisma by utilizing the 10 great powers of personality that have a major impact on the way people think and feel about others.

The first of these powers is the power of purpose. Men and women with charisma almost invariably have a clear vision of who they are, where they're going, and what they're trying to achieve. Leaders in sales and management have a vision of what they're trying to create and why they're doing what they're doing. They're focused on accomplishing some great purpose. They're decisive about every aspect of their lives. They know exactly what they want and what they have to do to get it. They plan their work and work their plan.

In more than 3,300 studies of leadership, and in every book and article I've read on the subject, the quality of purpose, or vision, was one of the qualities that was consistently used to describe leaders.

You can enhance your charisma by setting clear goals for yourself, making plans to achieve them, and working on your plans with discipline and determination every day. The whole world seems to move aside for the person who knows exactly where he or she is going. In fact, the clearer you are about your purposes and goals, the more likely people will be to attribute other positive qualities to you. They will see you as being an admirable human being. And when you have clear goals, you begin attracting to yourself the people and opportunities necessary to make those goals a reality.

The second personality power is self-confidence. Men and women with charisma have an intense belief in themselves and in what they can do. They are usually calm, cool, and composed in their personal lives and in their work settings. Your level of self-confidence is often demonstrated in your courage and willingness to do whatever is necessary to achieve a purpose you believe in.

People are naturally attracted to those who exude a sense of self-confidence, those who have an unshakable belief in their ability to rise above circumstances to attain their goals.

One of the ways you exude self-confidence is by acting on the assumption that people naturally like you and accept you and want to do business with you. For example, one of the most powerful ways to close a sale is simply to assume that the prospect has decided to purchase the product or service, and then go on to wrap up the details. One of the best ways to achieve success in your relationships is to assume that people naturally enjoy your company and want to be around you, and then proceed on that basis. The very act of behaving in a self-confident manner will generate personal charisma in the eyes of others.

The third personality power you can develop is enthusiasm. The more excited you are about accomplishing something that is important to you, the more excited others will be about helping you do it. The fact is, emotions are contagious. The more passion you have for your life and your activities, the more charisma you will have, and the more cooperation you will gain from others. Every great man or woman has been totally committed to a noble cause and, as a result, has had the encouragement and attracted the support of others—in many cases, thousands or millions of others.

The fourth personality power you can develop is expertise, or competence. The more knowledgeable you are perceived to be in your field, the more charisma you will have among those who respect and admire that knowledge because of the impact it can have on their lives. This is also the power of excellence, of being recognized by others as an outstanding performer in your field. Men and women who do their jobs extremely well and who are recognized for the quality of their work are those who naturally attract the help and support of others. They have charisma.

The fifth power of personality that gives you charisma in the eyes of others is thorough, detailed preparation prior to undertaking any significant task. Whether you are calling on a prospect, meeting with your boss, giving a public talk, or making any other kind of presentation, when you are well-prepared, it is clear to everyone. The careers of many people are put onto the fast track as a result of their coming to a very important meeting after having done all of their homework.

Whether it takes you hours or even days, if an upcoming meeting or presentation is important, take the time to get on top of your subject. Be so thoroughly prepared that nothing can faze you. Think through and consider every possibility and every ramification. Often, this effort to be fully prepared will do more to generate the respect of others than anything else you can do.

Remember that the power is always on the side of the person who has done the most preparation and has the best notes. Everything counts. Leave nothing to chance. When you do something related to your work or career, take the time to do it right the first time.

The sixth power that enhances your charisma is self-reliance. The most successful men and women in America are highly self-reliant. They look to themselves for the answers to their questions and problems. They never complain, and they never explain. They take complete ownership of projects. They volunteer for duties and accept accountability if things go wrong.

An amazing paradox of human nature is that when you behave in a totally self-reliant manner, others will often be eager to help you achieve your goals. But if you seem to need the help and support of others constantly, people will avoid you or do everything possible not to get involved with you.

One of the most admirable qualities of leaders, which gives a person charisma in the eyes of others, is the propensity to step forward and take charge. The leader accepts complete responsibility for getting the job done without making excuses and blaming anyone. When you become completely self-reliant, you experience a tremendous sense of control and power that enhances your feeling of well-being and generates the charisma that is so important to you in attracting the help of others.

The seventh personality power is image. There are two types of images you need to consider. First is your self-image, which, of course, has an enormous impact on the way you perform and the way others see you and think about you. Your self-image plays an important part in your charisma. The other type of image is the image or appearance that you convey to others. The way you look on the outside will strongly influence the way people treat you and respond to you. Successful men and women are very meticulous about how they appear to others. They take a good deal of time to think through every aspect of their external appearance to assure that it is helping them rather than hurting them.

Remember that everything counts. If an element of your image is not building your charisma and your respect in the eyes of another person, it is lowering your charisma and your respect in the eyes of others. Nothing is neutral. Everything is taken into the equation.

The three primary factors in personal appearance are clothes, grooming, and accessories. Select your clothes with care. Before you go to an important meeting, stand in front of the mirror and ask yourself, "Do I look like one of the most successful people in my field?" If you don't feel that you do look like one of the best people in your business, go back to the closet and change.

Note the personal appearance of the most successful people in your area of endeavor. How do they dress? How do they wear their hair? What kind of accessories do they have? Pattern yourself after the winners in your field, the people who have personal magnetism or charisma. If you do what they do, over and over, you will eventually get the same results they get.

The eighth form of personal power is character. Men and women who possess the kind of charisma that arouses the enthusiastic support of others are invariably men and women with high values and principles. They have very high ideals, and they continually aspire to live up to them. They are extremely honest with themselves and with others. They speak well of people, and they guard their conversation, knowing that everything they say is being remembered and recorded. They are aware that everything they do is contributing to the formation of others' perception of them. Everything about their character is adding to or detracting from their level of charisma.

When you think of the most important men and women of any time, you think of men and women who aspired to greatness, who lived their lives by a high moral code, and who had high expectations of others. When you act consistently with the highest principles you know, you begin to enhance your charisma. You begin to become the kind of person others admire and respect and want to emulate. You begin to attract people who can give you help and support and encouragement—people you admire. You activate the Law of Attraction in the very best way.

The ninth power of personality is self-discipline. Men and women of charisma are highly self-controlled. They are well-organized, and they demonstrate will power and determination in everything they do. They have a tremendous sense of inner calm and outer resolve.

The very act of being well-organized, having clear objectives, and setting clear priorities on your activities before beginning gives you a sense of discipline and control. It causes people to respect and admire you. When you then exert your self-discipline by persisting in the face of difficulties, your charisma rating goes up.

Men and women who achieve leadership positions, who display what others refer to as "charisma," are invariably those who possess indomitable will power and the ability to persist in a good cause until success is achieved. The more you persist when the going gets rough, the more self-discipline and resolve you have and the more charisma you tend to have.

The tenth power you can develop, which underlies all of the other powers that lead to charisma, is extraordinary performance, with the goal of achieving extraordinary results. These results then serve as an inspiration to others to perform at equally exceptional levels. People ascribe charisma to those men and women who they feel can most enable them to achieve their most important objectives.

We develop great perceptions of those men and women we can count on to help us achieve what is important to us. Men and women who make great sales or who establish admirable sales records develop charisma in the minds and hearts of their coworkers and superiors. They are spoken about in the most positive way. Men and women who are responsible for companies or departments that achieve high levels of profitability also develop charisma. They develop what is called the "halo effect." They are perceived by others to be extraordinary men and women who are capable of great things. Their shortcomings are often overlooked, while their strong points are overemphasized. They become charismatic.

In the final analysis, charisma comes from working on yourself. It comes from liking and accepting yourself unconditionally as you do and say the specific things that develop within you a powerful, charismatic personality. When you become determined and purposeful and set clear goals, and back those goals with unshakable self-confidence, you develop charisma. When you are enthusiastic and excited about what you are doing, you radiate charisma. When you take the time to study and become an expert at what you do and then prepare thoroughly for opportunities to use your knowledge, the admiration that others have for you goes straight up. When you take complete responsibility for and accept "ownership" of problems without making excuses or blaming others, the example of control you set leads to the perception of charisma. When you look like a winner in every respect, when you project the kind of image others admire, you build your charisma. When you develop your character by setting high standards and then disciplining yourself to live in a manner consistent with them, you become the kind of person who is respected everywhere. Finally, when you concentrate your energies on achieving the results you have been hired to accomplish, you develop the reputation for performance that leads to the perception of charisma.

You can develop the kind of charisma that opens doors for you by going to work on yourself and becoming the kind of person everyone can admire and look up to. That's what charisma is all about.

Questions to Ponder

• Do you share the thrill of victory with the entire company?

• Does your company pull together in times of pressure?

• Are you quick to dismiss failure and move on to better things?

• Does your company have class? Do others recognize it?

The 5th was recently built by Jack Nicklaus along a parcel of newly acquired land right along the cliff face. It's playing a little over 200 yards today, and as you can see hitting it right is deadly! Keep it left, and hit enough club to get it all the way back. . . . Yes, Sir, I think a 3-iron would be just fine.

You caught that a touch heavy, didn't you? Never mind, you're on the green, even though it's a long putt.

The course gets tougher from here on. It's here you have to look for that little extra motivation to kick in, sort of like a second wind . . . Do champions need to motivate themselves? . . . Good question. I've seen many talented players develop into champions and just as many slip into mediocrity. Motivation makes the difference; champions have it, the others don't.

CHAMPIONSHIP MOTIVATION

"It's my love of golf rather than natural talent that
has made me a great player"
Nick Faldo

Making the Effort

Champions are motivated to get out of bed at 6 a.m. and practice. That includes practicing in rain and wind, or putting on the carpet of a motel room. Jack Grout, the pro at Scioto Country Club in Ohio, observed that Jack Nicklaus was the only one out of 50 or 60 kids in the junior program who went out and practiced in the rain.

Champions are motivated to work longer and harder to improve their game and to make major adjustments, even if they result in temporary backward steps, in order to achieve long-term success. Ben Hogan and Nick Faldo are unquestionably two of the hardest workers ever to play the game. They have something else in common. Both decided to make substantial swing modifications at a stage in their respective careers when they were already considered to be great players. What motivated them to do something many would have considered unnecessary and possibly even dangerous? It was a commonly held determination to be the best, rather than settling for being merely *one* of the best. Ultimate perfection may be eternally elusive and terribly time-consuming, but the pursuit of it is, to some champions, the strongest form of motivation and well worth the effort.

Love What You Do

"Love what you do, and it won't seem like work. The practice and dedication you need to put into your job to be a champion can only be accomplished if you love your work."
Dennis Walters, golf's premier trick-shot artist.

You'd probably laugh if I asked you whether Greg Norman or Arnold Palmer ever got up in the morning cursing their luck because they had to go to work again. I'm sure it may have happened on one or two occasions when the weather was bad, their backs were sore, or they were already out of contention, but such occasions would be very rare. They *love* what they do! They eat, drink, and breathe professional golf, and that's one reason they have been so successful.

It is impossible to reach the pinnacle of any profession without a real sense of affection for your work. Even if you're not totally enthralled about what you do to make a living—be it selling, driving a truck, or computer programming—you'd better at least really enjoy it if you want to be successful. If you don't, you will never make the necessary commitment, both physical and mental, to reach the top. Am I suggesting you should go do something else if you don't like what you are doing at present? Exactly.

Can you imagine Jack Nicklaus winning 20 major championships if he didn't love what he did? Or Arnie still traveling many weeks of the year to play in tournaments, even though well into his senior years? Of course not!

Positive or Negative?

Motivation can be either positive or negative, or in some cases, both. Tour Qualifying School is a good example of the latter case. If you are one of the 40 or so players who annually make it through the hated and dreaded Q-School, you get your PGA Tour card. That means you are just a few short weeks away from teeing it up on TV on the regular tour for millions of dollars in prize money. Every Thursday morning you'll start even with stars like Greg Norman and Freddie Couples. Pretty positive, wouldn't you say? If, on the other hand, you fail to qualify, you face another year of scraping a living on the mini tours, moving from one dingy motel to another, hoping your old car doesn't break down in the middle of nowhere! Trying to avoid this fate definitely comes under the heading of negative motivation.

For many of the great players of the 1940s and 1950s, negative motivation was their initial driving force. Ben Hogan caddied, dealt cards, and sold newspapers. If he didn't make it playing golf, he had no Plan B. He knew what it meant to be hungry, and that drove him. The same is true of Snead, Nelson, or more recently, Calvin Peete. None of them had a family business or a college education to fall back on if he failed. Playing professional golf was their way out of poverty and motivated each of them to achieve greatness.

On the other side of the coin, Frank Stranahan, an amateur with private means that made it unnecessary for him to work for a living, played full-time on the regular tour in the '40s purely because he wanted to be the best. This positive motivator was all he personally needed to start his motor.

Human emotions like pride or sadness due to personal tragedy can sometimes provide the additional motivation needed to produce championship performance. Let's take a look at how champions get that extra edge by using both internal and external forces to fire them up.

The Clubs Don't Know How Old You Are

In 1984, just prior to the PGA Championship at Shoal Creek, Lee Trevino complained to his wife that he was too old to compete with the "flat bellies" anymore. Instead of sympathizing with him, Claudia cleverly appealed to his sense of pride. She gave him precisely the kick in the butt he needed by telling him, "Your clubs don't know how old you are." The logic of her remark was not lost on the Merry Mex. Positively reinforced, Trevino went out and won his sixth major championship, beating Lanny Wadkins and an even more mature Gary Player for the title.

Victory Born of Sorrow

The tragic early death of Gary Player's mother, when he was only eight years old, had a traumatic, yet motivating effect on him. It added to his grim determination to be the best. Player states, "All that I am and all that I have become is in some way a tribute to her. Golf has been a means for me, as it were, to settle some unfathomable debt. Throughout my adult life I have had the same dream. It happens about twice a year and never changes in any detail. I see my mother. I call her and try to tell her what I have achieved, how successful I have been, and how proud she can be of me. But she cannot hear me. My burning regret is that she never saw what I had made of myself."

Although he did not realize it at the time, Player now believes the loss of his mother bred the independence, determination, motivation, and self-discipline that would ultimately make him one of golf's greatest and most enduring champions. The tragic loss taught him another of life's great truths. His mother had died and there was nothing he could have done to stop it or change it. Life must be played as it lies, just like his ball. Said Player, "There is no point in protesting about bad luck or demanding why it had happened to me. The only task was to make the most of what was left and get on with it."

Champions often respond to negative situations by reaching deep within themselves for that extra focus and motivation that carries them beyond their problems and on to victory. This was certainly the case with Ben Crenshaw's victory in the 1995 Masters. Just prior to the tournament, Ben's long-time friend, mentor, and coach, Harvey Penick, passed away. Ben and another famous Penick student, Tom Kite, were pallbearers at Penick's funeral. The following day they began their preparation for the Masters. Ben sadly dedicated his performance in the tournament to his departed friend, and this motivated him to go out and win, playing better than he had for some time. Afterward, he said it was as if Harvey's spirit was out on the course with him. It was a memorable moment as Crenshaw tapped in his final putt to win, then covered his face with his hands and wept unashamedly, finally releasing his emotions.

Turning Negative into Positive

It was just after 1 a.m., Pacific Time, when the phone rang in Raymond Floyd's San Diego hotel room. When it rings at that time, it's seldom good news, and this was no exception. His wife Marie broke the news that their home of many years in Miami had just burned to the ground. The Floyds had lost everything, including golf trophies, memorabilia, and worst of all, the photographs recording his successes and many of the wonderful moments they had shared. Memories of ball games, fishing trips, friends, the kids growing up, and their wedding were reduced to ashes. "It was," he said, "the worst thing that ever happened in my entire life."

The Floyds decided then and there they would rebuild on the same spot, and Raymond started to discuss what he needed to do to get things started. At this point, his wife stepped in. She told him she would take care of getting the home built if he would go out and win a golf tournament. With a renewed sense of purpose, and in spite of being winless for over six years, Floyd entered the Doral Open, which would be played just a few miles away from the wreckage of his home. He won with a blistering score of 17 under par over the famed Blue Monster course, and told reporters afterward, "I count that victory as a team title. I had a tremendous urge to perform on behalf of my family. I was inspired. They needed some good news. We had to put the fire behind us."

Feel the Pain

Tom Kite's unusual method of negative motivation was to impose fines on himself for poor performance. As a collegiate golfer, if he had failed to hole a predetermined number of 10-foot putts during a practice session, he would leave $5 in the cup. That may not seem too tough for someone so high on the list of lifetime money winners, but it was a big deal during his college days when, like every student, he was always short of cash. It was particularly tough if he performed badly for two or three days in a row!

Putting Pride on the Line

Many great players wager among themselves in practice rounds to promote something approaching a tournament atmosphere. The amounts are usually fairly minor, and the money itself is not as important as the symbolic value of one great player beating another. If they win it's pleasurable—if they lose it stings. It's just one more motive to play hard and play to win.

The Competitors

When they are asked to select the tournament victory that thrilled them most, many golfers remember Jack Nicklaus winning the 1986 Masters by holing a long putt across the 15th green for eagle in the final round, then making birdies at 16 and 17 as well. We are well aware that the Golden Bear is motivated by the desire to win "majors." Was this his only driving force in the 1977 British Open, a tournament many believe to be the greatest ever? On this occasion, there was an additional reason he wanted to win. It was his competitive spirit.

After two rounds at Turnberry, a windswept links course on the west coast of Scotland, Nicklaus and an equally determined competitor, Tom Watson, were tied for the lead. The third and fourth rounds would become a head-to-head contest between Jack and Tom, the intensity of their struggle rendering the play of the rest of the field irrelevant. Even a stunning total of 30 on the back nine by none other than Palmer went largely unnoticed, except, of course, by Arnie's Army.

This was a case of Nicklaus, still the best in the world at 37, against his foremost challenger for the crown, Watson, who was 10 years younger. As the third round progressed, birdie was answered by birdie and great approach by incredible recovery. The drama was heightened by vivid flashes of lightning, splitting the threatening skies and occasionally causing brief interruptions in play. At the end of the day, both men had carded a 65 and were still tied. Neither giant showed any signs of folding under the pressure. Ben Crenshaw, their nearest challenger, had managed to stay within three shots of them by shooting a fine 66, but he would fall out of contention coming down the stretch on the final day.

Three shots behind after four holes of the final round, Watson fought back with birdies at 5, 7, and 8 to draw level. After the 12th, Nicklaus had regained a two-shot lead, but the fiery redhead from Kansas wasn't ready to concede, and he birdied 13 and 15 to tie for the lead yet again. As they stood together on the 16th tee, Watson turned to Nicklaus and remarked with a smile, "This is what it's all about, isn't it?" Nicklaus smiled back. They were both champions, and nothing else needed to be said.

At the par five 17th, Watson was on in two with a superb long-iron shot, and two-putted for *another* birdie. Nicklaus finally slipped, missing a three-footer to trail by one stroke with one hole to play. Beside the 18th green, the giant scoreboard was updated, showing Watson at 11 under par. The gigantic crowd roared, but it wasn't over yet.

On the final hole, after driving into deep, thick rough well to the right of the fairway, Nicklaus was faced with a seemingly impossible situation. Watson had already played a magnificent 7-iron approach shot, and his ball lay only a couple of feet from the hole. The greatest of golf champions did not surrender. From a near unplayable lie, Nicklaus used his great power to force an 8-iron shot to within 40 feet. Arriving at the green, Jack studied the line as carefully as ever.

Watson said to his caddie, "I expect him to make this." Sure enough, as if his very life depended on it, Nicklaus rolled in the putt for birdie and a total of 66. The spectators erupted again. Watson wasted no time. He replaced his ball and backed up five steps. Then, with Nicklaus holding up his arms for silence and the applause slowing and finally stilling, he stepped up to his ball and knocked it in for a birdie three, his second consecutive 65, and a new record total of 268, which shattered the old record by seven shots. Tom Watson had won the Open Championship for the second time and would take the title three more times in 1980, 1982, and 1983. The thunderous applause was for one winner, but even more, for two great champions who had been motivated by fiercely competitive spirit and the need to be the best—to give the golfing public an unforgettable experience.

At the awards ceremony, Nicklaus was as gracious as ever, even in defeat. "I gave you my best shot, and it just wasn't good enough. You were better." Later, sitting in his room on the top floor of the imposing Turnberry Hotel with his wife, Linda, and sipping champagne from a fluted glass, Watson looked out across the links. The sounds of a lone piper drifted through the window. Tom and his wife began to cry softly. It was at this moment that he fell in love with the game of golf.

That first putt didn't make it far enough up that rise to give you a good chance at two putts, Sir. Never mind. You dropped a shot, but that one's over, and the next is par five. Maybe you can get it back.

. . . Right, that's the 6th green perched way up on the cliff, 515 yards away. If you hit right, you're in the ocean, and the left is guarded by that heavy rough and that huge trap. I know it looks daunting, but on a day like this, the hole is reachable in two solid blows. Come on, Sir; let's get that stroke back! . . . Yes! Perfect! You just may be able to get home from there . . . How do champions motivate themselves? Well, they all do it a little bit differently.

Championship Motivation Techniques

"It's frustrating. It's demoralizing. It's all of those things, but most of all, it's fun."
Arnold Palmer

Let's be really subjective about this. Do you become excited about teeing up when you watch others playing great golf? I know I do.

Think carefully. What was the best putt you have ever stroked? What did it mean to you when you holed that putt? Whom did you beat? Did you win money, a trophy, respect?

What about the best shot you have ever made in your life? Take yourself back in time. Visualize the hole in detail. Relive the swing and see the ball going toward the hole. Relish the moment. Savor the sensation.

OK, back to reality. How do you feel at this precise moment in time? My guess is you feel pretty good, because you have just relived a powerful and happy moment.

Anchoring

The technique you have just practiced is called anchoring. Initially researched by Dr. Ivan Pavlov, anchoring is effectively employed by champions to heighten their motivation and quickly reach peak levels of emotional and physical performance. It involves recalling a stimulating event and using it to create a feeling in the mind that spurs you to action. Pavlov experimented by ringing a bell when about to feed hungry dogs. The sound aroused the pleasurable sensation in the minds of the dogs that they were about to be fed. In a very short time, Pavlov had only to ring the bell to start the dogs salivating wildly, despite the absence of food.

How does anchoring work for champions? Jack Nicklaus started every year by viewing movies of tournaments he had won in order to "psyche" himself for the upcoming golf season. He was actually using anchoring to remind him how good it feels to win. This helped motivate him into action and encouraged him to practice and sharpen his game so he could win again.

Other champions keep scrapbooks of their victories and prepare for each season by thumbing through them in an effort to recapture the sights, the smells, the taste of victory.

You already have some anchors, both positive and negative, built into your mind. Do you know what they are? Is there a particular hole at your course that you consistently play badly? It could require a shot over water, or might be the 1st or 18th. Just arriving at that particular hole may have the effect of immediately triggering anxiety in you because of your negative anchor. Your heart beats faster, you tense up a little, and sure enough, you make another bad shot.

For our purposes, we are interested only in positive anchors, such as a memorable experience that will serve to heighten your motivation, both short- and long-term.

Do this right now. Look at yourself in the mirror and think back to a time where you felt terrific about something that had just happened to you. Maybe you had won a tournament, broken 80, or beaten your boss. Recall how it felt to be a winner. Now, are you smiling as your mind focuses on this pleasant memory? Is your back a little straighter? Do you feel more relaxed or perhaps more excited than you did just a few seconds ago? You should, because you have just anchored on a pleasant experience. With just a little practice you can quickly learn to use past, positive experiences as driving forces to help motivate you to achieve and enjoy even better ones in the future.

You can use anchoring in a variety of ways to motivate yourself. Reading newspaper clippings about past successes could do it. Tour player Robert Gamez plays music on his way to the course. Listening to certain songs anchors him in a positive way and arouses in him a state of controlled enthusiasm.

You can do it merely by making the gestures you *customarily* make when you are energized and motivated. When Nicklaus makes an important putt, he raises both hands and his putter in the air. Ballesteros, on the other hand, clenches his fist and pumps his arm up and down at waist height, very much like tennis star Jimmy Connors. Raymond Floyd points his finger at the hole.

Each one of these idiosyncrasies is done *after* a positive event. The trick to motivation is knowing how to use a simple gesture *before* the event, thereby positively influencing the outcome. With a little practice, you will find you need only make the gesture in order to acquire in advance the mood that normally exists *after* a positive event has already taken place.

Champions are concerned only with the highest level of humanist Abraham Maslow's theory of motivation. Their basic needs for survival, such as food and shelter, have been satisfied without difficulty. So has their need for acceptance by their peers. Champions focus on self-actualization. That means the fulfillment of one's greatest human potential—simply stated, being the best they can be. To be a champion, you must have a consuming passion to be the best at what you do and the determination to never give anything less than a 110 percent effort.

Visualization Heightens Motivation

Setting motivational goals and dreaming dreams is all well and good, but what about the process that must be initiated and built upon, step by step, to make those dreams come true? How do you bring this process into focus and execute the necessary tasks, day by day, with passion and precision?

Jack Nicklaus said he has never hit a shot in tournament golf where he did not first visualize what he wanted to accomplish, visualizing the target, the flight of the ball, and the end result. Last but not least, he would visualize the swing he needed to make in order to achieve the desired result. To sum up the process, he set a goal, visualized the outcome, and followed up by visualizing the actions he would have to take to accomplish such a goal. With planning and preparation like that, it's hardly surprising that he was such a huge success. We can all take a lesson from Nicklaus in our business and personal lives.

Few people fortunate enough to have seen Jack Nicklaus playing in his prime can recall Jack missing a putt to lose a tournament. Other people lost tournaments, not Nicklaus. Although he has never been known as a great putter, no one ever made as many *crucial* putts as Nicklaus, nor even came close. On the last green, if you had a 10-foot putt to save your life, choosing a designated putter would be no contest. Jack just never missed to lose. Golf writer Dan Jenkins brought this to Jack's attention one evening while chatting about the "secrets" of the game. How was it that he never seemed to miss the really big ones? After considering the question for a moment, Jack responded in a matter-of-fact tone, "I never missed a putt in my mind."

Champions are Motivated to Be the Best

"The ability to use imagination is one of the most valuable assets a golfer can possess."
Jack Nicklaus

Most people judge their performance by comparing themselves to others at their club or office. With a small measure of success, they reach a comfort level; they become big fish in small ponds, and they stop growing. They never find the answer to the question "How good could I be?" because they never ask.

Champions push the outer limits; they judge themselves by the standards of the best in the world, not the best in their club, office, region, or state. They challenge themselves to perform beyond their own expectations. They are motivated by the pursuit of excellence. Champions never stop growing. They are, by nature, always seeking to reach greater and more ambitious levels of accomplishment.

Champions know that the better the competition, the higher their level of performance must be in order to win. Champions know that the tougher the competition, the greater the need for preparation and practice. Champions know that the harder the competition, the more they will be motivated for the contest by the desire for victory. It is a fact that in any sport, be it tennis, boxing, or golf, when a champion becomes dominant in the manner of Bjorn Borg, Muhammad Ali, or Jack Nicklaus, it raises the level of a few other top contenders to superstar status. Champions also know that the tougher it is to achieve that victory, the sweeter will be the taste.

For these reasons, champions *seek out* the toughest competition, not the weakest. Look at players like Tiger Woods, Greg Norman, and Nick Faldo. They organize their schedules around the majors and the tournaments that traditionally attract the strongest fields— events like the Players' Championship, Doral, the Memorial, and others. They don't do this because it's convenient or because they love the golf courses (although this *can* be a factor). They do it because they know the best players in the world are going to be there ready to compete. They know when they win one of these events, they have beaten the best of the best. They know that particular week they are not merely the best player in Florida or Ohio, but the best player in the world. Greg Norman did not promote the concept of a world tour so he could make a lot more money; he has all the money he will ever need and then some. He wanted to start a world tour so he could be sure he was teeing up with the world's best players every week, not just a few weeks out of the year.

Does it give you any satisfaction to beat a player who took up the game just a few weeks ago? Of course not! But suppose you defeat the club champion. Well now, that's really something to tell the boys at the office on Monday. Challenge yourself to reach new, higher standards on the course and in the office. Make a commitment to yourself to think like a champion. If you are not the best, find out who is. Compare yourself in business with the best in the world. Go head to head with your toughest competition and beat them fair and square for all the world to see. Only by doing this can you emerge from your own cocoon and compete in the big, wide world.

Great Champions Have Great Pride

Naturally, time eventually takes its toll, but no other athlete in any sport has come close to the level of performance Jack Nicklaus has maintained during the last four decades. How is he still able to compete with the best players in the world, more than 30 years after winning his first major golf tournament (the 1962 US Open) as a professional? The answer may sound too simple, but it's true. For Nicklaus, pride has proven to be wonderful motivation. He can't bring himself to accept anything less than being the finest player in the world. On the rare occasions when he performs below his best, he is personally and visibly embarrassed.

On the eve of the 1986 Masters Championship, a friend faxed Nicklaus an article clipped from an Atlanta newspaper. It opined that he was finished, washed up, too old, and that it was time for him to move over and make way for the younger players. Though many would say he had nothing to prove, especially to some hack sportswriter, he was unable to erase that article from his mind. In the most positive of ways, it made him mad. He felt obliged to show everybody he was still the greatest player in the world. By Sunday evening, with yet another green jacket adorning his ample shoulders, he had done so.

Maximize Your Motivation

Gene Sarazen described Ben Hogan as "perpetually hungry." Even after he had won almost everything in sight, Hogan himself said of his ferocious inner drive, "Whenever people said I couldn't do this or I couldn't do that, I have been determined to prove that I could."

Have you ever had someone tell you couldn't do something, even though you knew you could? How did it feel? Did it grate on you? Did it make your stomach turn? Did your face tighten up? Well, that's fine—preserve that feeling in a bottle. When an incident like that occurs in your life—and it happens to all of us—take action. Write down exactly what was said, and make copies. Post them on your refrigerator, inside your locker, or next to your bed. Feed off the energy you feel each time you look at those words. Prove them wrong because you are exactly the right person to do it.

Over the course of a player's career, there will be many sad moments and many happy ones. Some players find motivation in the negative ones; some are motivated by the happy ones; and some are motivated by both. Champions learn how to draw from every experience that extra atom of concentration, effort, and talent that allows them to drive on to victory. They use goals, anchors, wagers, visualization, music, clippings, pride, and personal events to motivate themselves to be the best they can be. Whatever the occurrence or stimulus, champions derive from it a reason for doing even better.

Y ou're so pumped you want to go for the green? . . . All right. You'l need a full 3-wood, and remember, this one has to climb about 100 feet to reach the putting surface . . . That's a solid blow, Sir, but it's a little bit left . . .

Well, that one was too bad. But you have a good lie and plenty of green to work with . . . Good out! . . . This four-footer is straight uphill. Just make sure you get it there! . . . Yes! Birdie number four!

Swing Thoughts

- Champions love what they do.

- Champions turn even anger and sadness into fuel for victory.

- Champions anchor on past successes to pave the way to future successes.

- Champions visualize success to enhance motivation and reach peak performance.

- Champions use pride to motivate themselves.

Back in the Clubhouse

As an executive or professional, once you know how to empower the people around you, how to motivate and inspire them, they will want to work with you to help you achieve your most important goals. Your ability to enlist the knowledge, energy, and resources of others enables you to become a multiplication sign, to leverage yourself so you accomplish far more than the average person and in a far shorter period of time.

There are three types of people you should empower on a regular basis. They are, first of all, the people closest to you: your family, your friends, your spouse, and your children. Second are your work relationships: your staff, your coworkers, your peers, your colleagues, and even your boss. Third are all the other people you interact with in your day-to-day life: your customers, your suppliers, your banker, and the people you deal with in stores, restaurants, airplanes, hotels, and everywhere else. In each case, your ability to get people to help you—to empower them to help you—is what will make you a more effective person.

The word *empower* means "putting power into," and it can also mean "bringing energy and enthusiasm out of." So the first step in empowering people is to refrain from doing anything that "disempowers" them or reduces their energy and enthusiasm for what they are doing.

With regard to the first group—those people closest to you—there are a few simple things you can do every day to empower them and make them feel good about themselves.

The deepest need each person has is for self-esteem, a sense of being important, valuable, and worthwhile. Everything you say and do in your interactions with others affects their self-esteem in some way. You already have an excellent frame of reference to determine the things you can do to boost the self-esteem and, therefore, the sense of personal power of those around you; give them what you'd like for yourself.

Perhaps the simplest way to make another person feel good about himself or herself is to continually express appreciation for everything that person does for you, large or small. Say thank you at every opportunity. Thank your spouse for everything he or she does for you. Thank your children for their cooperation in everything they do around the house. Thank your friends for the smallest of kindnesses. The more often you thank people for doing things for you, the more things those people will want to do.

Every time you thank people, you cause them to like themselves better. You raise their self-esteem and improve their self-image. You cause them to feel more important. You make them feel that what they did was valuable. You empower them.

And the wonderful thing about thanking people is that every time you say thank you, you like yourself better as well. You feel better inside. You feel happier and more content with yourself and your life. You feel more fully integrated and positive about what you are doing. When you develop an attitude of gratitude, when it flows forth from you in all of your interactions with others, you will be amazed at how popular you will become and how eager others will be to help you in whatever you are doing.

The second way to make people feel important, raise their self-esteem, and give them a sense of power and energy is through the generous use of praise and approval. Psychological tests show that when children are praised by the people they look up to, their energy levels rise, their heart rates and respiratory rates increase, and they feel happier about themselves overall.

Perhaps the most valuable lesson in Ken Blanchard and Spencer Johnson's book *The One Minute Manager* is their recommendation to give "one minute praisings" at every opportunity. If you give genuine and honest approval to people for their accomplishments, large and small, you will be amazed at how much more people like you and how much more willing they are to help you achieve your goals.

There is a psychological Law of Reciprocity that says, "If you make me feel good about myself, I will find a way to make you feel good about yourself." In other words, people will always look for ways to reciprocate your kindnesses toward them. When you look for every opportunity to do and say things that make other people feel good, you will be astonished at not only how good you feel, but also by the wonderful things that begin to happen around you.

The third way to empower others is simply to pay close attention to them when they talk. The great majority of people are so busy trying to be heard that they become impatient when others are talking. But remember, the most important activity in communication is listening intently to the other person when he or she is expressing himself or herself.

In summary, three general rules for empowering the people around you are appreciation, approval, and attention. Voice your thanks and gratitude to others at every opportunity; praise them for every accomplishment; and pay close attention to them when they want to talk with you. These three behaviors alone will make you a master of human interaction and will greatly empower the people around you.

It's certainly possible for you to get the cooperation of others by threatening or browbeating them, but you will get only minimal cooperation, minimal output, and minimal assistance. To move to the top of your field, you must appeal to people's inner motivations and drives, their deepest emotions.

What motivates people in the world of work? The biggest motivator is clarity. People need to know exactly what they are supposed to do. They need to know why they are supposed to do it and how it fits into the big picture. They need to know how it will be measured and when it is due. They need to know what standard of quality is expected and how their efforts affect the work of others. The greater the clarity a person has about his or her assignment and the order of priority in which parts of it are to be done, the happier and more empowered he or she feels right from the start.

On the other hand, the biggest demotivator in the world of work is not knowing what is expected. It is being in the dark about what is supposed to be done and in what order of priority. People are especially demotivated when they don't know why they are doing a task or how it fits into the overall goals of the company.

The more time you spend talking to your subordinates and inviting their feedback and comments on the work, the more empowered they will be to do the work well. Earlier in this book, we discussed the concept of ownership in a job. Your function is to transfer the ownership into the heart and mind of the employee. When he or she feels personal ownership for a job and the responsibility for doing it well, he or she will be empowered. This is one of the most important aspects of the art of management.

Another major motivator at work is consideration. Employees report that the best managers they ever had were people who cared about them as individuals and as friends. These managers took the time to ask them questions about their lives and to listen patiently while they talked about the problems and situations in their families.

The more the employees felt the boss cared about them and respected them, the more empowered and motivated they felt.

The flip side of this motivator is the demotivating feeling that the boss doesn't care. This is almost invariably expressed by the boss in a lack of recognition, a lack of appreciation, and a general failure to pay attention to the employee over time.

Remember, the amount of time you spend talking to and listening to an employee is a signal to that employee that he or she is important to you and to the company. This is why the very best bosses spend a lot of time walking around and chatting with their employees. They sit with them for lunch and coffee. They invite their comments and encourage open discussion and disagreements about work. They create an environment where people feel that the work belongs to them as well as to the company. In that environment, employees feel good about themselves and more fully committed to doing the job and doing it well.

To empower and motivate the third group of people mentioned at the beginning of this chapter—your customers, your suppliers, your bankers, and so on—you simply need to practice what we've already talked about. The most important of all is that you be a genuinely positive and cheerful person. You must be the kind of person from whom "never is heard a discouraging word." You must be easygoing, genial, friendly, patient, tolerant, and open-minded. You must make people feel comfortable being around you.

Remember, everyone is primarily an emotional creature. Everything people do or refrain from doing is triggered by their deeper emotions. Your job is to connect with their higher and more positive emotions so they feel so good about you, and so they will want to help you and please you in some way.

For example, whenever you go into a crowded restaurant, stand in a long line to board a plane, or go up to a busy hotel desk, instead of becoming impatient with the slow rate of service, put yourself in the employee's place, and ask him how he is.

Whenever I go into a busy restaurant, I always ask the waiter for his name. Then I address him by name, while observing sympathetically, "You seem to be working hard today."

From that moment on, the waiter always gives me special attention. Why? Because I took the time to empathize with his situation, rather than acting impatiently because of mine.

Try this approach with the people in your workplace. Observe their situation and empathize with how hard they are working, how many difficulties they have, how overloaded they are, and so on. It is amazing how much better people feel about you when you take that approach to them, rather than just thinking about yourself.

You always have a choice. You can either do everything yourself, or you can get others to help you do some of the work. Our entire economic structure is built on the principle of specialization. Specialization means that some people become very good at doing certain tasks, while other people become good at doing other tasks.

To achieve your full potential, you must contribute the greatest amount of value possible. You must concentrate all your energy on doing certain specialized tasks in an excellent fashion so you can be paid the amount you want to earn, and so you can move ahead at the rate you want to move ahead. But in order for you to specialize and do what you are best at, and more of it, you must delegate, relegate, and outsource virtually everything else.

Some non-management people feel that the subject of delegation does not apply to them. But even when you ask your child to bring you the newspaper, you are delegating a task. When you go out to lunch rather than making it yourself, you are delegating. When you go into a full-service gas station rather than filling your own tank, again you are delegating. You are in a process of continuous delegation from the time you get up in the morning until the time you go to sleep at night. The only question is your skill at it. Your ability to delegate effectively, which requires that you inspire and empower others to help you willingly, will determine how fast you move ahead. It will determine how much you earn in your job. It will determine the quality and quantity of your results. It will determine your ultimate financial success in life. And the key to all of this is your ability to empower others.

Questions to Ponder

• Do your employees love their jobs?

• Have you found out how you could make their work even more enjoyable? Astute managers know that recognition and pride are stronger motivators than money.

- What is your reward system for exceptional performance? Remember, exceptional performance doesn't only happen in the sales department!

The 7th is the shortest hole in championship golf, Sir; just 107 yards. But sometimes the sea's so rough the waves spray right onto the green. It's no trouble if you find the green. But if you miss it . . . This shot frightens you? Don't feel bad—it happens to the best of 'em. But the real champions accept fear and know how to deal with it.

Now just relax and make a smooth swing, Sir . . . Oh boy! You sure yanked that one left. I think it stayed up, but only just. You'll have one tough shot! . . . How do champions deal with fear? I'll tell you.

Conquering Fear

That Uncertain Feeling

We all know how it feels. Your round is going well; you're playing several strokes better than your handicap. Then you come to a perfectly straightforward par three—no more than a solid 5-iron with the flag in the middle of the dance floor. The only problem is the lake between you and the flag! You grip your club, set up for the shot, and suddenly it hits you like a Peterbilt truck. Fear! Nauseating, mind bending, paralyzing fear and anxiety about the different things that can go wrong and where your ball will finish. Unfortunately, you are already subconsciously determining your own fate. In your mind's eye, you can see your ball splashing into the lake, short and right of the green.

If you think it only happens to amateurs, you're wrong. Believe it or not, champions have to deal with identical fears—fear of failure, fear of choking, fear of looking bad in front of their friends and peers. On those lonely walks between shots, or waiting on the tee, it can invade their minds like a cancer. Bobby Jones once said, "I was always tense before I went out. I couldn't have done anything if I hadn't been. The days I didn't feel anything, I didn't score."

Yes, in the heat of battle, even the finest players question their swings, their putting strokes, and their ability to maintain a narrow lead in a tournament. One of the main reasons you almost never see a tour rookie win a major championship is the increased level of fear that exists in the majors. The thought of seeing your name on the same trophy with Nicklaus, Palmer, Hogan, and Jones certainly adds to the pressure and the fear. Aren't some of the players in the field better than they? Isn't this the most shots they have ever been under par? Can they actually break Nicklaus' 72-hole scoring record? Are they really ready to handle the fame and responsibility that goes with the green jacket?

There are actually two kinds of fear to be conquered on the road to victory. Anyone who has ever made it to the top in any field is familiar with the first; it's fear of failure. The second, while less well known, is equally damaging. It is fear of winning—of actually achieving your goals and getting to the top.

Fear of Failure

> "At the U.S. Open, the person I fear most in the last two
> rounds is myself."
> Tom Watson

Who has not at some time been afraid of failure, afraid of looking bad in front of his peers, friends, or clients? Who has never experienced the fear of struggling around the course on a bad day and shooting an embarrassingly high score, then having it posted for all his fellow club members to see? Who has never dreaded the possibility he'll top the ball off the 1st tee with a crowd of people watching, or shank it into the woods, or miss a crucial two-foot putt on the only hole where his partner needed help? Everybody has experienced fear of failure at some time.

Champions Confront Their Fears

How do champions develop the ability to deal with fear? Champions like Jack Nicklaus confront their fears head on rather than denying they exist. Denial of any problem aggravates the situation and leads to greater problems. Unfortunately, most people refuse to face their fears, believing it makes them appear weak. Instead, they deny, avoid, manipulate, and hide the truth from themselves and others. Champions accept that it is human nature to experience fear. It can be our best form of protection in times of great danger. To conquer *irrational* fears and get their minds back on track, they use positive attitude and plain old-fashioned reason.

Nicklaus confronts fear of failure by saying to himself, "Jack, what are you afraid of? You've obviously played well to get this far. You deserve to be in a position to win based on that good play. Why not just settle down, accept the challenge, and play the game one shot at a time?"

Incidentally, don't let anyone persuade you that talking to yourself, in a positive way of course, is a sign of mental illness. Many successful people use the technique to reinforce their strength of purpose.

Nicklaus has obviously found that confronting his fears by reasoning with himself has been an effective way of dealing with self-doubt, but others are not so skilled. They allow fear to take over their minds, their bodies, and their swings. They choke so badly you want to turn your head away to spare them, and you, further embarrassment. Fear is graphically evident every year at the Tour Qualifying School, where hundreds of talented players and would-be champions play for a precious handful of tour cards. Those who fail to get a card must scrape around for another long year on various mini-tours before getting another chance. Many of them tee the ball on the first hole, focusing on this frightening possibility, their minds dominated by negative thoughts about the pitfalls that lie ahead, waiting to rob them of their dreams. They anticipate failure and, consequently, they fail.

"I Don't Need It" Fear

Another type of fear of failure is the "I don't care" fear. In this case, the player involved adopts a nonchalant air about his shots, putts, and game in general, as if he is completely unconcerned with the outcome. If he turns in a sub-standard performance, he defends himself by saying he was just strolling around the course for fun and, if he really cared about trophies or prize money, he could quickly sharpen up his game to tour quality. He may tell you he doesn't like to travel, or he doesn't need the hassle and the pro-ams, and anyway he really doesn't need the money; he can make more selling real estate. He may tell you he is content to play the State Open and the local mini-tour and try to qualify for the occasional PGA Tour event that passes though. Of course, when he doesn't make it, he'll tell you he wasn't all that excited about qualifying anyway.

I have seen this fear a thousand times, and I assure you, every word that player utters is nonsense! His ego and his entire life are centered around his golf game, but he is so frightened he won't make it, he can't even admit it to himself, let alone his friends. He protects himself from having to concede that he doesn't have what it takes to be a champion by building excuses for his failure in advance. In doing so, he starts out with a self-inflicted handicap.

Fear of Success

While fear of failure afflicts 95 percent of those who wish to become champions, there is another kind of fear that cripples the other 5 percent and prevents them from climbing to the heights. This smaller group has beaten fear of failure, but hasn't yet overcome this more subtle fear—the fear of success. Fear of failure is easily detected, in yourself as well as in others, but fear of success is a far more elusive antagonist to recognize and defeat.

Some fear success because they believe they are not ready to be champions, even though the high quality of their play suggests otherwise. They fully understand that once they have competed and succeeded at the highest levels, they will be under enormous pressure to perform at that level again and again. They are afraid they will be unable to repeat previous fine performances, and they dread the humiliation they will experience in the event of subsequent failure. This, together with other responsibilities that go with being a champion, is too much for them. Instead of striving their utmost to reach the top of the championship pyramid, they sabotage themselves, usually without realizing it, just short of the prize.

Championship Responsibilities

Some players fear the responsibilities that come with championship status. Both the media and the public expect much more of champions, both on and off the course. They are in the spotlight, they are successful, and many people become jealous of their accomplishments. Before establishing himself as a great golfing talent and one of the world's best players, England's Nick Faldo was inundated by a deluge of merciless criticism in the ever charitable British tabloid press for his inability to win tournaments when he held the lead going into the final day. They labeled him, "El Foldo." Faldo didn't exactly help matters when he made statements such as, "I'd like to thank the press from the heart of my bottom!" It is to his credit that he has established his place in golfing history and today enjoys a much better, if occasionally shaky, relationship with the media.

Because of the microscopic attention to which they are subjected, champions are frequently the target of criticism and rumors. It's easy to avoid this type of responsibility and negative behavior by just being mediocre at whatever you do. Mediocre people are rarely the subject of faultfinding or envy, since there is little reason to notice them at all. Never be afraid to win. You had the self-discipline and the courage to work to reach your goals; you deserve whatever rewards and recognition victory brings. Ignore petty, non-constructive criticism and set new and grander goals.

Dealing with Criticism

"Jack Nicklaus plays a game with which I am not familiar."
Bobby Jones

Why were the fans so slow to take Jack Nicklaus to their hearts when he first burst on the golfing scene? Pure jealousy. He was young, he hit the ball a mile (and straight), he kept shooting very low scores, and he won majors when he was just out of school. How could he do that to Arnie! After a slow start, Nicklaus learned how to handle the pressure with skill and charm, and eventually won the fans over to his side by quietly doing what he did best. He kept making lower scores than anyone who had ever played the game! There was no denying he was the best, and he was comfortable with his supremacy.

Guilt Fear

Others experience fear of success because they're afraid of losing their friends. An example of this occurs when several young pros travel together on the tour for a period, sometimes with their wives, and form close relationships. Suddenly, one of them hits a winning streak, finishing in the top 10 twice in a row, then winning his first championship. You can be sure he's not going to be sleeping in the back of an RV any more. His friends, who cannot afford expensive hotels, will eventually drift away from their one-time buddy. Nothing will have changed in the way they feel about each other, but from this point forward, their lives will be going in different directions. The champion, no matter how much he wishes for things to be the same, will be isolated from his old friends and peers as he joins a new group. Only the very best friends will remain close. Because humans are social animals, this is too difficult for many people, so they choose instead to remain where they are in life, at a comfort level.

It's a fact of life that as you become a champion, the number of acquaintances you have dramatically increases while the number of good friends you have slowly dwindles. It's part of the price you pay for greatness. Birds of a feather flock together, and as you rise to greater heights, there will be fewer birds able to stand the altitude. The good news is that the birds that are left are your equals, and they are golden eagles. Your new peers are worthy of your friendship and loyalty.

That Crippling Comfort Zone

It is natural for many of us to rise to a level of comfort in our games, careers, or lives and then stop for a while to take a rest. Sometimes we don't realize we've leveled off, and at other times we talk ourselves into believing this is where we really wanted to be. The lure of the comfort level is appealing, and the fear of moving beyond it is great. Because the sensation of comfort is so powerful, many of us never again break out and strive to reach the next level with the same effort that propelled us upward to begin with. However, to become a champion, we must rise above our comfort zones again and again, breaking new ground each time, expanding our knowledge and experience and rising to new and ever greater challenges.

It stayed up, Sir, but you're not going to like the lie. It's sitting in a patch of ice-plant. About all you can do is shut the face on your sand iron and try to make solid contact . . . Well, you made it into the bunker. You can get up and down from there—just trust your swing . . . You quit on that one, Sir. Now take a moment to regroup and try again . . . That's the way! Tap it in for five and let's move on to number eight. That hole is history.

You can't believe you were four under and dropped two shots on the shortest hole on the couse? . . . Well, Sir, being in uncharted territory can be frightening, but champions have ways to handle it.

144

Breaking Through the Psychological Barrier

It's truly amazing how difficult it is for the human race to do what has never been done. For Chuck Yeager to fly a few miles an hour faster and break the sound barrier took years of research, cost millions of dollars, and was only achieved after several fine pilots had died in the attempt. Today, supersonic flight is routine. The sound barrier has been conquered by technology. Psychological barriers are an entirely different matter. The four-minute mile was considered by many to be beyond human endurance until Roger Bannister stunned the athletic world with his historic achievement. Nowadays, most of the field in top flight competition finishes faster than Bannister's once incredible time. Some athletic records are broken as athletes become bigger, stronger, and faster, but many barriers in the world of sports exist purely in the mind. Golf is a prime example.

Only a small minority of the world's millions of golfers ever break 100 on a regulation course. Those that do immediately begin to contemplate the near impossible feat of breaking 90. Having celebrated success in that goal, a smaller number dream of a round in the 70s. Only the greatest players aspire to the lofty heights of posting an 18-hole score under 70. Who selects these targets? What is their significance? Why not 92, 84, or 73? Specific numbers, of course, have no real importance, except as milestones on the way to something better. Strangely, though, just having the target score in our minds has the effect on most of us of increasing the difficulty of beating it. We find ways to fail when it seems success is within our grasp. Some cynic called it "snatching defeat from the jaws of victory."

Breaking Par

Think back. How many times have you arrived at the 17th or 18th tee with an excellent chance to shoot a new personal best score or win a tournament, only to have your game go bad just when you needed it most? How come you can get so close but can't break through? There are two reasons for this phenomenon.

First, we have never done this before; we are about to enter uncharted territory. Unfamiliar territory is always frightening, even when the rewards are high. It causes us to question our right to be there; in competition this means wondering whether we are good enough to win or even contend. This is where experience comes into play. You have to play yourself into a position to win often enough to overcome the fear that is born of your lack of experience.

One summer years ago, I played golf several times a week. I frequently arrived at the 9th hole at my club, a gentle dogleg to the right with little trouble and just over 400 yards from tee to green, needing a four or better to shoot one under par on the front side for the first time. That hole just refused to surrender! When I finally succeeded, it happened almost by accident, as I holed out from a greenside bunker. Having done it once, however, it no longer seemed so difficult, and I broke par for that side several times in the following month. Why did it take so long? Because I had never been there before. Eventually, I'd put myself in the position often enough to actually go ahead and break my own mental barrier. From that time on, although it was always a pleasant experience, breaking par was no "big deal."

When Jack Shot in the 80s

"The summer I was 12, I broke 80 for the first time. It was odd how it happened. I shot 80 eight straight times, and just as I was wondering what I had to do to break that barrier, I shot 74."
Jack Nicklaus

Even the great Jack Nicklaus scored in the 80s at one time; of course, he was only 11 years old. In his book *The Greatest Game of All*, Jack describes breaking his own mental barrier when he beat "old man par," as Bobby Jones called it, for the first time in his life.

The following year, Jack was playing golf with his father one evening when he shot 34 on the front nine, putting him in an excellent position to break 70 for the first time. To his dismay, as they walked off the 9th green, his father congratulated him on a great nine holes and announced it was time to go home for dinner. The young Nicklaus protested, but to no avail. His father said Mom was expecting them and they could finish the round after dinner. Both of them ate their food as quickly as they could swallow it and headed back to the course. Playing the par five 18th hole in near darkness, Nicklaus hit a long straight drive. He followed that with a 2-iron to the middle of the green, some 30 feet from the hole, just as the sprinklers came on. Making the eagle putt would give him a 69, and Jack Nicklaus seldom missed a putt that meant a lot to him. As he would do again and again during his unparalleled career when it really mattered, he rolled it in. To quote Jack, "The promised land!"

By regularly putting themselves in a position to win, overcoming fear of failure, and being ready to accept success, champions dramatically increase their chances of victory. Once that first winner's trophy is in the display case, others almost inevitably follow.

About "Choking"

Other than the dreaded "yips," no word strikes more fear into the heart of a professional golfer than "choke." In the early 1970s, one of greatest players ever, Tom Watson himself, had a reputation as a "choker." Then he won the 1975 British Open Championship at Carnoustie, in Scotland. It was the first of an incredible five times he would win the world's oldest major championship. That night, as he celebrated in a local pub with his friends, he was asked what was different this time compared to other times when he had come close but hadn't won. Tom's face lit up with his trademark, Huck Finn smile, and he said, "Sometimes you have to lose major championships before you can win them. It's the price you pay to mature. The more times you can put yourself in pressure situations, the more times you compete, the better off you are. It's a learning experience that's worth a fortune."

Nearly all great players would be quick to agree with him. With each adventure, good or bad, you expand your area of experience until that area encompasses the goals you set for yourself.

Play to Win

The second key to breaking through the "fear of success" barrier is playing to win. Often, when we see a possibility that we might win, we abandon the course of action or play that put us in a position to win in the first place, and opt for a series of safe, conservative shots. We start playing not to lose instead of playing to win. The results are seldom good.

The effect of this change of attitude on the human brain is enormous. In our minds, the concepts of winning and losing are in diametric opposition to one another; they can't readily co-exist. Once the brain is assigned a task, consciously or subconsciously, it does everything it can to complete that task. The "win" message is clear and unequivocal. The brain reacts by giving us an edge in terms of additional confidence and creativity. The "don't lose" signal is vague and indefinite, and any way you look at it, the word *lose* is a negative keyword. The brain is apt to function accordingly, eroding our confidence and stifling creativity, leading eventually to defeat.

Playing to win gives champions an edge, mentally *and* physically. When we play to win, the brain helps us to remain relaxed, and the adrenaline starts to pump, summoning up reserves of power. When asked to adopt a defensive position rather than a winning one, the brain is more likely to react by inducing tension and stiffness, neither condition being conducive to victory.

Arnie Changes Plans

Arnold Palmer relates in his book, aptly titled *Go for Broke*, that at some point in the middle '60s, he changed his overall game plan. He started trying to play golf in the style of Ben Hogan—conservative golf, precision golf, calculated golf. It just wasn't right for him. It wasn't the style of golf that had already won him seven major championships. After a lean year in 1965, Palmer privately reappraised his decision. "Ultimately, I began to wonder if I could win, if I was afraid to win."

At the start of the 1966 season, Palmer felt certain he had to win in order to prove himself again. After three rounds of the Los Angeles Open, he had built a seven shot lead. In the final round he unconsciously reverted to the "don't lose" mode of play. He went out worrying about his lead—concerned with how he could protect it rather than how he could increase it. With four holes left to play, the seven-shot lead had all but evaporated. Now he led by only one stroke. Finally, on the 15th tee, he shook himself mentally and went back to playing the kind of golf only Arnie could play. It was time to charge. Hitching up his pants, he ripped it down the fairway and went on to win the tournament. He would win five other tournaments that same year.

Over the years, Palmer resorted to all kinds of little tricks to help him play positively, shun negative thoughts, and avoid falling prey to "man's natural fear." One such trick was to look only at the leaders' scores when observing a scoreboard and ignore the names associated with those scores. In this way he avoided thinking about how *they* might play the remaining holes. Instead of second-guessing the competition, he just kept trying to make birdies and shoot the lowest possible score.

Mastering the Concept

In 1985, Curtis Strange was one of the hottest players in the world, but was still without victory in a major. At the Masters that year, after a horrible opening round 80, he had carded consecutive scores of 65 and was in a good position to win the tournament. Then he fell victim to Augusta's final nine, finding the bottom of the creek at 13 and 15 and finishing in second place behind Bernhard Langer of Germany. Let Curtis tell us what happened:

"I was more worried about losing than winning, and guess what—I lost. Now I just play the same game and allow the rest of the players to worry about winning or losing. When I stopped worrying about winning and losing, I started to win."

Having learned this valuable lesson, he became the dominant U.S. player of the late '80s, winning back-to-back U.S. Opens in 1988 and 1989. Curtis, however, has been bedeviled throughout his career by personal doubts and fears about his ability to win. The fact remains, when he played to win, he often did.

Perhaps the most audacious example of playing to win in recent memory was at the 1997 Tournament of Champions at La Costa Resort in California. Plagued by uncharacteristic rain, the tournament was shortened to 54 holes. That left the previous year's best player and reigning British Open Champion, Tom Lehman, pitted against young Tiger Woods in a sudden death playoff situation. After a lengthy delay, the two players took their position on the par three, playoff hole—almost 200 yards over water, with the flag cut back left dangerously close to the water's edge. Lehman, up first, was ready to strike a blow, but he hit it just a little fat and a little left into the water. Woods would surely play it safe. He should hit out to the right side of the green or even right of the green entirely; that's the safe play, right, away from the water. It was the smart play but wasn't the Tiger play. He got up and hit a 6-iron right at the flag, right over the water, six inches from the hole. Tiger only knew one way to play: play to win!

After the tournament, Tiger was interviewed by Curtis Strange. He asked Tiger if winning was the most important thing. "What's wrong with second or third?" Strange asked. With clarity and confidence, Tiger responded, "Second sucks!"

Once you have found a way to do well, the way you choose to do it, the way that works best for you, don't desert the methods that got you in a position to win. Play your own game. Don't let your competitors dictate how you will play. Remember the words of the great Bobby Jones. "Golf is a game played mainly in the six-inch space between your ears."

Use that space wisely and positively. Confront and overcome your fears with the burning desire to succeed that can crush any obstacle. Play to win—like a champion.

Jack Nicklaus calls the 8th the greatest par four in golf. At 425 yards, it's not one of the longest, but wait until you see the second shot! Two hundred yards from the top of the cliff and down over 100 feet to a tiny green that's still 50 feet above the ocean. First we have to get the ball in play. A good 3-wood will take you over the crest of the hill and keep you about 20 yards short of the cliff ... Good drive! That'll be in excellent position for the second shot.

I'd keep it left and let it fade back at the green if I were you, Sir. I think 3-iron is plenty ... That was a little quick, but it got up even if you caught it a tad thin. It may not have been your best shot, Sir, but anything that finishes in the middle of the green is a "keeper" on this hole ... This putt breaks a mile to the left! You'll have to aim several feet right just to get it close ... Okay!

Swing Thoughts

- Champions address and conquer their fears.

- Fear of failure is terribly powerful, capable of robbing you of the success that can be yours. Address it head on. Accept that putting yourself in a position to succeed means you can succeed.

- Champions break their psychological barriers by continually widening their field of experience until it includes victory.

- Fear of success is much more subtle, but must also be addressed before one can become a champion.

- When you are in a position to win, overcome fear of success by realizing that the ability and attitude that got you where you are entitle you to be a champion. You are ready; just stick to your guns.

- Champions play to win, they never play not to lose.

Back in the Clubhouse

Successful executives react and respond to fear more effectively than others. Perhaps the greatest challenge you will ever face in life is the conquest of fear and the development of the habit of courage.

Winston Churchill once wrote, "Courage is rightly considered the foremost of the virtues, for upon it, all others depend." Fear is, and always has been, the greatest enemy of mankind. When Franklin D. Roosevelt said, "The only thing we have to fear is fear itself," he was saying that the emotion of fear, rather than the reality of what we fear, is what causes us anxiety, stress, and unhappiness. When you develop the habit of courage and unshakable self-confidence, a whole new world of possibilities opens up for you. Just think: What would you dare to dream, be, or do if you weren't afraid of anything in the whole world?

Fortunately, the habit of courage can be learned, just as any other success skill is learned. To do so, we need to go to work systematically to diminish and eradicate our fears, while simultaneously building the kind of courage that will enable us to deal fearlessly with the inevitable ups and downs of life.

Syndicated columnist Ann Landers wrote, "If I were asked to give what I consider the single, most useful bit of advice for all humanity, it would be this: Expect trouble as an inevitable part of life, and when it comes, hold your head high. Look it squarely in the eye, and say, 'I will be bigger than you. You cannot defeat me.'" This is the kind of attitude that leads to victory.

The starting point in overcoming fear and developing courage is to look at the factors that predispose us toward fear.

The root source of fear is childhood conditioning that causes us to experience two types of fear: the fear of failure, which causes us to think, "I can't, I can't, I can't"; and the fear of rejection, which causes us to think, "I have to, I have to, I have to."

Based on those fears, we become preoccupied with the idea of losing our money, our time, or our emotional investment in a relationship. We become hypersensitive to the opinions and possible criticisms of others, sometimes to the point where we are afraid to do anything that anyone else might disapprove of. Our fears tend to paralyze us, holding us back from taking constructive action in the direction of our dreams and goals. We hesitate, we become indecisive, and we procrastinate; we make excuses and find reasons not to move ahead. And finally, we feel frustrated, caught in the double bind of "I have to, but I can't" or "I can't, but I have to."

Fear is also caused by ignorance. When we have limited information, we tend to be tense and insecure about the outcome of our actions. Ignorance causes us to fear change, to fear the unknown, and to avoid trying anything new or different. But the reverse is also true. The very act of gathering more and more information about a particular subject causes us to be more courageous and confident in that area. There are parts of our life where we have no fear at all because we feel knowledgeable and capable of handling whatever happens.

Another factor that causes fear is illness or fatigue. When we are tired or unwell, or when we are not physically fit, we are more predisposed to fear and doubt than when we are feeling healthy and happy and terrific about ourselves.

Once you recognize the factors that can cause fear, the second step in overcoming it is to sit down and take the time to objectively identify, define, and analyze your own fears. At the top of a sheet of paper, write the question, "What am I afraid of?"

Now, before you begin, here's an important point to remember: all intelligent people are afraid of something. It is normal and natural to be concerned about your physical, emotional, and financial survival. The courageous person is not a person who is unafraid. As Mark Twain said, "Courage is resistance to fear, mastery of fear—not absence of fear."

It is not whether or not you are afraid. We all are afraid. The question is, how do you deal with the fear? The courageous person is simply one who goes forward in spite of the fear. And here's something else I've learned: when you confront your fears and move toward what you are afraid of, your fears diminish and your self-esteem and self-confidence increase.

However, when you avoid the things you fear, your fears grow until they begin to control every aspect of your life. And as your fears increase, your self-esteem, your self-confidence, and your self-respect diminish accordingly.

Begin your list of fears by writing down everything, major and minor, over which you experience any anxiety. The most common fears, of course, are those of failure and rejection.

Some people, compelled by the fear of failure, invest an enormous amount of energy justifying or covering up their mistakes. And some people, compelled by the fear of rejection, are so obsessed with how they appear to others that they seem to have no ability at all to take independent action. Until they are absolutely certain that someone else will approve, they refrain from doing anything.

Once you have made a list of every fear you think may be affecting your thinking and behavior, organize the items in order of importance. Which fear do you feel has the greatest impact on your thinking or holds you back more than any other? Which fear would be number two? And so on.

With regard to your predominant fear, write the answers to these three questions:

1. How does this fear hold me back in life?
2. How does this fear help me? How has it helped me in the past?
3. What would be my payoff for eliminating this fear?

Some years ago, I went through this exercise and concluded that my biggest fear was the fear of poverty. I was afraid of not having enough money, of being broke, perhaps even of being destitute. I knew that this fear had originated during my childhood because my parents, who grew up during the Depression, had continually worried about money. My fear was reinforced when I was broke at various times during my 20s. I could objectively assess the origins of that fear, but it still had a strong hold on me. Even when I had sufficient money for all my needs, that fear was always there.

My answer to the question, "How does this fear hold me back in life?" was that it caused me to be anxious about taking risks with money. It caused me to play it safe with regard to employment. And it caused me to choose security over opportunity.

My answer to the second question, "How does this fear help me?" was that, in order to escape the fear of poverty, I tended to work much longer and harder. I was more ambitious and determined. I took much more time to educate myself on the various ways money could be invested. The fear of poverty was, in effect, driving me toward financial independence.

When I answered the third question, "What would be my payoff for eliminating this fear?" I immediately saw that I would be willing to take more risks, I would be more aggressive in pursuing my financial goals, I could and would start my own business, and I would not be so tense and concerned about spending too much or having too little. I would no longer be so concerned about the price of everything. By objectively analyzing my biggest fear in this way, I was able to begin the process of eliminating it.

You can begin the process of developing courage and eliminating fear by engaging in actions consistent with the behaviors of courage and self-confidence. Since anything you practice over and over eventually becomes a new habit, let's focus on some of the areas where you can practice to develop the habit of courage.

The first and perhaps most important kind of courage is the courage to begin, to launch, to step out in faith. This is the courage to try something new or different, to move out of your comfort zone, with no guarantee of success. John Ronstadt, a professor at Babson College who taught entrepreneurship for 12 years, conducted a study of those who took his class and later became successful. He could find only one quality they had in common: their willingness to actually start their own business in the marketplace. He called this the "corridor principle." He said that as those individuals moved forward, as though proceeding down a corridor, doors opened to them that they would not have seen if they had not been in motion.

It turned out that those who had completed his entrepreneurship course who had done nothing with what they had learned were still waiting for things to be just right before they began. They were unwilling to launch themselves down the corridor of uncertainty until they could somehow be assured that they would be successful—something that never happens.

The future belongs to the risk takers, not the security seekers. Life is perverse in the sense that the more you seek security, the less of it you have. But the more you seek opportunity, the more likely it is that you will achieve the security you desire.

One way to get the courage to begin, from which everything else flows, is to plan and prepare thoroughly in advance. Set clear goals or objectives; then gather information. Read and research in your chosen field. Write out detailed plans of action, and take the first step.

The second kind of courage is the courage to endure, to persist, to stay at it once you have begun. Persistence is a form of courageous patience, and it is one of the rarest types of courage. Courageous patience is the ability to stand firm after you have taken action and before you get any feedback or results from your action. When you plan your work and work your plan with persistence, even in the face of disappointment and unexpected setbacks, you will build and develop the quality of courage within you.

Whenever you feel fear or anxiety and you need to bolster your courage, concentrate your attention on your goals. Create a mental picture of the person you would like to be, performing the way you would like to perform. There's nothing wrong with thoughts of fear as long as you temper them with thoughts of courage and self-reliance. What you dwell upon, grows . . . so be careful.

The third type of courage is the courage to conquer worry—a form of negative goal setting. When you worry, you are dwelling upon, talking about, and vividly imagining exactly what you don't want to happen. If you worry long enough and hard enough about something, you are going to attract it into your life. The great tragedy is that even if the situation you are worrying about does not materialize, your health and your emotions will suffer just the same. And the fact is, most of the things people worry about never happen.

The only real antidote to worry is purposeful action toward a predetermined goal or solution. Since the conscious mind can hold only one thought at a time, when you get busy doing something to resolve your problem, you will not have the time or the mental capacity to worry. And before you know it, your worrisome situation will have been resolved.

The mastery of fear and the development of courage are essential prerequisites for a happy, successful life. With a commitment to acquire the habit of courage, you will eventually reach the point where your fears no longer play a major role in your decision making. You will set big, challenging, exciting goals, and you will have the confidence of knowing you can attain them. You will be able to face every situation with calmness and self-assurance, and the key is courage.

Questions to Ponder

- Have you addressed fear of change, failure, success, and responsibility in yourself and your staff?

- Have you identified and broken down any mental barriers that hold you back?

- Is your thinking sound? Why not find a better way?

- Do your actions demonstrate you are playing to win?

Now for the ninth. It's 450 yards, Sir, and the cliffs on the right come into play the entire length of the hole. On top of that, the fairway slopes from left to right. Most players try to keep the tee shot left, but as you can see, there are bunkers and heavy rough on that side. There's nothing for it but to trust your swing and hit a nice draw down the middle . . . Very fast on the backswing, Sir. You've pulled it way left . . . It missed the traps but the rough is petty thick over there. Let's see if we can find it. What do champions use on a tough hole like this? Confidence, Sir—it's the weapon of champions.

Confidence—
The Weapon
of Champions

The Importance of Confidence

"I'm going to make so much money this year, my cad-
die's going to make the top 10 on the money list."
Lee Trevino

It's been my experience, and that of many other interested observers, that most bad shots are the result of fear. When a player is already full of apprehension about his ability to play the required shot, and expecting the worst before he even addresses his ball, the outcome will invariably be a bad shot. You'll hear the same lament all over the world as the ball flies wildly into a water hazard or a bunker. "I *knew* I was going to do that!"

Players who have the confidence to stick to their game plan and trust their regular swings are the ones who become champions. Nobody becomes a champion in anything without first developing a high degree of self-confidence in his ability to perform. The key word here is "developing," since every champion in the world has been plagued by self-doubt and lack of confidence at some time. With high self-confidence in place, champions can win even when their swings are plagued by problems.

The "Yes I Can" Attitude

"It's easy to play like Jack Nicklaus when you're Jack Nicklaus."
Jack Nicklaus

During the 1973 Ryder Cup, Jack Nicklaus was paired with Tom Weiskopf, who had won that year's British Open at Royal Troon. Jack's wife, Barbara, was eight months pregnant. Although she had walked the course during the morning round, she announced as she stood on the first tee in the afternoon that she probably would not make it through the entire match. Jack responded, loud enough for his opponents to hear, "Don't worry; it won't be a long walk." Jack wasn't just talking; he meant exactly what he said.

On the 1st hole, Weiskopf had played an excellent approach shot to about 10 feet, while Nicklaus lay some 15 feet away on the same line. Jack startled Weiskopf, the gallery, and his opponents when he turned to Weiskopf and said, "Pick it up, Tom."

"You mean mark it." Tom said.

"No, pick it up. There's no way I'm going to miss this putt!"

A puzzled Weiskopf did as he was instructed and stood aside. Nicklaus made the putt, and they went on to win their match easily.

When Johnny Miller Was in the Zone

In 1974, Johnny Miller won eight tournaments on the PGA Tour. What could he possibly do for an encore in 1975? How about winning the first two tournaments he played in, shooting a total of 49 under par? (Yes, 49!)

After finishing 24 under par in the Phoenix Open, Miller was quoted as saying, "I'm hitting the ball so well it's almost a joke." Some of the other players were having difficulty seeing the humor in this situation. One commented, "Miller is playing so well he makes the rest of us look like monkeys." A reporter questioned Miller about his level of confidence, following yet another round in the low 60s. He replied, "I was standing out on the fairway with a 5-iron in my hand, 190 yards from the hole, actually thinking about holing the shot." That's the combination of confidence and visualization that elevated this great player to his maximum performance level. The following week, when the smoke cleared at the Tucson Open, Miller had recorded scores of 66, 69, 67, and a final round 61 for a total of 25 under par, nine shots ahead of his closest rival. Two weeks later he followed this feat with yet another first place finish in Bob Hope's annual 90-hole event in Palm Springs.

Miller was "in the zone." What brought him to this dizzying pinnacle of performance in the winter of 1975? He was fueled by unshakable confidence. Being young, handsome, and rich may have helped. Talent was undoubtedly important. But there were other key factors, developed over the preceding few months, that enabled Miller's self-confidence to reach such heights, namely:

1) His practice and tournament play were focused on getting himself in a position to win, building confidence in his physical abilities.

2) He liked the desert courses, and expected to do well on them.

3) He had been playing well enough to be rewarded with victory in previous weeks.

4) He was being told by the media, his peers—everyone in the world—how well he was playing, and this strengthened his own belief in himself.

5) He was visualizing perfect outcomes to all his shots.

6) He set no limits on how low a score he could shoot.

Boosting Your Confidence to Championship Level

How do you develop the confidence to hit your 3-iron over 205 yards of water, instead of playing safe to the left? Or change careers in midstream? Or make that big business deal a reality? Confidence is the result of habitually doing things well. It comes from being rewarded for doing those things well. It comes from the applause of the gallery, the headlines in the newspaper, the slaps on the back from your peers, and the thrill of holding up a trophy in victory. But how do you build that confidence when achieving your long-term goal may be several years away? How do you acquire the confidence to win before you have won?

If You Can Do It Once You Can Do It Regularly

Have you ever holed a 50-foot putt? Have you ever made two or more birdies in a row? Have you ever killed a drive over 250 yards, straight down the middle? Have you ever shot a round several strokes better than your handicap?

Many a player who has not yet reached championship level, when he shoots a great score, feels he has somehow played over his head.

When he hits a couple of long drives or sinks five putts in a row, he tells himself it was pure luck and not "the real him." In fact, what he is doing is demonstrating his true potential. If he can do it once, why should he entertain any doubts about being able to do it a thousand times?

If you shoot 68 once, you can do it again, and the first step is the realization that your true talent is probably greater than you think it is.

Practice Both Aspects of the Game

Nothing boosts confidence like quality practice. Striking balls solidly on the driving range will send you to the course feeling you can burn it up. That feeling is at least as important as having a good swing, mechanically. Look at the swings of Lee Trevino, Raymond Floyd, and Jack Nicklaus. They could hardly be more different, and yet, through practice, each has learned to place a high degree of trust and confidence in his method. Never forget that practice involves not only the physical aspects of the swing, but the mental as well.

Many observers believe Ben Hogan became an even better player after his car accident. Because of the reduced strength in his legs, he developed his course management skills to unheard of levels. He continued practicing just as much as he had before sustaining his injuries, but now he placed much greater demands on his mental capacity. Later, you'll meet others who, like Hogan, overcame physical handicaps with psychological strength in order to become champions.

Set Short-term Goals

To develop confidence, you must set short-term goals for yourself, *and be sure to write them down*. An early one might be breaking 100 *en route* to your long-term goal of shooting consistently in the 70s. Another might be to average 30 putts per round, or to hit a certain number of fairways or greens in regulation. For a tour player it might be making the cut and putting himself in position to shoot good rounds on Saturday and Sunday. Whatever your goal, it has to be in place so you have something to aim for, and also so you'll know when you reach it. More important, from the standpoint of building confidence, it has to be an achievable yardstick, so every inch of progress is noted by the brain and serves to increase confidence.

Reward Yourself

Once you have reached a short-term goal, reward yourself for your success. Give yourself a pat on the back, buy a new golf bag, or treat yourself to a week in Hawaii. The size of the reward for small successes doesn't matter, but make sure you do it. At the very least, be a one-person cheerleading team on your own behalf. There's no better feeling for a golfer than making a birdie, being congratulated for the achievement, and getting excited about the possibility of doing the same on the very next hole.

Several college golf coaches have their players play from the front tees a couple of times a month, so the players become accustomed to making birdie after birdie and shooting low scores. This quickly boosts the players' confidence and prepares them better mentally to shoot good scores in the heat of competition. Once you have been there, it's much easier for your brain to accept that you can go back and do it again under similar, if slightly different, circumstances.

Try building your own confidence by moving up from the back tees to the whites every now and then, to see how low a score you can shoot. If your home course is renowned for its difficulty, play another, easier course from time to time. All those good scores add up to increased confidence.

Look for Positive Signs

Self-confidence can also increase based on factors other than your own swing and the way you feel on a given day. For example, some players win often on certain courses. Mark O'Meara has made a habit of winning at Pebble Beach, while Sam Snead won at Greenbriar so many times they should have named the tournament after him. Johnny Miller, of course, was famous for playing some of his best golf on desert courses.

Certain tournaments also give certain players a feeling of confidence. Jack Nicklaus, Tom Watson, and Nick Faldo have always been at their best in major tournaments like the Open and the Masters. Walter Hagen was perhaps the world's finest match play champion, winning the PGA Championship five times before the format was changed from match play to stroke play.

The level of self-confidence of some players increases when the weather is bad. They believe playing in wind and rain, for instance, will give them an advantage over the rest of the field. Watson, Ballesteros, and Trevino are prime examples of excellent bad-weather players, because they have a wider variety of shots at their disposal and possess superior short games. They enjoy the ability to get up and down from almost anywhere, saving pars even when the elements are against them and others are having to settle for bogey.

Some players feel very confident with certain clubs, while they lack confidence with others. Some feel confident hitting a certain kind of shot or even playing a favorite hole. Even though they may not be enjoying a good day, they'll step up to the tee on a par five they like and rip it down the middle, setting themselves up for an easy birdie.

Search your mind for things, not associated with your basic physical ability, that build your confidence. What courses, holes, clubs, or tournaments have you felt good about in the past? Focusing on those positives will allow your confidence to grow around them.

Recruit Some Fans

One of the best ways for champions to enhance both the quality and quantity of their reserves of self-confidence is to surround themselves with others who believe in their ability. Excellent confidence boosters are to be found among family members, other players, and good friends. When a champion finds himself frequently in the company of someone who doubts his capabilities, he may have to remove that person from his list of friends. He cannot afford many acquaintances who make a practice of chipping away at his self-confidence.

Almost every professional caddie agrees that his primary responsibility is to maintain a high level of confidence in the player whose bag he carries. When their man is unsure or hesitant about the situation facing him, it's the caddie's job to reassure him that he has the right club and can successfully make the shot. You'll often hear a caddie say something like, "I like that club. It's perfect for this shot!" Nothing sucks the confidence out of a golfer faster than being second-guessed once he has reached a decision. When a caddie is not supportive, he won't be around for very long, and quite frankly, that's the way it should be. There are enough monsters out their waiting for a chance to devour you. You don't need to be surrounded by a bunch of "confidence thieves."

What Boosts or Destroys Your Confidence in Your Own Ability?

Do you play better when you set yourself a target score? Are you better when you find yourself in a tight spot? Does it help you to give yourself little reminders or a quiet word of encouragement under your breath? Do you feel that you are likely to score lower when you wear a cap rather than a visor? It doesn't matter. If it helps, use it!

Is your self-confidence diminished if your peers laugh at a bad shot? Is it threatened by a particular hole, the mere sight of water, or a specific course? Does tournament play or the pressure of a gallery cause you to lose confidence? Do you fold when the bet is pressed?

Knowing that you lack confidence in certain areas allows you to plan around your "confidence stealers." For example, if a tour player loses confidence in his driver during the course of a round, he'll complete play using a 3-wood or a long iron from the tee. This allows him to make good swings because he trusts himself to make a better shot with the shorter club. Likewise, if he doubts his ability to make a certain shot with his pitching wedge, a champion may vary his strategy. A shorter shot from the tee will leave him an approach shot he feels good about, perhaps with an 8-iron. He knows the practice ground is the place to fix problems.

Most amateurs, on the other hand, are so stubborn that they will continue to beat away with the driver, even after they have completely lost confidence in their ability to hit it well. They try all kinds of desperate and unproven, experimental swing corrections, which only succeed in magnifying the erosion of trust.

The champion's way is much more effective. Once you recognize the influences that increase or threaten your self-confidence, you can go to work emphasizing the former and take steps to eliminate the areas where you have problems. Identify situations that eat away at your confidence, then plan to use the techniques of champions to restore and strengthen it. Alternatively, devise a strategy for working around problem areas until you have the opportunity to practice and rebuild your confidence in that specific area or situation.

Here it is, Sir . . . You'll just have to pitch back on the fairway . . . Smart play. You still have 210 yards to the green. That huge greenside trap reminds me of some of the nastier ones at St. Andrews. It guards all but the extreme right-hand portion of the putting surface. This calls for your best shot. I recommend the 5-wood. You've been hitting that with a lot of confidence . . . That's a beauty, bang in the center of the green . . . Two putts is fine from there.

The 10th hole is slightly shorter at 436 yards, but it still runs southeast and presents the same difficulties from the wind and the cliffs on the right. Nor is the left any easier! The green's slightly larger than number nine, but just as close to the rocks and the beach below. You need to start it down the right center with a nice draw . . . Now that's a fine shot, Sir!

What techniques do champions use to build confidence? I can think of several.

Golf Is Not a Perfect Game, and Neither is Life

In the late 1950s, the incomparable Ben Hogan was sitting by his locker after a tournament. A young, but already charismatic Arnold Palmer had taken first place and had just completed giving an entertaining interview to the members of the press. The room emptied, and one remaining reporter noticed Hogan somewhat stiffly tying the laces on his street shoes. It was an uncommon opportunity to speak to the Hawk one-on-one.

"Excuse me, Mr. Hogan," said the reporter, in a more polite tone than was his habit. "I wonder if you'd care to comment on Arnie's statement that he only hit the ball dead solid perfect about 10 times in shooting 67 today?"

Hogan, who is almost universally recognized as the purest striker of the golf ball ever to play the game, looked up. "That many?" he murmured, with an expression of honest surprise.

Hogan strove constantly for perfection, although he understood how elusive it was. His definition of a flawed shot was one that wound up in poor position, regardless of how well it had been struck and how accurately the striker had judged all of the outside factors, such as wind. Along the way he came to understand, as had Jones and Hagen before him, that golf is a game of mistakes. He believed that no player hit more than a handful of perfect shots during a single round of golf. Having fully accepted this fact, the self-doubt that had plagued him for so long began to vanish. In 1946, when he returned full-time to the tour after serving in the U.S. Navy during World War II, a new, more confident Hogan emerged. He was ready for battle, believing he could play well enough to win all the time—not just some of the time. Hogan said the foundation of his newly increased self-confidence was that he had stopped trying to hit every shot perfectly. It had become clear to him that this over-ambitious goal was neither possible, advisable, or necessary to play winning golf. While Hogan continued to search for perfection, he had learned to live with the imperfections that exist in all of us.

Demanding absolute perfection can be very damaging to the confidence. Many a golfer's dream has been lost without trace in the search for the flawless game. Many otherwise excellent players never make it to the top because they waste so much time in pursuit of the perfect swing, or waiting for the course and conditions that exactly suit their games. It's all right to look for it on the range and in practice rounds, but in competition, focus on the goal. Remember, it doesn't matter how well you hit it or where you hit it, as long as you take fewer strokes to get the ball in the hole than your competitors.

Expect the Best

Rather than getting into an exhaustive debate about the power of positive thinking, let's leave it at this. You have to be optimistic. Champions condition themselves to expect the best things to happen to them. They tee up on the 1st hole expecting to shoot a good score. They approach difficult situations expecting to hit a good shot, and they keep expecting good things to happen throughout the round. What technique do they employ to maintain all their high expectations? In their thoughts they dwell on the good things that happen to them, rather than the bad. Sounds too simple? Well, let's take a little test. I want you to think about four things, and decide whether they give you a feeling of confidence.

> The best course you have ever played.
> The best round you have ever played.
> The best shot you made last time you played.
> The worst shot you hit during your last round.

Did you consider all four items? Notice, there were three positives and one negative. Do you feel better about your game? I sincerely doubt it. Next time you are in a situation where you need an infusion of confidence, ask yourself the three positive questions and forget about the negative one. You *can* control your mental processes. It takes practice, but you can do it.

Visualization

Champions not only establish specific goals to help fuel their ambitions, they also visualize how they propose to accomplish those goals and how they will feel when they have achieved them. They experience mentally how it will feel to walk up the 18th fairway at Augusta, receiving a standing ovation. They get goose bumps just thinking about slipping their arms into the sleeves of that green jacket. They become emotionally excited, as if it were really happening. This type of psychological training not only intensifies desire but also helps condition the body and mind to react the right way when the opportunity actually arises. It is a key way to induce the body to perform at peak levels, and peak performance is the only kind that interests champions, because it is the only kind that quickly moves them closer to their goals.

The ability to visualize the outcome of achieving your goals is critical in helping you reach them quickly. It is also vital in helping you build reserves of confidence, determination, and persistence. The sharper and more vivid the visual images, the easier it will be to occasionally accept defeat in a skirmish, but still go on to win the war.

For a champion, visualization takes two forms. The first involves the overall outcome of the event, namely, winning the championship. The second is visualizing each specific and individual course of action he must take on the way to his goal. For example, standing on the first tee, the player will mentally picture the exact spot where he wants his shot to finish. Next he will picture the flight of the ball, how high it goes, whether it fades or draws, where it lands, and how it rolls to the selected spot.

Once he has pictured the exact shot in his mind, he will visualize the course of action that will propel the ball to that spot in the manner he has already "seen" in his mind's eye. Depending on the player's swing keys, he might picture his takeaway, swing plane, hand position at impact, and follow through. This done, he addresses the ball with a wonderfully clear and positive picture, not only of a perfect end result, but also of the perfect actions needed to send it to its destination. The clearer the visualization, the more confidence the player will have that he can successfully make the shot, even under pressure.

Winning in Advance

Gary Player's most vivid memory of the 1965 U.S. Open, where he became the first non-American winner in over 45 years, was something only he could see. On top of the giant scoreboard that listed past winners was the name of the 1964 champion, Ken Venturi.

Yet right above his name in bold letters, before the tournament had even started, Player could see another name. It was the name of the 1965 champion. Said Gary, "Make no mistake about it. The name on top of that board was mine."

Visualization is a powerful confidence-building weapon, so use it to your advantage.

Fake It 'Til You Make It

One of the miraculous qualities of the human brain is the way it reacts to the information you give it. If you tell it you are the best putter in the world, it has to believe you. Some players, when suffering a temporary loss of confidence, try to fake it until it returns. They maintain a positive attitude in their unspoken inner dialogue, telling themselves they are great putters, ball strikers, and players. They remind themselves that the law of averages is going to take effect and pretty soon the putts will start to drop.

Bear in mind that trying to fake yourself into being confident is not the same as being over-confident. Every day on golf courses all over the world, hundreds of people attempt, with complete confidence, to hit a 3-wood shot 230 yards over a lake, even though the best 3-wood they ever hit in their lives carried only 210 yards . . . downwind! That's over-confidence, and it's just plain stupid.

"I Am the Greatest"

> *"Serenity is knowing that your worst shot is still going to be pretty good."*
> *Johnny Miller*

Nobody who saw him will ever forget Muhammad Ali, thundering out at the end of every fight, "I am the greatest! I am the best that ever was!" Whether they liked him or not, few disagreed with him. Golfers rarely make such public announcements. After all, it's a gentleman's game. Still, a key ingredient of champions is a belief in themselves—a belief that deep down inside they have the talent and ability to be the best. Some, for reasons of social acceptability, are afraid to admit they think they're the best, or even that it is their goal to be the best. Our society frowns upon those who boast openly. Nevertheless, most truly great players acknowledge their greatness, and all of them acknowledge their quest.

Champions have no problems with compliments. They do not become shy or embarrassed, or insist they don't deserve the recognition. They receive the acclaim with thanks and move on, accepting it as honestly offered and believing themselves to be worthy of the praise. In short, they are comfortable in the position to which they have risen. They don't continually ask themselves, "Why me? Am I really this good? Am I playing way above my level? Will I lose it soon?" Champions accept and embrace success with open arms. Being the best is their reason for living.

The desire for greatness must be burning within at all times, and those seeking greatness must use their time wisely in pursuit of success. We all start out on a level playing field. All of us have days consisting of 24 hours. It's how champions employ their time that defines them. Each word, action, and thought can move a champion closer to his goals. Every hour spent on the range, the putting green, or the course can give a player that minute edge, helping to raise his game to championship level. By the same token, each hour spent aimlessly watching television or playing cards in the clubhouse bar can erode a champion's foundation and impede his progress.

The breeze has picked up a little, so I think you might want one club more. Hit your 3-iron, and bring it in a little from right to left . . . Good shot, Sir! . . . Hold on, it's turning a little too much. It caught the trap . . . Good explosion shot from that position. You're about due to make a 20-footer . . . Yes! What a great par! Excited, Sir? I'll never be too old to be thrilled by a shot like that . . . You say you could see it going in before you hit the putt? Well, then I'm not surprised you holed it.

Swing Thoughts

- A champion has confidence in his clubs, his swing, and his ability.

- Confidence is the weapon of all champions, and it can be learned and developed, just like a good golf swing.

- Champions develop confidence by:
    A)   Practicing both the physical and mental aspects of the game.
    B)   Setting short-term, measurable goals so they can clearly see each small increment of progress.
    C)   Rewarding themselves for their successes, heightening the desire for more.
    D)   Visualizing success, both overall and in detail.
    E)   Thinking positively.

- Champions can speed up the process by faking confidence until they actually feel it.

- Champions accept the honest praise of friends and fans, which can increase their confidence to even higher levels.

- Champions keep the game in perspective and don't allow their self-confidence to be damaged by an occasional sub-standard performance.

Back in the Clubhouse

A young woman wrote to me recently, telling me that her whole life had taken a different turn since she had heard me ask the question, "What one great thing would you dare to dream if you knew you could not fail?" She wrote that, up to that time, this was a question she had never even dared to consider, but now she thought of nothing else. She had realized, in a great, dazzling flash of clarity, that the main thing separating her from her hopes and dreams was her lack of belief in her ability to achieve them.

Most of us are like this for most of our lives. There are many things we want to be and have and do, but we hold back. We are unsure because we lack the confidence necessary to step out in faith in the direction of our dreams.

Abraham Maslow said that the story of the human race is the story of men and women "selling themselves short." Alfred Adler, the great psychiatrist, said men and women have a natural tendency toward feelings of inferiority and inadequacy. Because we lack confidence, we don't think we have the ability to do the kind of things others have done, and in many cases, we don't even try.

Just think: What difference would it make in your life if you had an absolutely unshakable confidence in your ability to achieve anything you really put your mind to? What would you want and wish and hope for? What would you dare to dream if you believed in yourself with such conviction that you had no fear of failure whatsoever?

Many people start off with little or no self-confidence, but as a result of their own efforts, they become bold and brave and outgoing. And we've discovered that if you do the same things that other self-confident men and women do, you will experience the same feelings they have and get the same results.

The key is to be true to yourself, to be true to the very best that is in you, and to live your life consistently with your highest values and aspirations.

Take some time to think about who you are and what you believe in and what is important to you. Decide you will never compromise your integrity by trying to be or say or feel something that is not true for you. Have the courage to accept yourself as you really are—not as you might be or as someone else thinks you should be—and know that, taking everything into consideration, you are a good person.

After all, we all have talents, skills, and abilities that make us extraordinary. No one—including yourself before you discover them—has any idea of the highest limits of your capabilities or of what you might ultimately do or become. Perhaps the hardest thing to do in life is to accept how extraordinary you really can be and incorporate this awareness into your attitude and personality.

In developing unshakable levels of self-confidence, your self-esteem and self-regard are important starting points, but they are not enough. People have tried positive thinking and wishing and hoping for years with only mixed results. To develop the deep-down kind of self-confidence that leads to victory, you need positive knowing, not just positive thinking.

Lasting self-confidence really comes from a sense of control. When you feel very much in control of yourself and your life, you feel confident enough to do and say the things that are consistent with your highest values. Psychologists today agree that a feeling of being "out of control" is the primary reason for stress and negativity and for feelings of inferiority and low self-confidence. To get a solid sense of control over every part of your life, you must set clear goals or objectives; you must establish a sense of direction based on purposeful behavior aimed at predetermined ends.

Being true to yourself means knowing exactly what you want and having a plan to achieve it. Lasting self-confidence comes when you absolutely know that you have the capacity to get from where you are to wherever you want to go. You are behind the wheel of your life. You are the architect of your destiny and the master of your fate.

Instead of being preoccupied with the fear of failure and loss, as most people are, you focus on the opportunity and the possible gains of achievement. With a clearly defined track to run on, you become success-oriented, and you gradually build your confidence up to the stage where there is very little you will not take on.

Another essential way to build your self-confidence, to develop positive *knowing* rather than just positive *thinking*, is to become very good at what you do. The flip side of self-confidence is "self-efficacy," or the ability to perform effectively in your chosen area.

You can raise your self-confidence instantly by the simple act of committing yourself to becoming excellent in your chosen field. You immediately separate yourself from the average individual who drifts from job to job and accepts mediocrity as the adequate standard.

Some years ago, a young man named Tim came to one of my personal development seminars. He was shy and introverted. His handshake was weak, and he had tremendous difficulty making eye contact. He sat in the back of the seminar room with his head down, taking notes. He seemed to have few friends, and he didn't socialize very much during the breaks. At the end of the seminar, he told me he was in sales and hadn't been doing very well up to that time. But he had resolved to change, to go to work on himself, to overcome his shyness, and to become very good at selling for his company. He then said goodbye, and I wished him the best of luck as he went on his way.

A year later, he came back to take the seminar again. But this time, he was distinctly different. He was calmer and more self-assured. He was still a little shy, but when he shook hands, his grip was firmer and his eye contact was better. He sat toward the middle of the seminar room, and he interacted quietly with people around him. At the end of the seminar, he told me he was starting to move up in his sales force and had had his best year ever. He was determined to do even better in the year to come.

About 14 months later, Tim came back to the seminar. This time, he brought five people from his company, all of whom he had convinced to come to the seminar, and he had offered to pay their tuition if they weren't satisfied. He walked right up to me and shook hands firmly, looking me straight in the eye with a strong, self-confident smile. He asked if I remembered him, and I told him I remembered him very well. He said he had brought something he wanted to show me. He took out of his pocket a letter from the president of the national corporation he worked for—one of the biggest companies in the country—personally congratulating Tim for the great selling job he had done in his territory in the past year.

It turned out that Tim had gone from No. 33 to No. 1 out of 42 salespeople. His income had risen from $26,000 a year to $98,000, and he had increased his sales volume at a faster rate than any other salesperson in the country. He was still quiet, but he had a wonderful air of power and purposefulness about him. He had taken the steps and paid the price to build himself into a fine, confident young man. He had made the decision to do whatever was necessary to overcome his shyness and to develop the kind of personality he admired in others. He was—and is—in every sense of the word, a self-made man.

Perhaps the most wonderful result of developing a high level of self-confidence is the positive impact your personality will have on your relationships. There are two mental laws that are always operating and that determine much of what happens to you in your interactions with people. The first is the Law of Attraction, which says that you will inevitably attract into your life people who are very much like you. The second law is the Law of Correspondence, which says that your outer world of relationships will correspond, like a mirror image, to your inner world of personality and temperament.

In combination, these laws simply say that as you change in a positive direction, you will find yourself surrounded by people who are very much like the new person you are becoming. As you get better, the quality and quantity of your relationships will get better. You will meet nicer, more self-confident, more interesting, and more enjoyable people. You will find yourself getting along better with members of the opposite sex, including your spouse. You will find yourself doing better at your job, or even in a new job, and getting along better with your boss and your coworkers. Your attitude of confidence and calm assurance will make you more attractive to people. They will want to be around you, to open doors for you, to make opportunities available to you that would not have arisen earlier when you didn't feel as terrific about yourself.

Often, people lack self-confidence in their relationships with others because they judge themselves poorly in comparison. Perhaps you have experienced moments when you were afraid people would not like you or accept you the way you want them to. Well, there is an important mindset you can adopt to improve your ability to interact with others in a more relaxed and confident fashion.

It's important to remember that no one can affect your thoughts or feelings unless there is something you want from him or something you want him to refrain from doing. As soon as you begin to practice detachment and decide in your own mind that there is nothing you want or expect from another person, you will find that that person's ability to shake your self-confidence is greatly reduced. The people who are the most successful in human relationships are those who practice a calm, healthy detachment from others and don't allow the behaviors of others to determine how they think and feel about themselves.

As you can see, it is our fears and doubts that, more than anything else, undermine our self-esteem and self-confidence and cause us to think in negative terms about ourselves and our possibilities. As Abraham Maslow said, we begin to "sell ourselves short" and see all the reasons why something might not be possible for us. We magnify the difficulties and minimize the opportunities. We become preoccupied with the possible losses we might suffer and the possible criticisms we might endure. Our fears and doubts paralyze us, preventing us from acting boldly, lowering our self-confidence, and causing us to think and talk in negative terms. In fact, this probably describes the great majority of mankind. Most people are so preoccupied with their fears that they have time for little else, and this preoccupation manifests itself in much of what they say and do.

The only real antidote to doubt, worry, fear, and all the other negative emotions that sabotage our self-confidence, is action. Your conscious mind can hold only one thought at a time, positive or negative. When you engage in systematic, purposeful action, using and stretching your abilities to the maximum, you cannot help but feel positive and confident about yourself.

Act as though it were impossible to fail. Act as though you already had a high level of self-confidence. Continually ask yourself, "What one great thing would I dare to achieve if I knew I could not fail?" Whatever your answer, you can have it if you can dream it and if you have the self-confidence to go out and get it.

Questions to Ponder

- How can you set yourself up for some easy victories to build your confidence?

- Do you keep a list of names of clients whose business you have won, competitors you have beaten, and successes you have enjoyed? Look at this list when you need a boost.

- How can you build confidence in key members of your staff?

- What effect would greater confidence have on your sales people, buyers, and other key staff members?

- Do you invariably reward successes with cards, a genuine pat on the back, and thanks for a job well done? We all *mean* to do these things, but how often do we do them?

That was a great sandy par on the 10th. Now it's time to move back inland and contend with the trees again. Don't worry; we'll be seeing the ocean again before long! The 11th tee is over by those bushes, and the hole goes uphill, 389 yards, over that ridge . . . OK, Sir. Try to keep it down the left side, so you'll have a better angle at the green; it's a very small one . . . Perfect drive!

Now, although the hole's cut in the middle, you'll want to aim to the right side of the green; the ball kicks left . . . Look out, Sir! It's going left . . . Oh, oh! That one's plugged under the back lip of the trap. Well, you'll just have to make up for it. This is your chance to show these gentlemen what you're made of. You've already made a couple of great recoveries, so I know you can keep it together . . . How do champions keep it together? Well, it's a question of attitude, Sir!

ATTITUDE IS EVERYTHING

Overcoming Problems

"I'd like to see the fairways more narrow. Then everybody would have to play from the rough, not just me!"
Seve Ballesteros

During a round of golf, any number of things can go wrong, from a bad swing to a bad bounce. Tony Lema once hit a near perfect shot on the 12th at Augusta, only to have it hit the flagstick and bounce back into the water. Sometimes the weather can be the biggest challenge. At many British Opens, for example, rain and strong winds have made normal par impossible, even for the best players in the world. At times like that, a champion sets his own par and plugs away tenaciously in spite of the severe conditions, meeting every challenge as it arises.

All truly great champions are excellent problem solvers. Since it's impossible to achieve success in any area without encountering obstacles along the way, only those who overcome these challenges ever become champions. There are two important keys to overcoming every obstacle that confronts you, and we will start with one that is a vital characteristic of any champion. It is attitude.

The Haig

"I don't want to be a millionaire, I just want to live like one."
Walter Hagen

Although he played in another era, with different equipment on different golf courses, it is entirely possible that no one in history was as good a player from trouble as the legendary Walter Hagen. Hagen was a dashing combination of Bobby Jones, Lee Trevino, and Arnold Palmer, amassing 10 major championships during a career that occurred in a period before the inauguration of the Masters. The PGA Championship was, until 1958, a match play event. Hagen competed in it seven times between 1916, when the tournament was introduced, and 1927. He won five times, in 1921, '24, '25, '26, and '27, and in 1923 took Gene Sarazen to the 38th hole before losing to him. He was undoubtedly the finest match play golfer in history.

In a celebrated, 72-hole, head-to-head match in 1926, Hagen beat the great Bobby Jones with 11 holes up and 10 to play. Hagen pull-hooked his drive on the 1st hole and sent his ball crashing into the woods. Finding it on some hardpan, he rifled a long iron through a narrow opening in the trees, over the green, and into a patch of swamp. He then blasted out of the mud and sank the putt for par without so much as touching the fairway. Jones, meanwhile, split the fairway with his drive and made a regulation par. Thus the tone of the match was set; Jones down the middle, Hagen hitting repeatedly into trouble, but always recovering, sometimes miraculously, to make par or birdie. Even the unflappable Robert T. Jones admitted that after a while it began to "get his goat."

Hagen, ever the swashbuckling hero, pocketed almost $8,000 for winning the match, which was the largest check ever seen in golf up to that time. He then spent $1,000 out of the proceeds on a set of platinum, diamond-studded cuff links, which he presented to Jones as a gift.

Why was this champion so capable in the face of adversity? It can be summed up in one word—attitude. Hagen learned early in his career to accept those breaks that did not go his way. He knew that for every bad bounce there would be a compensating good bounce sooner or later. He just had to keep trying until it arrived.

Additionally, Hagen knew that in this most fickle of all games there would be plenty of occasions when he did not feel well, swing well, or play well. His ability to accept this fact meant Hagen was not prone to second-guessing his method and fiddling constantly with his swing. He declared, "A tournament golfer has to learn. He only has his game at the time; it may be far from his best, but it's all he has, and he might as well harden his heart and make the most of it."

Hagen once said, "I have never played a perfect 18 holes. There is no such thing. I expect to make at least seven mistakes a round. Therefore, when I make a bad shot I don't worry. It's just one of seven." He also observed that the bad shots of the past are best forgotten, and that the only shot that matters is the one you are about to play.

The worst defeat he ever suffered came at the hands of British pro Archie Compston. In another of Hagen's famous 72-hole challenge matches at the Moor Park Club, just outside London, he was beaten 18 and 17. Compston played magnificent golf, and Hagen was far from his best, being fatigued from a long ocean voyage. Nevertheless, it was hard to justify such a huge margin of defeat. In spite of this, Hagen was photographed after the match, smiling and looking as if he had just won a major championship. The following week he did so, beating Compston and the rest of the world to capture the British Open at Sandwich. The following year, after a disastrous 10 and 8 loss in the Ryder Cup matches, he bought his caddie a new suit and took him to Muirfield, where he won his fourth Open Championship. Surely no player in golfing history enjoyed more comeback victories.

By accepting in advance that he would inevitably hit some bad shots, have bad rounds or bad weeks, and encounter difficult problems, Hagen always had a mental edge over his opponents. When faced with a problem, he never wasted time and energy dissecting the reasons the problem had occurred; there would be time enough to do that later, on the practice ground. The task at hand was to solve the problem, quickly and efficiently, and get the round back on track.

There's No Such Thing as "Can't"

"I always travel first class. That way, I think first class, and
I am more likely to play first class."
Raymond Floyd

You can face up to and solve any problem if you first identify it and then put your mind and body to work on it. Just because you have sliced for 15 years doesn't mean you have to continue slicing for the rest of your life. If you have the physical ability to hit a ball, then you have the ability to stop slicing. In the worst cases, it may take an entire summer of hard work to straighten that banana, but it can be done. In most cases, a slice can be cured in a matter of days. One PGA teacher I know has a very simple and effective way of correcting this most common of problems. He starts by showing the student how to hook a chip shot. Now, if you can hook a chip shot you can hook a pitch shot and so on up the scale until you get to the drive. It's the same grip and basically the same swing. It's just a question of working up to it in stages.

When I was a youngster, I went through a phase of blocking the ball dead right off the tee, and it was ruining my game. Nothing I tried seemed to help. Eventually, I went to my old pro and asked him for help. He watched me hit a few balls—dead right. He told me to hook the ball. I hit a few more shots—dead right. He asked me if I was listening and told me once again to hook the ball. Again I hit it dead right. I was becoming convinced it was the only shot I could hit, as if some genetic flaw had suddenly appeared in my body causing all my shots to fly to the right. I was very frustrated and completely consumed with negative thoughts.

"I can't do it," I said.

"There's no such thing as can't," he said. "You're a capable golfer. If you want to hook the ball, what must you do?"

"Swing inside to out, closing the clubface slightly in the hitting area," I answered.

"Exactly! Now, you are obviously swinging in to out. That's why the ball is starting out to the right from the moment it leaves the clubface. All you need to do to make the ball hook is close the clubface a little."

"But I can't seem to do that," I protested.

"That's ridiculous," he said. "If you don't feel able to do it as you swing, do it at the address instead. That'll make it go left."

I addressed the ball with the clubface slightly closed and hit another shot. This time it went straight. Then I hit a few more, each one with a small but noticeable amount of draw.

"Now start off with the clubface square and roll your wrists at impact," the pro suggested.

I proceeded to hit a series of duck hooks!

"OK," said the pro. "Now you know how to hit it left, why not hit it straight, or with just a slight draw, by rolling your wrists a bit less?"

By the end of the session, I had cured the chronic problem that had plagued my game for several months by doing what I already *knew* how to do. I had let my problem progress to such an advanced stage that I had lost confidence in my ability to solve it myself. I had concluded there must be some complex physical reason why the ball would not do what I asked of it, or that some major portion of my swing's operational department had shut down, so that hitting it with a slight draw had become permanently impossible. With the help of my golf pro, I found I had always known how to solve the problem, but had failed to take the necessary corrective action largely because of a negative attitude. In the game of golf, a negative attitude is about as helpful as a brain tumor. Whenever you see the warning signs that you are developing one, take massive and imme-diate remedial action.

Building a Positive Attitude

Most of us like to think of ourselves as fairly positive people. In adversity, however, the truth is that most of us quickly gravitate toward the negative. This change in focus is far more harmful than most people realize and actually cripples the brain's creative power to generate solutions. That's why it is crucial to build and maintain a positive outlook.

Reframe Negative Situations into Opportunities

A common technique used by champions to help them maintain a positive attitude is called reframing. The brain, being the wonder-ful mechanism that it is, will react to each situation based on what you tell it. If you tell it your ball is in a bad lie and your chances of hitting a good shot are zero, the brain will accept this input, bounce it around in the physical action department, then cause your muscles to live up to your expectations and act in a fashion corresponding to the information; i.e., it will help you make a bad shot.

If, on the other hand, you take a different approach when you find your ball in a bad lie, the results can be significantly better. This time, let's look at the lie and tell the brain, "It would really impress the other guys if I can find a way to hit it on the green from here." The message is absorbed by the brain, and transmitted to the physi-cal action department along with instructions to make an extra effort and provide all available resources to accomplish the task at hand. The possibility of producing a better shot this time, based solely on the way you communicated with your own brain, is at the very least a lot better than your chances of winning the lottery.

Three to One Odds in Your Favor

Curtis Strange reframes his attitude in this way. "When you hit a bad shot, you still have three ways to make par. You can hit a good chip, make a good putt, or hit a mediocre chip and a mediocre putt and still make par. Of the four things that can happen after a bad shot, only one of them is bad." If you keep this in mind, the odds are much better that you will react by refocusing and making a confident shot.

When Things Go Wrong, There Is Always Next Week

There are, of course, times when one bad hole can end your chance to win a tournament, but it doesn't ruin your next round, your next tournament, or your career. Tom Weiskpof once took 13 strokes on the 12th at Augusta, a par three. A few weeks later, Weiskopf shot a record equaling 63 in the first round of the U.S. Open at Baltusrol.

Arnold Plamer made 10 on a par five one year at the Los Angeles Open by hitting three consecutive shots out of bounds trying to get home in two. A reporter asked him how he made 10. "It was easy," he said. "I missed a 20-foot putt for a nine." Arnie may have been mad as hell, but he knew there was another tournament scheduled for the next week, and he was going to win it.

Don't Allow Circumstances
Beyond Your Control to Control You

Many times during a round, you are faced with circumstances that are beyond your control. There's nothing you can do about wind, rain, bumpy greens, divots in the middle of the fairway, and footprints in sand traps. When faced with challenges such as these, the average player often loses focus and starts to complain about misfortune. Champions avoid such self-destructive behavior at all costs.

Where the weather is concerned, it is wise to remember that the rain falls on everyone, just as the sun shines on everyone. You will be playing in the same general conditions as your opponents. Champions accept that adverse conditions cause all scores to rise, not just theirs.

As for bad breaks, like unlucky bounces or finding your ball in a divot, remind yourself that a bad break coming before a good one just means the course owes you one. Unfortunately, it is human nature to accept good breaks with little gratitude and to curse bad breaks as being the work of the devil. It's hardly surprising that the talk at the "19th hole" seldom focuses on the ball that hit a tree and bounced back in bounds, or the skulled chip that skidded across the green, hit the pin, and went in. Instead, the average player remembers the well-struck shot that spun back into a trap, or the spike mark that knocked his birdie putt off line. One famous old Scot from the early days of professional golf was asked why he didn't brush away a wormcast from the line of his putt. He replied dourly that, in his experience, it was just as likely to help the putt find the hole as cause it to miss!

Start to keep a mental record of all the good bounces you get, the topped shots that still reach the green, and the poorly struck putts that find their way into the hole anyway. Then, next time you get a bad break, balance it against a good one and continue on your way. By maintaining a positive attitude, you will free yourself from the bondage of negativity and give your mind the space to generate a solution. Champions remind themselves that bad breaks and good breaks tend to equal out, if not during the same round, certainly over the course of a four-day tournament.

Back to Basics

Champions always master the basics of their profession, so they can immediately check those vitally important fundamentals when part of their game starts to go wrong. Grip, setup, and alignment are always the first areas they check in order to get back on track. If the greatest players in the world can develop flaws in things that are second nature to them, so can you. Every profession has its basic skills, and we should all seriously evaluate our performance in these areas before looking for more complex answers to our problems. Never be above going back to basics. It may seem embarrassing or beneath your dignity, but that's often where the problem lies. Don't let your attitude get in the way.

The Last Word on Attitude

Consider for a moment these great champions—Hagen, Jones, Hogan, Palmer, Trevino, and Nicklaus. Do you find negativity anywhere? Of course not. In order to be a champion, you must be in control of your attitude, and it must remain positive. Without this trait, you cannot draw on your reserves of determination, persistence, and creativity when you need them.

Negative thoughts are a self-fulfilling prophecy. If you tell your brain a situation is hopeless, it becomes true. Give it a glimmer of hope, and it will do everything it can to get you out of a jam. Champions use this knowledge to their advantage to forge ahead while others become bogged down in a swamp of self-pity.

I know you're upset about leaving the first shot in the bunker, but there was little else you could do from that buried lie, Sir. After that, you did well to settle yourself down and concentrate on making a good shot. It was a great up and down. That's a bogey, but it's only one shot, and it could've been much worse.

Swing Thoughts

- Attitude is the key ingredient in any recipe for success.

- Anticipating in advance that things may go wrong helps you keep a healthy attitude.

- Champions use reframing to maintain a positive attitude.

- Champions do not allow circumstances beyond their control to control them.

- Losing one battle doesn't mean you lose the war. Champions take problems in stride and live to fight another day.

- When things start to go wrong, champions go back to the fundamentals.

Back in the Clubhouse

Playing a round of golf is like taking a trip. When I was 21 years old, a friend of mine and I decided to go off to see the world. Many of our friends were going to Europe and hitchhiking around with backpacks. We decided to be different and go to Africa instead. It never occurred to us to ask why no one else was going to Africa. We found that out later, much to our great regret.

We started out from London, and we rode bicycles across France and Spain. The labor was excruciating, the progress was slow, and the pleasure was nonexistent. In Gibraltar, we sold our bicycles and invested our last few dollars in an old Land Rover. We crossed from Gibraltar to Tangier and made our way through Morocco, over the Atlas Mountains, and into Algeria. We were on our way in Africa. Still, there was one obstacle between us and the greenery we were anxious to see, and it was that darn old desert. To get to our destination in Africa, we had to cross the Sahara Desert. (For a full account of this adventure, see my book, *Success Is a Journey*.)

Our Land Rover broke down many times, but we finally got it repaired and set off to cross the Sahara. We had no idea how serious and how difficult this adventure was to be. As we moved south across the desert, we encountered endless problems, any one of which could have ended our trip and probably our lives. It was during this desert crossing that I learned one of the most important lessons in my life about attitude.

The French, who had controlled Algeria for many years, had marked a path across the desert with black, 55-gallon oil drums. The drums were spaced exactly five kilometers apart. As we drove and came to an oil drum, the next drum, which was five kilometers ahead, would pop up on the horizon, and the last oil drum, which was five kilometers behind, would fall off the horizon, as if shot in a shooting gallery. Wherever we were, we could always see two oil drums at a time—the one we had just left and the one we were headed toward. To cross one of the greatest deserts in the world, all we had to do was to take it "one oil barrel at a time." We did not have to cross the entire desert at once. We had to cross it only one oil barrel at a time, and that would be sufficient.

For me, crossing the Sahara was a metaphor for life. In order to maintain a positive mental attitude under all circumstances, all you really have to do is to take it one step, one oil barrel, at a time. As

Thomas Carlyle said, "Our great business is not to see what lies dimly at a distance, but to do what lies clearly at hand."

A positive mental attitude is indispensable to success and achievement. You can foster and maintain a positive mental attitude by focusing on doing what lies clearly at hand, by taking the step that appears immediately in front of you. That will automatically lead to the next step, and the next, and so on, and eventually you will find yourself at your goal.

But there is much more to a positive mental attitude than this. You can have a positive attitude that disappears in the face of adversity, or you can have an attitude that is so strong that no matter what happens to you, you remain positive, cheerful, and optimistic.

Your degree of self-confidence is what determines how positive your attitude really is, and self-confidence is based on your belief in yourself and your ability. It is based on faith, or knowing that things are going to work out well in the long run, no matter how distressing they appear to be in the short run.

Let me give you an example. A friend of mine was called by the Internal Revenue Service and told that he was to be the subject of a tax audit. The IRS agent wanted all his tax receipts and returns for the past three years brought in for examination. My friend's first reaction was panic. He immediately became anxious and afraid of all the things that could happen.

However, he caught himself and began to apply his mind to keep his attitude calm and positive. First of all, he thought, have I done anything that is unacceptable under the existing tax law? As he thought, he realized that he had made every effort to file accurate tax returns. He then asked himself who else should be involved in the audit. As he thought, he realized that his accountant, who had prepared his tax returns, should be involved in explaining them.

Now he was calm and collected. He phoned his accountant and apprised him of the situation. The accountant explained to him that every year the IRS audits a certain percentage of tax returns at random. The fact that the IRS had chosen to audit him had nothing to do with whether or not his returns were accurate. It was simply routine procedure. The accountant also explained that if my friend wanted to send him, the accountant, to the meeting with the IRS agent, my friend didn't need to appear.

Now my friend was completely relaxed. He gathered the necessary documents and turned them over to his accountant, who had

had ample experience in dealing with the IRS. The accountant sat down with the IRS agent and went through everything, from beginning to end. When it was over, the IRS agent thanked the accountant and said that, based on the tax returns, everything was in perfect order, and there would be no need for a reassessment or for any additional payments or penalties. The audit was over, and life went on.

Right from the beginning, you can choose to be positive and constructive in dealing with any adversity. You can sit down and think through the situation and then begin to deal with it one oil barrel at a time.

Of course, this isn't as easy as it sounds. We all are faced with four obstacles that tend to get in the way of our maintaining a positive mental attitude. These obstacles are fear, worry, anger, and doubt.

When things are not working out the way we had expected, our immediate response is to become fearful and uneasy. We are afraid we will lose our money, waste our effort, or forfeit our emotional or physical investment in what we have done. If we are not careful, we start thinking of our potential losses rather than focusing on our potential gains.

Fear triggers worry, and we begin to use our power of imagination to create all sorts of negative images that cause us unhappiness and insomnia and make us unable to perform effectively.

Fear and worry create anger, or what has been called the "victim complex." Instead of moving constantly forward in the direction of our dreams, we begin to react and respond and to blame other people and other situations for our problems.

Surrounding these negative emotions is the mental quality of doubt. Doubt is a fertile breeding ground for the other three negative emotions. Therefore, to eliminate these obstacles to positive thinking, you need to systematically use your mind to get rid of the weakening emotion of doubt.

How do you do this? It's simple. The only real antidote to fear, worry, anger, and doubt is positive action toward the achievement of some worthwhile ideal.

Psychologists tell us that the key to dealing effectively with life is what they call "cognitive control." The cognitive control method is based on the assumption that you can think about and concentrate on only one thing at a time, either positive or negative. Successful people are no different from you or me. They have one outstanding characteristic, however. They consciously choose to think about what they want, rather than what they don't want. And as a result, they are continuously taking action toward their goals, rather than spending their time thinking and worrying about the inevitable challenges and difficulties that face them every day.

Dr. Karl Pribram, the respected neuropsychologist, has found that human beings have holistic mental pictures stored within their brains. Those pictures, imagined in complete detail, set up a force field of energy that begins to attract into your life the people, ideas, things, and even circumstances that are consistent with that image.

If you visualize a positive outcome, if you think about it and see it and feel it and sense it in every respect, you begin to exert a powerful magnetic force that brings the desired goal or outcome into reality. In effect, you control your life and your destiny through the vivid mental images you hold in your mind on a continuous basis.

You are the architect of your personality and character. Your goal, your desire, is to be as successful, happy, and prosperous as you possibly can in every aspect of your life. Therefore, the systematic development of a positive mental attitude is something you need to work on every hour.

There are six things you can do to assure that your attitude is the very best it can be under all circumstances.

First, whatever challenges you face, focus on the future rather than on the past. Instead of worrying about who did what and who is to blame, focus on where you want to be and what you want to do. Get a clear mental image of your ideal successful future, and then take whatever action you can to begin moving in that direction. As the *New Testament* says, "Let the dead bury the dead." Let the past take care of itself, and get your mind, your thoughts, your mental images on the future.

Second, whenever you're faced with a difficulty, focus on the solution rather than on the problem. Think and talk about the ideal solution to the obstacle or setback, rather than wasting time rehashing and reflecting on the problem. Solutions are inherently positive, whereas problems are inherently negative. The instant you begin thinking in terms of solutions, you become more positive and constructive.

Third, assume that something good is hidden within each difficulty or challenge. Dr. Norman Vincent Peale, a major proponent of positive thinking, once said, "Whenever God wants to give us a gift, he wraps it up in a problem." The bigger the gift you have coming, the bigger the problem you will receive. But the wonderful thing is that if you look for the gift, you will always find it.

Fourth, assume that whatever situation you are facing at the moment is exactly the right situation you need to ultimately be successful. This situation has been sent to you to help you learn something, to help you become better, to help you expand and grow. One of the affirmations I use continually is: "Every situation is a positive situation if I view it as an opportunity for growth and self-mastery." That is a wonderful affirmation. You cannot say it without thinking positive thoughts, feeling positive emotions, and seeing positive actions you can take.

Fifth, in every challenge, look for a valuable lesson. Assume that every setback contains a lesson that is essential for you to learn. Only when you learn this lesson will you be smart enough and wise enough to go on to achieve the big goals you have set for yourself. Again, since you can think about only one thing at a time, if you are busy looking for the lesson, you cannot simultaneously think about the difficulty or the obstacle. And—surprise, surprise—you will always find the lesson if you look for it.

Sixth, whenever you have a goal that is unachieved, a difficulty that is unresolved, or a problem that is blocking you from getting where you want to go, sit down with a pen and paper and make a list of every thing you could possibly do to resolve the situation. The more you think on paper, the more you will take control over your conscious mind. When you are writing down possible solutions, your mind will be more positive. As you write, you are taking advantage of the power of visualization, and all kinds of insights and ideas will come to you. By the time you stand up, ready to take the first step you see, you will be happy, eager, and enthusiastic about beginning to achieve your goals.

A positive mental attitude is indispensable to your success. You can be as positive as you want to be if you simply take actions consistent with achieving your goals rather than actions that cause you to feel the negative emotions of fear, worry, anger, and doubt. If you do what other successful people do, if you use your mind to think, to exert mental control over a situation, you will be positive and cheerful most of the time. And you will reap the benefits enjoyed by all successful people.

Questions to Ponder

- How is your attitude toward yourself? Your staff? Your customers?

- Do you quickly recognize when your attitude begins to deteriorate?

- Do you anticipate problems in advance?

- Are there things beyond your control that you can't seem to let go, that affect your attitude?

- When all else fails, do you go back to the basics of your business?

- Can you or can't you?

The 12th is a pretty straightforward par three . . . It's 205 yards today. The green is shallow, and it can be tough to hold, but if you're short, the bunkers guarding the front come into play. If the wind stays where it is now, it's a 3-iron shot. Ignore the flag, tucked away over there in the front left corner—it's just trying to tempt you! Aim for the middle of the green and make a smooth swing . . . Get down, now—blow wind—settle. The wind died the moment you hit your shot, Sir. It sailed clear over the green and landed in the pine trees. That's going to be a real problem. It'll be a challenge just to make bogey from there. You'll have to be creative and dream something up. How would a champion handle a problem like this? It all comes down to creativity.

CREATIVITY—
SURE SIGN
OF A CHAMPION

Now What Do You Do?

Let's test your ability to handle difficult situations against that of the four champions who faced these specific problems in tournament play. You'll be up against some pretty tough competition, so put on your best game face and let's get the show on the road. Here's how the game works. I'm going to put you in some tough spots. You must escape with a combination of your clubs, your skill, and your creativity. It's up to you whether you play the ball or take a drop and add a penalty shot to your score. Take whatever action you think is appropriate to deal with each situation. Ready? Don't take too long; you might get hit with a penalty for slow play.

• Your ball pitched on a hard spot and bounced over the green, right up against the wall of the clubhouse. You have an unobstructed line to the flag, but your ball is only four inches from the wall, so you have no stance.

• Your ball is pin high, only it's stuck in the branches of a tree, 15 feet above the ground.

• Your ball has bounced into a greenside trap and has rolled into a paper bag, discarded by an opponent's caddie after he had eaten his lunch.

• Your ball is under a low hanging tree with branches about two feet off the ground. Taking a normal swing, you can only move the club back 18 inches. The green is 180 yards away.

Now, ladies and gentlemen, let's hear your appreciation for our other contestants, a truly international foursome. From South Africa, Mr. Gary Player; from Germany, Mr. Bernard Langer; Mr. Walter Hagen himself, from the United States of America; and from Spain, Mr. Seve Ballesteros.

Up Against the Wall

The scene is the final hole of the 1974 British Open, on the Royal Lytham and St. Anne's Golf Course in Lancashire, England. Gary Player is standing on the 18th fairway and is in the lead. He selects a club, then changes his mind and selects another, stronger club. Due perhaps to a sudden surge of adrenaline, his ball lands near the back of the green and bounds right up against the clubhouse wall.

The crowd claps and cheers as Player walks up to the green. He raises his cap in appreciation, but when he reaches his ball, he cannot entirely conceal his anxiety about the situation he faces. The crowd falls silent as Player studies the situation. The ball is only inches from the red-brick wall. If he were Bob Charles, the New Zealand left-hander who had won the 1963 Open at Royal Lytham, he would have an easy chip. Being right-handed, however, he's in bad shape. He studies the situation carefully, running all the options through his champion's mind. Finally he is ready. Selecting his putter he plays a left-handed shot with the back of the club safely onto the green, 10 feet from the hole and into the record books as the 1974 British Open Champion, beating Britain's Peter Oosterhuis by four shots.

Try Your "Tree" Iron

While competing in a tournament on the European Tour, German player Bernhard Langer's ball lodges in the branches of a tree, some 15 feet above the ground. Since the rules of golf state that you must clearly identify your ball before declaring it unplayable, he decides to climb the tree. Someone in the crowd suggests he take his "tree" iron. He smiles, but selects his wedge before beginning the climb. When he eventually reaches the ball, he decides he can play a shot. Balancing on one limb and bracing himself against another, Langer plays his ball onto the green and makes the putt for a par.

It's in the Bag

During a tournament, Walter Hagen's approach shot lands inside a paper bag that has blown into a bunker. Hagen asks for a drop, but is told he isn't entitled to one since the ball is in a hazard. He must either play the ball as it lies, in the bag, or take a penalty stroke. Hagen is none too thrilled with either option, but as he draws on his cigarette, an idea comes to him. With the gallery and the official looking on, he discards the still smoldering butt onto the bag, which instantly bursts into flames. The bag all but gone, he pitches out and makes par.

Super Seve

Seve Ballesteros has birdied the last four holes he has played. This feat, although impressive in itself, becomes exceptional when you take into account the fact that he has driven his tee shot into the trees on all four holes. Now he has missed yet another fairway, and his ball has come to rest directly beneath a tree with low branches, only two feet above the ground. Seve's imagination comes into play once again. Having studied the situation for a few moments, he takes his stance beside the ball *on his knees!* This unusual stance allows him to swing the club on a low, flat plane, preventing the club from hitting the low branches of the tree. Incredibly, his 4-iron approach shot finds the putting surface, and he makes the putt for his fifth consecutive birdie.

Well, how did you fare against the champions? Their creativity is boundless. Here are just a few more examples of famous instances where imagination has been allied with talent to produce winning golf. Whom else should we start with except Seve, the golf magician?

The Parking Lot Open

"No matter how tough a shot your opponent faces, assume he'll make it. That way you won't be shocked if he does."
Dean Beman

Seve Ballesteros has won many championships using the creative talent that has been his trademark and made him famous. One of the best examples of his special ability in this department was the 1979 British Open, where he won in spite of hitting his tee shots just about everywhere except on the fairways of the Royal Lytham and Saint Anne's Golf Course.

Standing on the 16th tee, Ballesteros had already hit both of the fairways he would hit with his driver that day. The question was not so much whether he would miss the fairway, but by how much. With his usual swashbuckling swing, Seve sent the ball far to the right of his intended line. At a point some 260 yards down the fairway, the ball sailed over the heads of the large crowd, by now 20 or 30 people deep, lining the right side of the hole. The ball finally came to rest in an overflow parking lot, where it rolled under a car. It may have been one of the wildest shots in the long history of championship golf, missing the center of the 16th fairway by almost 100 yards. It was still in bounds—nobody was expected to hit a shot that far from the fairway.

After his ball had been retrieved from beneath the car by a tournament official, he was awarded a free drop under Rule 24, and he studied his approach shot. Incredibly, the position from which he now had to play gave him a very good line into the flag. So, despite going where no man had gone before, it was no great surprise to his fans, who are accustomed to such heroics, when his second shot arched towards the flag. He was left with a makeable 20-foot putt. Make it he did, and after a couple more wild drives on 17 and 18, followed by two more remarkable recovery shots, Seve's victorious scorecard was signed, sealed, and delivered.

To the casual observer, Ballesteros may have appeared to be the luckiest man alive that week, constantly putting his ball in previously unexplored territory, seemingly with no regard for the way the architect had laid out the golf course. In fact, Ballesteros had developed a strategic plan for accomplishing his goal. It was bold and it was brash, but it was creative, and he did win.

While practicing for the tournament, Ballesteros had realized that almost all the trouble spots, from the deep-set fairway bunkers to the heavy rough, were situated between 240 and 270 yards from the tee. Most players would be playing 3-woods and 1-irons and threading the middle of the fairways. Ballesteros decided it would make little difference whether or not his ball finished in the fairway if he could hit his driver over 270 yards, since he would be beyond the traps and the heavy rough. The sparse rough from which he would have to play was really not much of a handicap, especially considering the shorter yardage he would have left to the flags, compared to his competitors.

Seve's drive on the 16th was labeled by most observers one of the worst they had ever seen. They had no way of knowing Ballesteros was *aiming* for the parking lot! It was part of the creative approach he employed in winning his first major championship, and typical of the imaginative and daring style that has made him a legend.

Hinkle's Pine

At the 1979 U.S. Open, an unusual thing happened on the 8th hole. A 30-foot black spruce tree grew overnight, just off the front of the 8th tee! Now before you check the cover of this book to make sure you didn't pick up an omnibus edition of the *National Enquirer* by mistake, allow me to explain.

Lon Hinkle, one of the tour's longest hitters, may not have made as indelible a mark as some of the more famous champions, but he certainly possessed some of the necessary traits. His game featured very powerful tee shots and an enviable degree of creativity. During a practice round, Hinkle realized the 8th hole, a 528-yard par five, could be made much shorter and easier by playing his tee shot down the adjacent 17th fairway. During the first round, Hinkle did just that by firing a 1-iron through a gap in the trees, ahead and to the left of the 8th tee, straight down the 17th fairway. From there he played an unobstructed iron shot onto the 8th green for an easy birdie. This led to a solid round that placed him atop the first round leader board. Word quickly spread through the field about Hinkle's creative approach to the hole, but the USGA was "not amused."

That night, while the unsuspecting players slept, the "powers that be" drove onto the course under cover of darkness. Armed with a back hoe, a tractor, and an army of men, they dug a huge hole not far from the 8th tee. In it they placed the aforementioned 30-foot black spruce tree, effectively plugging the gap in the treeline between the adjacent fairways and preventing the players from making a mockery of the 8th hole by taking the short cut. To the best of my knowledge, this is the only occasion in U.S. Open history where the course was altered in the middle of a championship. But Hinkle may have had the last laugh. He still smashed his tee shot on the 8th down the 17th fairway by the simple expedient of hitting it *over* the tree. Although he finished 20 shots behind the eventual winner, Hale Irwin, the 1979 championship will be remembered by many as "The Hinkle's Pine Open."

Barnes Wallace to the Rescue

That same year, Hinkle won the World Series of Golf at Firestone Country Club by hitting another very creative shot. Trapped in the trees to the right of the 16th hole, Hinkle faced a pond between him and the green. Due to overhanging branches, he could not play a normal approach shot, and playing safe would almost certainly cost him a stroke and the tournament. He borrowed the solution from Barnes Wallace, the inventor of a bomb that bounced on the surface of a lake on its way to the target, and made famous in the 1960 movie, *The Dambusters*. Taking a straight-faced iron, Hinkle fired a shot that skipped across the pond and onto the green, saving par and winning the tournament.

Take the Low Road

Many years ago at the Bing Crosby Tournament at Pebble Beach, a fierce wind was blowing off the Pacific. On the short 7th, a mere 107-yard par three played downhill to a tiny green perched on a cliff, most players were taking sixes and sevens. Player after player watched in melancholy horror as their efforts were blown off course, missing the miniature target and being dashed on the rocks and swallowed up by the hungry ocean below. Sam Snead, having seen the problem others were having, and trying to protect a good round, knew he had to find a way to keep the ball out of the wind. Since the tee is elevated some 50 feet above the green, this was not an easy task. Snead answered the challenge by banging the ball down the cart path with his putter, and ending close to the edge of the green. Then he chipped on and made par as an amazed gallery watched in awe.

In another time and place, Johnny Miller hit his drive through the fairway and into a small clump of trees. His ball came to rest next to a large tree trunk, giving him no room to swing. He also used his putter to hit the ball left-handed through a tiny gap in the trees some 10 or 12 yards in front of him. The ball took off like a rocket and flew 160 yards, pitching just past the pin and actually backing up five or six feet, leaving Miller a "tap-in" birdie putt.

Necessity is the Mother of Invention

Champions and scientists have some things in common. Although their laboratories are the driving range, the carpet, the golf course, or the beach, champions experiment with numerous different shots, each of which is designed to fulfill a specific purpose. They hit shots over trees, under trees, around trees, and even through the branches of trees. They work on low shots that spin. They try high hooks and low slices. When it rains, they hit shots from puddles, just to determine the best way to do so. They experiment. They invent, test, and eventually perfect a dazzling array of shots, which are then available to them whenever the appropriate situation arises. As you watch a touring pro practicing on the range, you may wonder what he is doing as one shot curves viciously to the right while the next is a low hook. He is experimenting, creating a shot he can later use to make a birdie from a spot where others may make double bogey.

Many champions of yesteryear learned their craft behind the caddie shack, using an old, abandoned club to pitch into water buckets or cut up shots over nearby trees. By experimenting with every conceivable shot their fellow caddies could dream up, players like Ben Hogan and Byron Nelson grew up to be two of the best shotmakers in the history of the game.

Lee Trevino is another who practiced and experimented with passionate intensity. A great shot maker even in his youth, and with every club in the bag, he is remembered by old hands at Tennison Municipal in Dallas as the guy who played golf for cash with a taped up Coke bottle as his only club! In case you were wondering, he did this by tossing the ball in the air and striking it like a baseball coach conducting infield practice—only harder.

Gene Sarazen, Inventor

Before Gene Sarazen invented the sand wedge, most golfers played recovery shots from sand with a 9-iron. Because the blade was so sharp, this required enormous skill, leaving little or no margin of error for any but the most talented player. Sarazen came up with his idea for a sand wedge while he was a passenger on an airplane one day. He noticed how the wing flaps affected the flight of the plane when they were extended. When the aircraft landed, he called the Wilson sporting goods company and asked them to send him six niblicks (9-irons). Then he went to the local hardware store and bought all the solder they had in stock. For the next few days, Sarazen spent all his waking hours experimenting with the 9-irons by adding mass in different shapes and amounts to the sole of the club. He realized immediately he was on to something, and he kept on soldering and filing and trying again until he got it right. The result was the world's first true sand wedge, and so far as bunker play was concerned, a greatly improved Gene Sarazen.

Champions are always being asked to test new club designs, and they are happy to do so. It isn't just for the sake of change, but to check whether a different look, style, or feel might give them the edge they are constantly seeking. Some, like Arnold Palmer and Tom Kite, have workshops in their homes where they can bend a hosel a few degrees, grind down the sole of a wedge, or lengthen the shaft of a putter. Some of the greatest advances in the scientific arena have appeared to many to be pure luck. Penicillin, for example, was first discovered as a mold on top of another experiment. Luck may indeed be a factor, but continuous experimentation and long hours of hard work invariably predate the fortunate happenstance. The same is true in the world of golf. Part of being a champion is the lifelong quest for minor improvements, in any aspect of the game, that will one day contribute to victory.

It might work, Sir. I can't say I've seen too many players pull off that shot, but as long as it doesn't come back and hit you, it's worth a try. You'll have to hit it pretty hard if you want it to ricochet off that tree and onto the green . . . Well I'll be! What a wonderful shot! Hit the flag—stop. That's too bad. It was a wonderfully creative shot. It's a shame it ran into the trap, and it certainly didn't need to finish in that footprint. The putter, Sir? If you say so. Good luck with this one . . . Well, I didn't think you had a chance, but you can't argue with success. Let's sink this for a world-class bogey . . . That's what they call a good all-around putt, but they all count! There's no pictures on the scorecard—only numbers! I'll tell you what, Sir, you deserved the little round of applause you got from those gentlemen for your recovery shot out of the trees.

Swing Thoughts

- Champions direct all of their talent and energy into creative problem solving, not problem enlarging.

- Champions focus on the desired outcome, not the problem itself.

Back in the Clubhouse

Peter Drucker says that the primary jobs of management are marketing and innovation. I began studying creativity more than 20 years ago. I thought it was an ability that was possessed by a few especially intelligent people, such as artists and writers and scientists. But as I delved further into the subject, I came to a remarkable conclusion: I am a genius! Not only that, but you, too, are a genius! In fact, probably 95 percent of the population has the capacity to function at exceptional levels. Creativity is as natural to human beings as is breathing. Everyone is creative to a certain extent. People are highly creative because they decide to be highly creative. It's no miracle. Creativity is like any human faculty; it can be developed with practice and strengthened with constant use.

If you improve things in small ways, you are engaging in small acts of creativity. If you make major breakthroughs and improve parts of your life in extraordinary ways, you are demonstrating high levels of creativity. And the amount of creativity you use in your life is largely up to you.

If creativity is improvement, in what areas do you want to use it? The answer is simple. You want to use your innate creativity to improve the areas of your life that are most important to you. You can use your creativity to improve your relationships, to increase your income, to improve your business, and to assure yourself higher levels of health and happiness. With that definition, you can see clearly that you have opportunities to be creative from the time you get up in the morning to the time you go to bed at night.

Creativity is like a muscle. If you do not deliberately and consciously flex your creativity on a regular basis, it becomes weak and soft. It loses its strength.

If people criticize you for your ideas, or if you have concluded that you are not particularly creative, you will tend to be more passive and submissive and look to others for new and better ways of solving problems and achieving goals. However, if you start to practice creative thinking of the type that I'm going to share with you, you will be absolutely amazed at how smart you really are.

I used to think you had to be highly intelligent to be creative. Then I found that intelligence is not just a matter of IQ. There are many people with high IQs who got excellent grades in school, but who are doing poorly at life. They are working at jobs they don't like and earning salaries that are far below their potentials. They probably haven't come up with a creative idea in years.

Intelligence is a way of acting. If you act intelligently, you are intelligent. If you act stupidly, you are stupid. That's all there is to it. You can decide to be highly intelligent and highly creative simply by doing the things that highly intelligent and highly creative people do. If you do these things over and over, you'll soon get the same results. People around you will be talking about how bright and full of ideas you are.

There are three basic qualities of genius. (But since you are a genius, you probably know what they are and apply them regularly.)

The first quality of genius is open-mindedness. People who are fluent, flexible, and adaptive in their thinking are far brighter than those who are rigid, mechanical, and straitlaced. The more open you are to new ideas and possibilities, to new approaches and solutions, the more creatively you will function.

Most people tend to fall into what are called "thinking traps." They assume that there is only one right answer to a problem; in reality, there could be several right answers. They jump to conclusions, assuming that because one thing happens, it is the reason why another thing is happening; there may be no relationship at all between the two events. Sometimes people think the problem has to be solved immediately; often, the problem can be deferred for some time and will solve itself if left alone. People think certain problems have to be solved without spending any money; often, if the solution is important enough, it is a good idea to spend money on it.

Another thinking trap people fall into is the belief that they have to solve the whole problem; sometimes, solving just one part of the problem is enough for the time being. A final thinking trap is the belief that it is your problem and you are the one who must solve it; often, it is someone else's problem, and the very best thing for you to do is to turn it over to that person and refuse to get involved.

The second quality of genius is the ability to concentrate sin-gle-mindedly on one thing at a time, on one problem at a time, and to stay with it until it's solved. Highly creative people practice focusing on single questions and single problems, while uncreative people diffuse their mental energies by trying to do several things at once. They work on this and work on that. They pick something up and put it down. They move on to something else and then come back. Often, they are scatterbrained, and if they do come up with ideas, their ideas are shallow and poorly thought out.

The difference between diffusion and concentration in creativity is the difference between gentle sunlight and sunlight concentrated through a magnifying glass. It is the difference between ambient light and a laser beam. It is the difference between a small flame and a welding torch. Your job, in increasing your creativity and enhancing your intelligence, is to concentrate your powers where they can do the most good.

The third quality of genius is the ability to approach problems systematically. People who throw themselves at their problems often become frantic and confused. They take a haphazard approach to thinking, and then they are amazed when they find themselves floundering and making no progress.

In his book *Innovation and Entrepreneurship*, Peter Drucker points out that innovation must be a systematic process. It must be planned and organized. It is too important to be random and haphazard.

Questions to Ponder

• Do you hold contests designed to produce creative ideas?

• Do you offer worthwhile rewards for valuable ideas?

The 13th is 400 yards uphill, but it doesn't play as long as it looks. It's a birdie opportunity if your drive avoids the string of traps up the left side and your approach shot stays below the hole . . . That one'll play just fine . . . What do champions do to help them make good decisions, Sir? Well, there are several steps.

CHAMPIONSHIP PROBLEM-SOLVING

Solving Problems Systematically

While creativity is an important aspect of solving problems as they arise, having a system for approaching those problems can also be invaluable. Not only will it give you a place to start, but it will help you think under pressure. It can help you think like a champion.

Step 1: Define the Problem

The first step in championship problem solving is to make sure you determine the exact nature of your problem. Many a tournament has been lost by the player who attempts an impossible shot from the rough in the vain hope of making birdie when bogey will win the day. The six or seven he winds up making takes him right out of contention. Precisely defining the problem is an art in itself.

Golf teacher Tommy Armour, author of the timeless masterpiece of instruction *How to Play Your Best Golf All the Time*, was a master at finding a player's problem, and no one was better at accurately defining it. One day a club member approached him to schedule a lesson.

"What seems to be your problem?" questioned Armour.

"I can't get backspin on my long-iron shots, like the pros do," he said.

"How far do you hit your 3-iron?" asked Armour

"About 175 yards," replied the member.

"Then why on earth would you want to put backspin on the ball?" asked Armour.

Ben Hogan had a similar laserlike approach to problem solving. He believed in breaking the problem down to its simplest form. Late in 1992, he sat down for lunch with one of his greatest admirers, Nick Faldo, who had recently won his third British Open. Both men realized they had similar attitudes to hard work, practice, and determination. For his part, Faldo was fascinated by Hogan. He found himself in total agreement with everything the Hawk said. At one point during lunch, Faldo asked Hogan for any advice he might have on how to win the U.S. Open. Hogan remained silent. As their meeting was about to end, Faldo again asked if there was one secret that could help him win that elusive U.S. Open. "Shoot lower scores," responded the great champion.

Step 2: Gather All the Data

At the 1937 U.S. Open, held at the Philadelphia Club in the days before giant leader boards were to be found beside many of the greens, Sam Snead came to the final hole thinking he needed a birdie to win. It was his first year on the PGA Tour. Going for a long drive on the par 5 in order to reach it in two, he hooked his ball into the left rough. Now he attempted to power the ball out of the rough and cold topped it into the face of a steep bunker, well short of the green. Although the face of the bunker was five feet high, and still thinking he needed a birdie, Snead elected to hit an 8-iron rather than a wedge. The ball failed to clear the top of the bunker, lodging in the long grass on the lip. From an almost impossible stance Snead then hacked the ball into a greenside trap and was rewarded with yet another bad lie. Now he blasted the ball to 40 feet and three-putted for an eight. He finished an agonizing two strokes behind the winner, Ralph Guldahl. Although he won 135 times worldwide, 84 times on the PGA Tour, and captured seven major titles, the U.S. Open crown would elude him throughout his career.

Snead's loss in the 1937 Open is only one example of players losing championships because they made crucial decisions and played crucial shots based on inaccurate or incomplete information. Countless others have faltered for similar reasons. Even in the 1990s, in spite of electronic scoreboards, Swedish star Jesper Parnevik handed the British Open to Nick Price by going for a birdie on the last hole, thinking he needed that to tie, and making bogey instead. He admitted afterward that he had failed to look at the scoreboard.

Before attempting a difficult shot, carefully weigh the various possibilities. Determine the risk involved. Balance the price of failure against the reward for success. How far into the round are you? Don't ruin a good round early by playing a shot that could get you into even deeper trouble. How good, or bad, is the lie? What is your opponent's position? What other trouble exists on the hole? Will the weather conditions have any effect? Finally and most important, do you have the necessary skill to make the shot? Far too often, golfers turn minor problems into huge problems by taking ill-considered risks that instantly lead to situations that neither their game nor anyone else's can handle.

Only after you have carefully considered all the data should you decide what you are going to do.

Step 3: Generate Solutions

Simple solutions are often the best. When you have made a mistake and your ball lies in a position that makes reaching the green impossible, squarely face up to the facts. Take a drop or chip back out onto the fairway. One extra shot will never ruin a round, but four or five on one hole can kill it.

When simple solutions don't seem to fit the circumstances, it is time to be creative. By maximizing their powers of creativity, champions can extract themselves from situations others would find hopeless. You may be able to invent a shot within your capabilities that will get you out of a tight spot, even if you have never tried it before.

Step 4: Avoid Making the Same Mistake Twice

After you have played the shot, analyze the results to determine if you made the correct choice of action. If you did, that's great; if not, decide what went wrong and why you failed so you can modify your approach to similar or identical situations in the future. Remember, experience is gained as a result of making mistakes. Champions store their mistakes and the reasons for them in their memory banks so they can take positive action to avoid repeating them.

Champions have the ability to assess a problem accurately, accumulate the correct data, consider possible solutions, select one of them, and act on it quickly and decisively. Once you have decided on the action you will take, there can be no halfhearted efforts. The shot must be executed with all the confidence and poise of one played from the middle of the fairway. If you are to be successful, you must not approach the shot with any doubt in your mind about club selection, the ball's intended flight, or any other distracting influences.

T he flag's back left. A punched 5-iron is the shot to play. That'll get it chasing up the green and moving left with the slope . . . You've hung it out to the right, Sir. It's a very difficult putt from there; there's almost no way to stop your first putt by the hole . . . That's what I meant. Nine feet past the hole was about as close as you could get it, but at least you have the line coming back up the green. Remember to hit it firm—it's directly uphill and into the grain . . . Good putt, Sir. It caught the left edge, but the speed was perfect; it had to fall. Nice four!

Swing Thoughts

- Champions employ the four-step problem-solving method:

  1. Accurately define the problem.
  2. Gather all the data.
  3. Generate creative and unusual solutions. They are often the best.
  4. Execute the shot, analyze the results, and store that information for future use.

Back in the Clubhouse

Here is a 10-step method you can use to think systematically. With this method, you can develop your creativity to genius levels.

1. Change your language from negative to positive. If a sale falls through, you can say something like, "This is an interesting challenge. It is an opportunity for me to improve my sales effectiveness so this doesn't happen again in the future."

The more positive your language is, the more confident and optimistic you will be when approaching any difficulty, and the more creative and insightful you will be in identifying solutions and breakthrough ideas.

2. Define your situation or difficulty clearly. What exactly is the challenge you are facing? What is causing you the stress and anxiety? What is causing you to worry? Why are you unhappy? Write it out clearly in detail.

Sometimes what you are worrying about is what is called a "cluster problem." It is a series of small problems clustered together. You need to sort them out and define them separately.

3. Ask, "What else is the problem?" Don't be satisfied with a superficial answer. Look for the root cause of the problem rather than getting sidetracked by the symptom. Approach the problem from several different directions.

For example, if your business is slow, you could ask, "What exactly is the challenge facing me?" Your first answer might be that sales are down. But what else is the problem? How else could you phrase your answer to make the problem more amenable to a solution?

Here are some different ways of answering that question. You could say that sales are down. You could say also that you are not selling enough. Or you could say that people are not buying enough. Or you could say that people are buying too much of your competition's product. Or you could say that people are not buying your product the way it is currently produced or packaged. Or people are not buying your product the way you are selling it, or for the reasons you think they should, or in the quantity you need them to buy for you to be financially successful. In each case, by changing your definition of the problem, you change your possible approach to the solution. You expand your possibilities. You become more creative. You unlock more of your inner genius.

4. Ask, "What are my minimum boundary conditions?" What must the solution accomplish? What ingredients must the solution contain? What would your ideal solution to this problem look like? Define the parameters clearly.

5. Pick the best solution by comparing your various possible solutions against your problem on the one hand, and your ideal situation on the other. What is the best thing to do at this time under the circumstances?

6. Before you implement the decision, ask, "What's the worst possible thing that can happen if this decision doesn't work?" I remember once spending all the advertising money of the company I was working for on a single advertising campaign. I was convinced that, even at a low rate of return, sales would more than justify the expenditure. I failed to ask that question about the worst possible outcome. I got blindsided by the "fallacy of large numbers," which is that if you advertise to an enormous number of people, the odds are that you will get a certain number of sales. What happened was that I got no sales at all from the advertising. As a result, I almost ruined the business. I should have asked, "What effect would there be on the business if the advertising did not work at all?"

In fact, before you make any expenditure of money or effort in trying to achieve your goal, you should evaluate what would happen if your decision were a complete failure.

7. Set measures for your decision. How will you know that you are making progress? How will you measure success? How will you compare the success of this solution against the success of another solution?

If you decide to sell or market your product or service in a particular way, how will you know that you have made the right decision? How will you define a success? Make it measurable. Then monitor it on a regular basis.

8. Accept complete responsibility for implementing the decision. If you don't have time to follow through yourself, you might want to delegate responsibility for the implementation of the action steps. Many of the most creative ideas never materialize because no one is specifically assigned the responsibility of carrying out the decision.

9. Set a deadline. A decision without a deadline is a meaningless discussion. If it is a major decision that will take some time to implement, set a series of short-term deadlines and a schedule for reporting. If you have a one-year goal to increase your income, break down the goal into months, and then break down the months into weeks. Break down the weeks into days and the days into hours. Then discipline yourself to do the things you need to do, every hour of every day, to assure that you achieve your weekly and monthly goals and your annual goal on schedule. With the deadlines and sub-deadlines, you will know immediately if you are on track or if you are falling behind. You can then use your creativity to alleviate further bottlenecks or choke points.

10. Take action. Get busy. Get going. Develop a sense of urgency. The faster you move in the direction of your clearly defined goals, the more creative you will be, the more energy you will have, the more you will learn, and the faster you will develop your capacity to achieve even more in the future.

The world is full of creative individuals who have wonderful ideas. But almost all of them fall short when it comes to implementation. And this is where you can excel. The future belongs to the creative minority who not only think like innovators, but also take action and put their ideas into effect.

You can solve any problem, overcome any obstacle, or achieve any goal you set for yourself by using your wonderful creative mind and then taking action consistently and persistently until you attain your objective. Success is the mark of a creative thinker, and when you use your ability to think creatively, your success can be unlimited.

Questions to Ponder

- Do you empower others to solve small problems before they become large problems?

- Do you encourage unusual solutions to your company's problems?

The 14th heads further inland and plays 555 yards. It's uphill after you reach the dogleg to the right. The right side is guarded by a trap you can barely see, so the best line for your drive is left of center. The second shot is where this hole gets interesting; it goes straight uphill and gets progressively narrower, with out-of-bounds on both sides of the fairway.

We've caught up with that group that teed off about 30 minutes ahead of us. Looks like we'll have to wait for a minute or two. Now's the time when you really have to stay focused, Sir. Don't lose that concentration! . . . How important do I think it is to stay focused? Very important, or better still, **vitally** important! It makes all the difference where champions are concerned.

IN THE ZONE

Focus on the Task at Hand

"Concentration is a fine antidote to anxiety. I have always felt that the sheer intensity Ben Hogan applied to shot-making specifics was one of his greatest assets. It left no room for negative thoughts. The busier you can keep yourself with the particulars of shot assessment and execution, the less chance your mind has to dwell on the emotional 'if' and 'but' factors that breed anxiety."
Jack Nicklaus

Great champions have desire, confidence, vision, and goals, but they also possess another special quality that allows them to live that vision and reach those goals before many others have traveled halfway along the road to success. It's a quality that will instantly improve your performance in any task you undertake. It is the ability to focus. Its basis is so obvious, you may be tempted to dismiss it, in spite of what it can do for you, without even trying to take advantage of its power. Resist that temptation!

Golf is played one shot at a time; it's played in the present tense; it's a matter of right here and right now. The ability to focus one's thoughts and actions solely on the task at hand until completion is one of the keys to golfing success. When an acquaintance asked Ben Hogan to name the shot he believed to be the most important in the game, he politely replied, "The next one."

Champions have an innate ability to focus all their attention on the shot they are about to play, denying themselves the luxury of thinking about the next shot, the next hole, or the next day. They can quickly and accurately define the desired result of a particular shot and focus themselves entirely, both physically and mentally, on the actions necessary to achieve that result. All other thoughts are excluded during the process. They don't allow other players, crowds, cameras, low-flying blimps, or noisy announcers to distract them from their purpose while they are actually in the process of executing the shot.

Commitment to a Single, Defined Purpose

If ever a game was based on concentration and commitment, golf is that game. Unlike most sports, the ball doesn't move while you are trying to hit it. It just sits there and ignores you. It isn't a game requiring lightning reactions, like tennis, where you must move your racket to the flight path of the ball largely by instinct. Golf is a thinking man's game. Those long walks between shots allow plenty of time for the mind to wander away from the purpose at hand. Time to look at the scoreboard, thinking how you could be several places higher if only a couple of birdie putts hadn't lipped out. Time for recriminations about the bad swing you made on the previous hole that cost you a shot. Time to look at the water hazard ahead and remember how you underclubbed and dumped your ball in it yesterday. During a slow-paced round, there is even time for your mind to drift away from golf altogether, becoming involved with personal or business problems.

Without excellent focus, time can become a dangerous enemy. Golf demands total commitment to a single purpose, 70 or so times a round. Those who lack this commitment don't become champions. Arnold Palmer was once asked what it was that gave him an edge over the other players. He was probably expected to cite his long, straight drives or his deadly putting in clutch situations. At the pinnacle of his career, no player was better on the greens. His response surprised quite a few observers. It was, "Concentration."

This commitment to a single definite purpose demands no supernatural powers, no superhuman strength, and no awesome talent. Anyone can do it. Champions, however, do it better and more consistently than most.

A Lesson from Tiger: Focus on Core Business.

As Tiger Woods sank his last putt to win the 2000 U.S. Open by 15 shots, prompting some to suggest that the USGA ought to "tigerproof" courses or "flight" future tournaments. But consider this: while David Duval takes time off to go snowboarding or Phil Mickelson reminisces about how great it is to spend time at home with his daughter, Tiger Woods just practices and tries to get better. While Nick Faldo opens golf institutes with Marriott across America, Colin Montgomery is doing the same across in Britain. Meanwhile, Tiger just practices. While Ben Crenshaw, Tom Watson, and Mark O'Mera design golf courses, Tiger just practices. While Greg Norman races to set a record for the most businesses run by a golfer, Tiger just practices.

Strangely enough this single-minded focus seems to be working. Tiger seems content, at least for the moment, to let others handle the minor business of capitalizing on his name to the tune of $100 million a year. He knows that the money will keep rolling in only if he continues to play great golf. While he does have a host of endorsements, he does not own car dealerships and real estate developments like Arnold Palmer or his own golf club manufacturing company like Jack Nicklaus. He does not own Vineyards, a turf company, and a boat building enterprise like Greg Norman. He does not, as yet, design golf courses—although the mere addition of his name would mean an instant $2 to $3 million. Instead, he just plays golf and practices, staying focused on the only goal that matters to him—being recognized as the best golfer who ever played the game.

Concentration

> *"I had to learn to concentrate—to ignore the gallery and the other golfers and shut my mind against everything but my own game."*
> *Ben Hogan*

In the 1947 Masters, Hogan was paired with Claude Harmon, one of the most respected of all golf instructors. When they reached Augusta's devilish 12th hole, the pivotal point in Amen Corner, Harmon had the honor. He stepped up to the tricky, nerve-racking, 155-yard shot and knocked it in the hole. It was the first hole-in-one in Masters history. The crowd erupted in admiration and delight, but Hogan didn't say a word, not "Great shot," or "Well done," or even "You lucky son-of-a-gun!" Then, when the noise gradually subsided, he fixed his steely glare on the green and played a fine shot a few feet past the cup. As they marched onto the green, the crowd gave Harmon a standing ovation, and the roar continued until he had removed his ball from the cup. Hogan's eyes never left his own ball as he paced around the cup to study his line. Finally, he stroked a smooth putt right in the middle of the hole.

As the two players made their way to the 13th tee, Hogan turned to Harmon and finally spoke. "You know, Claude," he said, "that's the first two I've ever made on that hole. What did you have?" Now, that's concentration!

Hogan was involved in a similar incident, this time playing in a threesome that included the long-hitting George Fazio. Fazio holed his second shot, a magnificent 7-iron, for an eagle on a very long par four. When they had completed the round, Hogan handed Fazio his score card to check. Fazio immediately noticed that Hogan had marked him down for a par four at the 9th hole instead of the eagle two he actually had. He pointed out the error to Hogan, who said, "George, the 9th is a 460-yard par four. How could you have had a two?" Only after the third player in the group had attested to George's amazing shot did Hogan correct the score and sign the card.

Hogan was so focused during play that when close friends spoke to him from just a few feet away, wishing him luck or offering words of encouragement, he would have absolutely no recollection of any contact upon finishing his round. Although no other player can match the level of concentration displayed by the Hawk, Nicklaus comes close. Not far behind these two, you can list many other great players, champions like Faldo, Palmer, Player, Jones, and Nelson. Even Lee Trevino, known as the "Merry Mex" for his clowning and apparent lighthearted approach to the game, is an absolute model of focus and concentration when he is planning and playing his shots.

Developing Concentration

Having championship concentration means being totally absorbed in one specific, current objective. It means the five senses—sight, smell, taste, hearing, and touch—are all working in unison to achieve a common purpose. It requires you, as you approach your task, to clear your mind of any extraneous thoughts that might invade your own, private zone and interfere with your performance.

How do we develop this championship concentration and put it to work for us? Although it comes naturally to a select few, most of us can achieve enormous improvement through conscious effort. One player I know, whose hobby is astronomy, thinks of concentration as being similar to looking through a telescope. He scans the skies looking for something interesting, then adjusts the focus of the telescope to zone in on a particular star or planet. This system works well in preparing to undertake any task, including making a golf shot. Consider the distance, the contours of the green, traps, hole position, and weather conditions. Then, having compiled and reviewed all the information, zone in on the hole. Now, with nothing else in mind, just hit it!

When working on the range, select a spot where the temptation to talk to other players will not interfere with your practice. Don't just stand out there, mindlessly hitting ball after ball, without a goal. That's nothing more than mild exercise. Select a target. Plan on hitting that target using a variety of different shots. Play from different lies, both good and bad. Change clubs and change targets. Above all, don't let your concentration lapse. If you find it impossible to maintain focus or recover it when you lose it, it is the wrong time for you to practice. Take a break until you are ready to apply your mind to the task.

The "Pre-Shot Routine"

Using the same routine as you prepare to hit every shot, every time, in practice and on the golf course, can help you get into the zone. All champions use this technique. The pre-shot routine functions like a switch, turning off all distractions and interruptions and allowing players to sharpen their focus. Jack Nicklaus's pre-shot routine, for example, includes picking a spot a few inches in front of the ball over which he wants the shot to fly. Once he has selected his spot, he focuses not on a target that is 200 yards away but on the spot that's just a few inches away.

Set a Specific "Micro-Goal" and Stick to It

Concentration can only reach its peak state when the mind is confident it has adequate and accurate information and is allowed to focus all its efforts on a single, clearly defined task. Once you have gathered the relevant information and analyzed the data, it will help you to focus if you set a goal for the *precise* outcome of the shot. By setting a "micro-goal," such as hitting a high fade with a 6-iron that will travel 170 yards and finish a few feet short and right of the pin, your mind can concentrate on doing exactly that. It's when we give our mind vague, indefinite instructions that it starts to wander instead of maintaining focus.

What If You Lose It?

"When the mind leaves the body, the body seldom does what you want it to do."
Andrew Wood

Many golfers allow their minds to wander all over the universe during the hours they spend on the course. Champions have the ability to concentrate for longer periods than the average player, enabling them to produce their best efforts more of the time. Even champions, however, are subject to lapses. Fortunately, they know how to recognize the symptoms of loss of concentration so they can reaffirm their motivation and re-focus before their game deteriorates. That's when those pre-shot routines and micro-goals are really valuable.

What breaks your concentration? Noise, personal problems, business responsibilities, anxiety? The important thing is to identify those occasions when your mind drifts away from its current task and make a conscious effort to quickly return your focus to the job at hand. You might find it interesting and beneficial to note each time your concentration is broken. Once you perceive a pattern of distractions that tend to regularly invade your thoughts, you can take appropriate actions to address and correct the problem.

Overcoming Boredom

It is also not uncommon for a player to lose concentration through boredom, even in the middle of his round. While this may seem unlikely to the average golf addict, the guys on the tour are playing at least 90 holes week after week. In normal circumstances, champions are motivated to perform. They know what they want to achieve and why. It matters more to them than anything else. Their goals are foremost in their mind. In the middle of an indifferent performance, however, when a player is well down the leader board or in danger of missing the cut, boredom may start to creep into his game. Few things affect concentration like boredom. Even a good player can easily become detached and lethargic. To avoid this pitfall, champions find innovative ways to restore their concentration. They'll endeavor to get inside their opponent's approach shot, for example, or to come up with a different way to play a tricky pitch shot. The key is to bring some sort of competitiveness or creativeness into the process and get the mind back on track. They have to remind themselves that it isn't over 'til it's over.

Destiny in the Balance

"If you pick up a golfer and hold it close to your ear like a conch shell, and listen, you will hear an alibi."
Fred Beck, author of 89 Years in the Sand Trap

When a player loses concentration, it's almost inevitable that the resulting shot is not going to be pretty. You can tell a lot about a player by the way he handles the situation after a lapse of concentration that results in a bad shot or a bad round.

On the PGA Tour, nearly all of the caddies are professional. They carry those huge, logo-covered bags for a living, and some of them, depending of course on the ability of the man whose name is on the bag, do pretty well at it. These tour caddies do much more than just carry the bag. They assist with club selection on the tee and indicate the best line to follow in order to be in optimum position for the approach shot. They are the keepers of the notebook that contains all the yardages. They chart flag positions and calculate distances from the present position of the ball to the front edge of the green and to the flag. Many of them are called upon to help "read the greens," assessing speed, slope, and especially "break" or "borrow" on the impending putt. One might even call them "tour guides." In addition to their more obvious duties, they are also responsible for encouraging their players, boosting their confidence and helping them maintain concentration. In some cases, following a misjudged shot or putt, they are blamed, and on rare occasions, verbally abused.

One of the closest comparisons that can be drawn between golf and life in general is that champions always take responsibility for their own actions. Golfers don't have teammates to back them up or make up for their mistakes. Football, baseball, and basketball players can perform poorly from time to time but still find themselves on the winning team. In golf, nobody else can make your 3-foot putt for you. Your competitors can't make you hit your tee shot out of bounds. Although many players have mentors or coaches these days, they don't perform the same function as a Vince Lombardi or a John Wooden. They can't exhort their player to go out and destroy the competition. Only the player himself can conjure up the motivation to perform at championship levels. Champion golfers don't win tournaments for the Gipper, they win them for themselves.

Golfers understand that they are in charge of their own destiny. They don't blame bad luck, society, the economy, racism, their parents, the government, the PGA Tour, or anyone else for a sub-standard performance. Only *they* can hole that putt on the 18th green to win the Masters, and they are personally at fault if they choke and make six. Champions learn this early in life, and the trait of responsibility remains with them forever.

On the First, I Drove It in the Rough

"You face a situation that you fear you cannot cope with, so you give yourself an excuse for possible failure by getting mad at the course or the injustice you've suffered."
Jack Nicklaus

"Bartender! I'll have a Heineken, please. Hi, Charlie; how are you? Grab a stool. Bartender! Make that two."

"I'm fine, thanks," says Charlie. "How about you; how was your game?"

"Let me tell you, I had a lousy day out there. On the 1st tee, someone moved in my backswing, and I flinched and drove it in the rough. When I got to the ball, it was sitting deep down in long, wet grass. I tried to hit the green with a 5-iron, but the club turned in my hands and I pull-hooked it way left. When I found it—you won't believe—it's sitting in a divot the size of Joe Robbie Stadium. I hit a great recovery, but it took a bad bounce and ran over the green into the back trap. It wound up in someone's footprint, and I took two to get out. I had a 10-foot putt for a six. My first putt was dead center, but it hit a spike mark right in front of the cup and lipped out. I had a tap-in left, but they'd cut the cup on an angle and the stupid thing spun out. So I made 8 on the first. On the 2nd tee . . ."

You've heard enough, haven't you? You've had to sit through a blow-by-blow account of a friend's round, even though he shot 95. When did you start to lose interest? I'll bet it was the moment he opened his mouth.

Nobody cares how rough you had it out there today; and nobody cares how rough you had it in life, except maybe you and your Mom. So to quote a famous Eagles' song, "Get over it!" If you are to become a champion, it's up to you. Champions realize their fate is in their own hands. Destiny awaits you, but you must take action. So start by developing a game plan that will enable you to direct that action and make the right things happen. It's up to *you*.

You'll need to be very careful with your third shot. This green is extremely difficult. Stay away from the huge trap that guards the left side. The hole is cut in the traditional championship position, back left, only about 15 feet from the edge of the green. On the right side, the green slopes severely from front to back—a drop of at least eight or 10 feet. If you leave your approach shot, two putting is almost impossible . . . Wedge is enough club, Sir, but be sure you don't hold back . . . OK, that'll do nicely . . . About 20 feet, I should think . . . Give it two cups to the right . . . Nice smooth roll. Stone dead for another par . . . Thank you, Sir! But remember, although I told you where you needed to play that approach shot, you're the one who put it there. Good job!

Of course, it's always nice to know I've been able to help. It's certainly better than being blamed when something goes wrong! . . . Believe me, it happens all too often. Funny thing about champions, though; they never blame their mistakes on others.

Swing Thoughts

- Champions know they must focus on a single action to achieve the desired result.

- Champions start by eliminating all possible distractions, so they can maintain focus.

- Champions develop a pre-shot routine they follow every time to put them "in a zone."

- Champions recognize when they have lost concentration and quickly regroup.

- Champions recognize the signs of boredom and eliminate it by challenging themselves in new and creative ways.

- Champions accept responsibility for their own success or failure, because they know their destiny is in their own hands.

Back in the Clubhouse

Back in the real world, focus, concentration, and getting in the elusive "zone" where great things happen is basically a function of time management. Perhaps the greatest single problem people have today is "time poverty." Working people have too much to do and too little time for their personal lives. Most people feel overwhelmed with responsibilities and activities, and the harder they work, the further behind they feel. This sense of being on a never-ending treadmill can cause you to fall into the "reactive/responsive" mode of living. That is, instead of clearly deciding what you want to do, you continually react to what is happening around you. Pretty soon, you lose all sense of control. You feel that your life is running you, rather than that you are running your life.

On a regular basis, you have to stand back and take stock of yourself and what you're doing. You have to stop the clock and do some serious thinking about who you are and where you are going. You have to evaluate your activities in the light of what is really important to you. You must master your time instead of becoming a slave to the constant flow of events and demands on your time. And you must organize your life to achieve balance, harmony, and inner peace.

Taking action without thinking first is the cause of every failure. Your ability to think is the most valuable trait you possess. If you improve the quality of your thinking, you improve the quality of your life—sometimes immediately.

Time is your most precious resource. It is the most valuable thing you have. It is perishable, it is irreplaceable, and it cannot be saved. It can only be reallocated from activities of lower value to activities of higher value. All work requires time, and time is absolutely essential for the important relationships in your life. The very act of taking a moment to think about your time before you spend it will begin to improve your personal time management immediately.

I used to think time management was only a business tool, like a calculator or a cell phone. It was something you used so you could get more done in a shorter period of time and eventually be paid more money. Then I learned that time management is not a peripheral activity or skill. It is a core skill upon which everything else in life depends.

In your professional or business life, there are so many demands on your time from other people that very little of your time is yours to use as you choose. However, you can exert a tremendous amount of control over how you use your time at home and in your personal life, and it is in this area that I want to focus.

Personal time management begins with you. It begins with your thinking through what is really important to you in life. And it only makes sense that you organize it around specific things you want to accomplish. So you need to set goals in three major areas of your life.

First, you need personal and family goals. These are the reasons why you get up in the morning, why you work hard and upgrade your skills, why you are concerned about money and sometimes feel frustrated by the demands on your time.

What are your personal and family goals, both tangible and intangible? A tangible family goal could be a bigger house, a better car, a larger television set, a vacation, or anything else that costs money. An intangible goal could be to build a higher quality relationship with your spouse and children or to spend more time with your family going for walks or reading books. Achieving your personal and family goals is the real essence of time management and its major purpose.

The second area is your business and career goals. These are the "how" goals, the means by which you achieve your personal, or "why," goals. How can you achieve the level of income that will enable you to fulfill your family goals? How can you develop the skills and abilities to stay ahead of the curve in your career? Business and career goals are absolutely essential, especially when balanced with personal and family goals.

The third type is your personal development goals. Remember, you can't achieve much more on the outside than what you have achieved on the inside. Your outer life is a reflection of your inner life. If you wish to achieve worthwhile things in your personal and career lives, you must make sure you develop into a worthwhile person. You must build yourself if you want to build your life. Perhaps the greatest secret of success is that you can become anything you really want to become to achieve any goal you really want to achieve. But in order to do it, you must go to work on yourself and never stop.

Once you have a list of your personal and family goals, your business and career goals, and your self-development goals, you can then organize the list by priority. This brings us to the difference between priorities and "posteriorities." In order to get your personal time under control, you must decide very clearly upon your priorities. You must decide on the most important things you could possibly be doing to give yourself the greatest amount of happiness, satisfaction, and joy in life. But at the same time, you must establish "posteriorities" as well. Just as priorities are things you do more of and sooner, "posteriorities" are things that you do less of and later.

The fact is, your calendar is full. You have no spare time. Every moment is extremely valuable. Therefore, to do anything new, you will have to stop doing something old. In order to get into something, you will have to get out of something else. In order to pick up something, you will have to put down something. Before you make any new commitment of your time, you must firmly decide what activities you are going to discontinue in your personal life.

If you want to spend more time with your family, for example, you must decide which activities you currently engage in that are preventing you from doing so.

A principle of time management says that hard time pushes out soft time. This means that hard time, such as the time you spend at work, will push out soft time, such as the time you spend with your family. If you don't get your work done at the office because you don't use your time well, you almost invariably have to rob that time from your family. As a result, because your family is important to you, you find yourself in a values conflict. You feel stressed and irritable. You feel a tremendous amount of pressure. You know in your heart that you should be spending more time with the important people in your life, but because you didn't get your work done, you have to fulfill that responsibility before you spend can time with your spouse and children.

Think of it this way. Every minute you waste during the workday is time your family will ultimately be deprived of. So concentrate on working when you are at work so you can concentrate on your family when you are at home.

There are three key questions you can ask yourself continually to keep your personal life in balance. The first question is, "What is really important to me?" Whenever you find yourself with too much to do and too little time in which to do it, stop and ask yourself, "What is really important for me to do in this situation?" Then, make sure the things you are doing are the answer to that question.

The second question is, "What are my highest-value activities?" In your personal life, this means, "What are the things I do that give me the greatest pleasure and satisfaction? Of all the things I could be doing at any one time, what are the things I could do to add the greatest value to my life?"

And the final question for you to ask, over and over, is, "What is the most valuable use of my time right now?" Since you can do only one thing at a time, you must constantly organize your life so you are doing only the most important thing at every moment.

Personal time management enables you to choose what to do first, what to do second, and what not to do at all. It enables you to organize every aspect of your life so you can get the greatest joy, happiness, and satisfaction out of everything you do.

Questions to ponder

• Do you finish one task before starting another?

• What about the people who work for you?

• Do you remove all possible distractions before starting work?

• Do you quickly recognize the signs of boredom or loss of concentration? What do you do to combat these problems?

• Do you accept total responsibility for all your successes and failures, in business and in life?

The 15th is one of the tightest driving holes on the course. Your tee shot must be threaded between the trees. It's 406 yards, and it plays shorter since it's downhill, but it's OB left and right. The best shot is to hit it parallel with Seventeen Mile Drive on the right and draw it back toward the center. That takes that big pine on the left out of play . . . Oh, you pushed that one, Sir. Luckily, it hit a tree and stayed in bounds, but I'm not sure if you have much of a shot.

What does a true champion do in a tricky situation like this? This is where champions shine the brightest, staring adversity right in the face. They never give up. This is when the strength of their determination comes to the front. Now, take your 6-iron and punch it low, to the left of the tree trunk, below those branches . . . That's the way, Sir. Good shot; just in front of the green. You can still make par from there.

How important is determination to a champion? Understanding the power of determination is as important as any lesson champions have to learn. It's about what to do when things really go wrong and your dreams of success start to fade away before your very eyes. It's about continuing to believe in yourself, deep down in your heart, even when others tell you that you can't overcome your problems. We have a few moments while that group ahead finishes the hole, so let me share a couple of memories with you. They're about the rock hard determination a champion needs in order to succeed in spite of the odds—to reach the highest goals despite pain, fear, injuries, and the negativity of others. These stories are about golf, but they could just as easily be about a business collapse, a failing relationship, or life in general. Did you ever rebuild your swing, Sir? Well, this is about rebuilding your body and your mind—staring defeat squarely in the eye until it blinks and looks away.

DETERMINATION— THE CHAMPIONSHIP DIFFERENCE

"I've always made a total effort, even when the odds seemed entirely against me. I never quit trying. I never felt that I didn't have a chance to win."
Arnold Palmer

The Hawk

When things go badly for them, many people throw in the towel. They quit, stop trying, and blame life, fate, or bad luck. They blame their parents, family, upbringing, education, and social circumstances. Yet some people, a special few, let nothing deter them. They do very little differently than people who fail, except in one critical area. They don't accept failure as an option. They know the only time you fail is when you stop trying. All the setbacks they encounter along the way are merely obstacles and challenges, and given enough determination, none of them is insurmountable.

Consider a boy who was nine years old when his father killed himself with a shot to the head from a revolver. The boy's name? Ben Hogan. His first exposure to golf was as a 12-year-old caddie, where he sometimes had to fight other caddies for the chance to carry a bag and earn a few cents. He started out as a lefty because someone gave him a left-handed set of clubs, then later switched to the right side, playing cross-handed for a while before adopting more orthodox techniques. He didn't graduate from high school, so there was no comfortable golf scholarship to start him on his way to the PGA Tour. He never won an amateur golf tournament. In spite of all this, he decided to become a golf pro.

In 1930, age 19, he declared himself to be a pro, prior to playing in a tournament in San Antonio, Texas. He didn't make the cut. Two years later, he tried his hand at the PGA Tour and was soon forced to go home because he couldn't win enough to support himself. He tried again in 1934, helped by a $225 check from a Fort Worth businessman, and fared much the same. He was, in his own words, "a terrible golfer." Finally in 1937, after working for literally thousands of hours on the practice tee to improve his game, he joined the tour for good. The $1,400 he and his wife, Valerie, had set out with had diminished to $85 when he rented a cheap room in Oakland to play in that week's tournament. Emerging from the hotel after breakfast to drive to the course for the first day's play, he found his aging Buick on blocks; the wheels and even the jack had been stolen. He hitched a ride with another contestant and rushed to the first tee without warming up. In spite of these distractions, he won the princely sum of $385. It was, he said, the biggest check he had ever seen or would ever see in his life. He would later recall that check, rather than his numerous Masters, Open, and PGA Championships, as his greatest thrill. Are you getting the feeling this was a determined man? Just wait a moment.

Hogan finished 1939 in seventh place on the money list, but he was still without an individual victory on the PGA Tour. This was to change the following year. In 1940, he won his first tour event on Donald Ross's masterpiece, Pinehurst No. 2, and then won again the following week. This started a record stretch of 56 consecutive tournaments in which he received a check. He was the year's leading money winner, cashing checks for more than $10,000. Hogan had arrived. He won five tourneys in 1941 and was once again the leading money winner, with $18,358. In 1942, Hogan lost in a playoff with Byron Nelson for the Masters title, a major championship eluding him yet again. Then, in 1943, his career was interrupted by World War II, and he was drafted into the U.S. Army. In August 1945, with the war in Europe over and the end of the Pacific war in sight, Capt. Hogan returned to his peacetime profession. In his second tournament, he won at Knoxville. He would win five of the 11 tournaments in which he played that year and finish second or third in the other six. Between August 1945 and August 1946, he would win 18 tournaments, an incredibly dominant performance. But his most important victory was in the 1946 PGA Championship, his first major. Hogan took home $42,556 that year.

The new Hogan won seven times in 1947 and 11 times in 1948, including another PGA Championship and the U.S. Open at Riviera Country Club in Los Angeles, which became known as Hogan's Alley. After winning two of the early tourneys on the West Coast swing in 1949, he decided to take a rest and set off with his wife for a new home in Fort Worth. It would be some time before he would see his new house, and 11 months before he would play golf again.

On the night of Feb. 9, 1949, he was driving his brand new, black Cadillac on Highway 80 just outside of the small town of Van Horn, Texas. Suddenly, out of the fog ahead, Hogan saw giant headlights coming at him on the wrong side of the road. The lights belonged to a 20,000-pound Greyhound bus. The driver, frustrated by being behind schedule after following a slow truck for miles, had decided to pass. It was the wrong time and the wrong place. There was nothing either driver could do to avoid the impact. At the last second, Hogan instinctively threw himself to the right, in front of his wife, to protect her. His action probably saved both their lives, since the steering column of his Cadillac was driven straight though the back of the driver's seat, where he had been sitting a split second earlier. The engine was driven into the driver's side, crushing his legs. Although many people were on the scene, it took an agonizing 90 minutes for help to arrive. Then he faced a 150-mile drive to the nearest hospital in El Paso. His injuries were massive, and for a while, he was not expected to survive. Even later, as his condition began to slowly improve, doctors told him he would never play golf again. To make matters worse, a blood clot developed and a second emergency operation had to be performed. He was on his back in bed for six weeks.

As soon as Hogan could stand, he started to retrain his body to play golf and actually completed a round in December. As 1950 opened, he began the painful process of rebuilding his life and his game and, incredibly, lost the Los Angeles Open to Sam Snead in a playoff, after a 72-hole tie. At the awards banquet, famous golf writer Grantland Rice said of his effort, "Courage never goes out of fashion." The Hawk actually won at Greenbriar a few weeks later, and then, at the Merion course near Philadelphia, he won his second U.S. Open, his fourth major title. The next season, in 1951, he won three out of the five tournaments in which he competed, including the Masters and another U.S. Open crown, this time at Oakland Hills, near Detroit, where he shot a final round 67.

Although he was already held in awe and admiration by golfers around the world, his crowning performance was yet to come. In 1953, at the age of 40, he played in only six tournaments and won no less than five of them. Of these five, three were majors. Hogan took the green jacket at Augusta for the second time with a 72-hole total of 274, a mark that would stand for 12 years. A few weeks later, he won his fourth U.S. Open at Oakmont by a five-shot margin. Then, after being pressured by friends to compete in the Open Championship at Carnoustie, in Scotland, he crossed the Atlantic.

Hogan prepared himself in typical fashion, with long hours of practice and careful analysis of the course. He opened with a round of 73, and local wags suggested that was what their grandmothers shot. He silenced them with successive rounds of 71 and 70, then closed with a 68 in howling wind and pouring rain, endearing himself to the knowledgeable Scottish fans and earning the fondly bestowed title "The Wee Ice-mon." He and his wife returned to a ticker-tape parade in New York City, to accept recognition for his remarkable achievements. Who knows? He might also have won the PGA that year, thereby completing the modern grand slam, had it not been scheduled the same week as the British Open.

Hogan never had a manager, sports psychologist, or coach. His total career earnings would barely make the top 60 on this year's money list. Yet, in spite of all the setbacks and failures, Ben Hogan is regarded as the purest striker of the ball in the history of the game. Only Jack Nicklaus, Bobby Jones, and Walter Hagen have won more major tournaments.

Ben Hogan took lots of small steps. After his near-fatal car crash, he learned to walk again, step by painful step. Later he hit practice shot after shot, until he had raised his skills to a new level. He took small steps and kept taking them again and again, overcoming every obstacle, until his golfing performance became a symbol of excellence. He became a legend in his own time.

The golf writers of the day dubbed Hogan "The Hawk" for his steely eyed concentration and determination. He was once asked what achievement in his long and distinguished career gave him the most satisfaction. Was it winning four Opens or three majors in one year? Was it the comeback from a near-fatal car crash? "No," said

Hogan. "I get the greatest satisfaction from knowing that I went dead broke out on tour more than once and still came back and made it on my third try."

—T hat was a fine chip and a great save. You sure hung tough on that one, Sir. Good par!

Swing Thoughts

- Champions are never discouraged by the negativity of others. You don't fail until you stop trying, and only you get to make the call.

- Champions go out of their way to help others become the best they can be.

Back in the Clubhouse

Here's a question for you that applies equally to golf and personal life: What are you made of? What are you *really* made of? When push comes to shove, when the rubber meets the road, when the chips are down, what lies at the very core of your character?

You learn what you are really made of only when things go wrong and you are tumbled, end over end, by some adversity or setback that hits you like a Mack truck coming out of an alley. Since your behaviors on the outside are the real indicators of who you are on the inside, only by observing how you behave when things go wrong can you tell what you really have inside you.

Let's make one thing clear at the beginning. Life is a continuous succession of both small and large problems. They never end. No sooner do you get control of one situation when you are hit by another. Life is a process of "two steps forward and one step back." When you become a great success, you simply exchange one type of problem for another. Before, you had small problems with limited consequences; now you have large problems with enormous consequences. No matter how smart and clever and careful you are, you'll face challenges, difficulties, and sometimes heartbreaking adversities every day, week, and month of your life.

And thank heaven for that! You couldn't possibly have become the person you are today if you had not had to contend with adversity on your way up. Perhaps your chief aim in life is to develop a noble character, to become an excellent human being, to become everything you are capable of becoming. Only by contending with challenges that seem to be beyond your strength to handle at the moment can you grow more surely toward the stars.

The starting point in dealing with any difficulty is to relax. Clear your mind. Get into a state where you're calm and cool and in full control of your emotions and senses. Back off mentally, and become as objective as possible. Look at the problem with a certain amount of detachment, as if it were happening to someone else. When you can analyze your adversities clearly, you can see opportunities to turn them to your best advantage.

One of the rules for dealing with adversity in life is that you are only as free as your well-developed alternatives. You are only as free as the options you have. Only when you can switch and do something else can you be flexible in dealing with your current situation. If you have not developed an option or an alternative, you will become anxious and even panicky when you are threatened with a sudden loss or reversal in a particular area of your life.

For example, if you are in business, look into the future and imagine that your biggest customer goes broke or starts buying your product or service from someone else. If that were to happen, what would you do? How would you compensate for the loss of business? What could you do right now to ensure that it doesn't happen? How could you increase the quantity or the quality of your service or your product in such a way that your major customer would never think of switching? How could you develop additional customers so you wouldn't be so dependent upon a single purchaser?

If you are in sales and your goal is to earn a certain amount of money so you can enjoy a certain quality of lifestyle, you have to look down the road in your sales work and ask, "Where will my sales come from? How many prospective customers do I have who can generate the business I need to make my numbers?" And ask yourself, "What would I do if I lost my best customer? What would I do if I lost my biggest prospect?"

When I was a boy, I read a story that contained one of the most important messages about adversity I've ever learned in my life.

In the story, a young man went up to Alaska and worked with an old Indian trapper, learning how to lay traps, clean pelts, live in the bush, and take care of himself in the wilderness. At the end of his apprenticeship, the old Indian gave him some advice. He said, "Remember this. Whatever you do, when you travel, always use two logs crossing."

He was referring to the best method for crossing the many small rivers and streams the young man would come upon between the small town where the Indian lived and the distant wilderness where he would be trapping.

The young man went off on his own and trapped throughout the summer until he had all the furs he could possibly carry. When the leaves began to turn, he began his long hike back to the small town where he would trade his furs for enough money to live on for the winter and to outfit himself again for the spring. He did everything exactly right, as he had been taught, until he came to the last, fast-running stream remaining between him and civilization. In his eagerness to get back to town, he tried to cross it on a single log that stretched from one bank to the other.

Alas! He lost his footing and fell into the stream. He had to throw off his pack to avoid drowning. He lost everything. His whole year was wiped out. He arrived in town wet, bedraggled, and exhausted. There he met the old Indian, who looked at him, shook his head, and said, "You forgot to use two logs crossing."

The moral of the story is clear. To contend with adversity in your life, you have to develop alternatives. You have to expand your range of choices. You can never afford to put all your hopes on a single person or a single possibility. You, too, must use two logs crossing.

Questions to Ponder

- Is your desire and determination to succeed as great now as it was five or 10 years ago?

- Are you still willing to pay the price?

The 16th heads back toward the ocean, so it might play a bit longer than the 400 yards you see on the card. Keep your drive down the left; those bunkers you see on the right were deepened for the 1984 U.S. Open, and you can't get home from there . . . That's one of your best, Sir . . . Did Hogan's story inspire others? You bet it did!

INSPIRING DETERMINATION

> *"I hate to lose at anything, even checkers, chess,*
> *pool—you name it. I feel if you ease up in any game,*
> *it breeds a quitting attitude."*
> Tom Watson

More on Determination

The trait of determination is so critical to championship performance that it requires added attention. Determination, or perseverance, can literally mean the difference between success and failure in countless cases. Athletes have demonstrated its importance throughout history. Beyond Ben Hogan, other golfers have had to persist against great odds. Here is another story of championship determination.

The Bobby Nichols Story

When champions use their innate determination to achieve their goals, they also help others by setting an example to be followed. The greatest champions take it a step further; they go out of their way to help others. Ben Hogan was a case in point. He once said he believed he had a purpose in life, and it was to give courage to those who are sick or broken in body. In one case, by writing an encouraging letter to a young boy he had never met, Hogan did more than just give him courage. He helped inspire another champion.

Bobby Nichols was born and raised in Louisville, Kentucky. Like many players of his generation, his first introduction to golf was as a caddie at the local club when he was 10 or 11. He started out with just one club, playing a single hole over and over again. He quickly showed some aptitude for the game, which was no great surprise since he was already showing considerable promise in other sports, particularly basketball and football. Around the time he was 14, Bobby really started to take golf seriously. His heroes were Sam Snead, Byron Nelson, and of course, Ben Hogan. Bobby studied their swings and imitated aspects of each of them, and this "modeling" technique seemed to work very well for him. He developed a fine, fluid swing and won the state caddie championship at the age of 15. Bobby discovered that he loved winning and the feeling that came with it. Now it was time to dream big dreams.

Then came the night of Sept. 4, 1952, a date that would be forever imprinted on the mind of Bobby Nichols. He was 16 years old, without a care in the world, and was spending the evening with four of his friends. They were in an automobile, and they were traveling at high speed. Just after 8 p.m., the speedometer inched above 100 miles per hour, and the car failed to make the next bend. When they finally came to rest, four boys and a girl lay trapped in the twisted wreckage. Firefighters, police, and paramedics arrived and quickly fought to extricate them. A doctor at the scene indicated that no time should be wasted on Nichols, since he wasn't going to make it anyway. A priest performed last rites on the 16-year-old boy.

Two days later, Bobby was still clinging to life, but the medical prognosis was not good. He was still unconscious, and in addition to a variety of minor injuries, he had a broken pelvis, a damaged spine, a collapsed lung, a bruised kidney, a brain concussion, and he was paralyzed from the waist down. The doctor advised his distressed parents that, if he lived, he would probably never walk again. His dreams of golfing greatness had apparently ended in a head-on collision with a utility pole. For 13 tension-filled days, friends and family maintained a vigil beside Bobby's hospital bed. Suddenly he opened his eyes, looked around, and asked two questions: How long had he been asleep, and had he missed football practice? He quickly learned the answer to the second question when he discovered, to his horror, that he couldn't move his legs. Bobby Nichols went home a month later. At least he was alive.

Take any active teenager and make him lie in bed, in traction for 100 days, incapable of doing anything physical, and the result will almost certainly be the same. Bobby soon became discouraged. His condition seemed hopeless. A couple of dedicated teachers, including his golf coach from St. Xavier's, Brother Jerome, visited him regularly. They tutored him and encouraged him when he talked of playing golf again. For his mother, this was a form of torture, for as soon as his visitors left, Bobby would ask her to bring him a club, even though he couldn't sit up without help.

The weeks dragged by, and Bobby's spirits sank even lower as it became more and more apparent that he might not recover. Then Brother Jerome conceived an idea that just might help. He knew Bobby idolized Ben Hogan, who had gone through a similar terrible experience. Perhaps the great golfer would be kind enough to write the boy a few words of encouragement. There was nothing to lose, so he wrote to Hogan asking for his help, and the Hawk quickly responded. When Bobby's mother handed him the letter with his idol's name above the return address, he thought it was a practical joke, but when he opened the letter, he found it was genuine. Hogan had written:

Dear Bobby,

I received a letter the other day from Brother Jerome at Saint Xavier's High School, telling of your misfortune and asking me to drop you a note. I was delighted to receive his letter, although it wasn't necessary for him to tell me to write you. I would have done that anyway, knowing of your accident. I don't know if there is anything I can say to you that would console you mentally or physically, since I know you have been through everything. I always figured that no one ever went through life without some things happening to them, some of them minor, some major. Those of us who have had minor things just don't have to work as hard recuperating as the people like you who have the major things.

I don't have to tell you that the human body probably is the greatest machine ever known, plus the fact that given the chance, it will heal any sickness or hurt. It is the determination and will of a person to do the exercises that will get him well, and, as you certainly know, there are no shortcuts.

I don't want to sound like a preacher, and I hope you understand my thought for you. I am terribly sorry for your misfortune, and you shall be remembered in my prayers.

My best wishes for a complete and speedy recovery.

I am sincerely,

Ben Hogan

The letter had an effect no doctor could ever have hoped to achieve. By the time he had finished reading it, Bobby Nichols was determined to walk, to play golf, and to be a champion. Only days after receiving the letter, he sat up unassisted for the first time. A few weeks later, he was out of bed, on crutches, practicing his putting and chipping. One small step led to another until, after several months, the happiest day Bobby had experienced for a long time finally arrived, and he threw away his crutches.

Hogan's letter was to provide inspiration more than once over the course of Bobby Nichols' career. "As you know," said Bobby, "golf is not a fair game. You could be playing your best and nothing happens; then one day something does. The letter and its message helped me get through some rough times." It's framed now, together with the original envelope in which it came, and occupies a place of pride in his game room in Fort Myers, Florida. Still weak and sore, Bobby's first complete round after the accident was an 82, but to him it felt like a 62. In the summer of 1953, less than a year after the crash, Bobby shot three under par on the back nine to help his high school team win the state championship. He was officially back in business. Now he could afford to dream again. Playing on the PGA Tour was still a long way off, but Bobby Nichols had persevered and won the toughest fight of his life.

After leaving Texas A&M University in 1958, Bobby worked on the oil rigs of west Texas, as well as being employed as an assistant in a golf shop. After six months of military service, he returned to the golf shop and worked on his game. By the 1960 season, he felt ready to try the tour. At that time, a new entrant needed two or three professionals to sponsor him for membership in the PGA. Then, once he received a card, he could go out and try to qualify for one of the few available spots in each event on the Monday prior to the actual tournament.

In his first year on tour, Bobby made over $16,000 and easily made the top 60 players, exempting him from having to qualify every Monday. It would be one more year before he finally broke into the winners' circle by capturing the 1962 St. Petersburg Open. He also won in Houston that year, finished a strong third in the U.S. Open and sixth in the PGA Championship—a sign of things to come. That year *Golf Digest* named him golf's most improved player, and the Golf Writers of America honored him with the Ben Hogan Award, presented annually to a golfer who had overcome a major physical handicap.

During his first four years on tour, Nichols worked diligently to improve his game and practiced as hard as anyone ever had. Then, 12 years after the near-fatal crash, the 28-year-old Nichols realized one of his lifelong ambitions when he was paired in a tournament with his idol, Ben Hogan. It was the 1964 PGA Championship at the Columbus Country Club in Ohio, right in Jack Nicklaus' back yard.

Nichols opened the tournament with a course record 64 in the first round. He followed that with a solid 71 in the second round and a scrambling 69 in the third, giving him a one-shot lead over Arnold Palmer going into the final round. That evening, looking at the giant scoreboard, he was excited to see that Hogan had shot 68 and had moved up in the standings. Under the PGA's complicated pairing system, they would be playing together in the final round. Unlike many tour players, Nichols was not intimidated by the thought of playing with Hogan. In fact, he looked upon it as a break—perhaps even a sign that he was meant to win. He found this to be a comforting thought to sleep on the night before the final round of a major championship.

The next day, Bobby Nichols stood on the 1st tee of the Columbus Country Club. He had never felt such intense pressure in his entire life. Thousands of people had come to watch the final few groups comprising more than a few well-known players, including Arnold Palmer, Jack Nicklaus and Ben Hogan. Bobby kept thinking how badly he wanted to win; how badly he wanted to show that newspaper in Louisville that he had what it takes to be a champion; how badly he wanted the endorsements that would accompany the championship and provide security for his wife, Nancy, and their new baby. He also thought how badly he wanted to show Mr. Hogan that his encouragement and support had been well-placed. All of these things were in his mind as he teed his ball for the most important round of his life.After a good drive and a solid approach shot, Nichols nervously three-putted from 12 feet. With 17 holes to play, he was even with Arnold Plamer. On the 2nd tee, his lack of concentration persisted, and he sent a huge hook bounding into the woods on the left side of the fairway toward the out-of-bounds stakes. Suddenly, he snapped out of his reverie as the ball hit a tree and bounded back onto the fairway. Inspired by this lucky break, he played a perfect 4-iron shot, leaving himself an easy birdie putt. Another birdie at number three put him one shot ahead of Palmer again. After parring the 4th, 5th, and 6th holes, he bogeyed 7 and 8 and finished the front nine dead even with Palmer. The gallery was 100 percent Arnie's Army as Nichols came to the 10th tee. He could hear them telling one another, "Nichols is going to choke," or, "He's about to blow up." He could hear them saying that Arnie was charging and quickly found out from the vocal crowd that Palmer had just eagled the 10th. He knew he needed a birdie at worst to stay in contention. The 10th was a 536-yard par five, with a large ravine guarding the left side of the green. The long-hitting Nichols hit his tee shot as hard as he had ever hit a drive in his life. It traveled straight as a bullet, 300 yards down the center of the fairway. From there, ignoring the ravine, he went for the green in two with a 3-wood, leaving his ball 40 feet from the cup. His long eagle putt rolled toward the hole, broke several feet, and fell into the cup, dead center. He was confident now that the championship was his. Birdies at the 15th and 17th gave him a three stroke advantage over Palmer and Nicklaus.

Nichols also set PGA Championship records by leading the tournament after all four rounds and setting a new, low, 72-hole score of 271. It was his crowning achievement in a professional career that would span four decades. Even more, it was a dramatic demonstration of the power of persistence and determination to succeed, no matter what obstacles one encounters in life. Later that evening, Hogan came up to Nichols and congratulated him again. "You know," he said, "I would never have gone for the green on the 10th the way you did." Nichols recalls, "It made me feel proud, not just winning the PGA, but hitting a shot Ben Hogan wouldn't have attempted and having him acknowledge it as being well done."

When asked what he did to motivate and inspire himself in the face of adversity, Nichols said, "I focus on all the good things: my family, my health, and the fact that I have been fairly successful. I look at the good things that have happened, and that helps when things don't go well. I also think of all the people who have had things much worse than I have and try to put life in perspective. Often people become obsessed with golf or with business and lose their perspective. Keeping the big picture in mind helps you stay motivated in the face of small setbacks."The No. 1 key to success, though, is discipline. I had parents that weren't strict but had discipline. I knew right from wrong. I feel that discipline carries over to whatever you do, whether it be golf or anything personal."

There's the green, nestled down in a hollow between those two large trees . . . It's only a 9-iron from here. Go right at it, Sir, but be sure you clear the huge trap in front of the green . . . That's about 15 feet short of the cup. Nice shot!

. . . Just outside the right lip . . . Perfect! Never a doubt on that one! You're back to one over—you can still shoot that 72!

Swing Thoughts

- Champions know the past is not a mirror image of the future.

- Champions have guts and determination.

- Champions do not let obstacles stand in their way.

Back in the Clubhouse

We can avoid tragedy by following a four-step method for dealing with any adversity. Dale Carnegie created this model more than 50 years ago, and it's still one of the most powerful mental tools anyone can use when confronted with problems or worries of any kind.

1. Define the problem clearly.

What exactly is the problem? What exactly are you worrying about? Write out the definition of your problem. Make sure it's a single problem. If it's more than one problem, write out clear definitions of all the problems that together constitute what you are worrying about now.

2. Determine the worst possible outcome.

Ask, "What's the worst possible thing that can happen in this situation?" Be frank and honest with yourself. You might lose your money, your relationship, your customer, or someone or something else that is really important to you. If everything fell apart, what is the worst thing that could occur?

3. Resolve to accept that the worst may occur.

Having identified the worst possible outcome, you now can go through the mental exercise of pretending it is going to happen, no matter what you do. The remarkable thing is that as soon as you stop resisting the worst possible outcome, you'll relax, your mind will clear, and your ability to deal with the situation will improve dramatically.

4. Begin immediately to improve upon the worst, which you have already accepted is going to happen.

Throw all of your mental resources into the battle to minimize the problem or resolve the difficulty. Concentrate on the future. Don't worry about what happened, why it happened, and who was responsible. Think only about the question "What do I do now?" How can you minimize the consequences? What's the first step you can take? And the second step? And the third step? And so on.

Successful people are not people without problems. They are people who respond quickly and positively to their problems. They think them through in advance; they anticipate them. And when they can't, they use the four-step method to resolve whatever difficulty they face. They define the problem clearly. They define the worst possible thing that could happen as a result of the problem. They resolve to accept the worst, should it occur, and then they concentrate all of their energies on making sure the worst doesn't happen.

In dealing with adversity effectively, your ability to ask questions is essential. As long as you are asking questions, you are expanding the range of options and possibilities that are open to you. As long as you are asking questions, you are keeping your mind calm and cool and objective. You are not allowing yourself to get caught up emotionally, which shuts down large parts of your brain and your creative powers.

Many problems and adversities arise because of misunderstandings and incorrect information. One of the smartest things you'll ever do in facing any adversity is to ask yourself, "Who else may have had this problem, and what did he or she do?" Ask around. Don't be afraid to admit you're in a bind. If you made a mistake or dropped the ball and found yourself in a difficult situation, don't be afraid to go to someone and admit you need help. You'll be amazed at the valuable advice you can get from someone who has already experienced the difficulty you're going through.

In dealing with adversity, perhaps the four most important words you can remember are these: "This, too, shall pass." Whatever it is, however difficult it appears, say to yourself, "This, too, shall pass."

Remember, too, that you are never sent a difficulty that is too big for you to handle. Whatever problems or adversities you face, you have within you the resources to deal with them. You have the creative ability to find a solution to your problem. You have within you, right now, everything you need to deal with whatever the world can throw at you.

One of your main jobs in life is to become an expert in dealing with adversity, to triumph over difficulty, to rise above the challenges of day-to-day life. Keep your thoughts on where you're going, not on where you've been. Keep your eyes on your goals, and keep your chin tilted upward toward the sunshine. Resolve in advance that you will meet and overcome every difficulty, and then, no matter what happens, don't give up until you do.

Questions to Ponder

• Do you have the resolve to face near failure three or four times before achieving your goals?

With the wind blowing in your face, the 17th is the toughest par three in the world. At least, it ranks right up there with the 16th at Cypress Point and the 12th at Augusta. It's 218 yards to an hour-glass green that's just a few paces wide and surrounded by bunkers. If you hit it left, the Pacific's definitely in play, and there's not much hope of getting it up and down if you miss the green on the right side, either. I'd go with that magic 5-wood of yours again, Sir. Just hood it a little so the ball doesn't balloon . . . Go ball, go! . . . The wind gusted just as you hit it. It caught the trap and fell in the sand. You should have a good lie.

Excuse me, Sir? I didn't hear because of the wind . . . Oh! You enjoyed those stories about Hogan and Nichols, but what do you do when you can't come back? Good question! Maybe I can tell you something about that as we walk up to the green.

BEATING THE ODDS

What If You Can't Come Back?

What if something happens that is even more damaging than the injuries sustained by Ben Hogan and Bobby Nichols—something so bad that the victim of the tragedy must accept that he will never recover sufficiently to play competitive golf again? What if all the surgery, will power, and positive energy in the world just aren't enough to enable him to walk again? What if all your dreams are smashed in a split second, without warning? It happened to Dennis Walters, and the way he dealt with the tragic consequences of his accident is a truly amazing story.

The Dennis Walters Story

Dennis Walters started to play golf at the age of seven. He passed a golf course on his way to school each morning and was fascinated by how high and far the players hit the ball. Seeing that little white ball traveling 250 yards made a big impression on him. Deep within him was born a passion for golf that has never diminished over the years. By the time he was 12, golf was the only sport he really cared about. Sam Snead, Ben Hogan, and Tony Lema became his heroes. At the age of 13, he had already broken 80 on a regulation length course, and he had decided to make golf his career.

After numerous wins as a junior, including the state junior championship, Dennis graduated from high school and set off to study business administration at North Texas State University. He fondly remembers his college golf days as some of the happiest he has ever spent. The thrill of playing competitive, tournament golf week after week against such up-and-coming players as Ben Crenshaw and Bill Rodgers was his life's blood.

As a young man, fresh out of college, Dennis Walters had all the traits of a champion. He had been dreaming big dreams since childhood, and he was ready to take action in his quest to make those dreams come true. That year, he had finished 11th in the U.S. Amateur Championship and had led his school to its fourth consecutive collegiate championship. His consuming desire was to play on the PGA Tour alongside Palmer, Player, and Nicklaus, and the future looked bright for the 24-year-old athlete. He decided to spend a few months in South Africa, playing on the Sunshine Tour with a friend to sharpen their competitive edge among the ranks of professionals. While he was there, he played several rounds with Gary Player and the great Bobby Locke, as well as competing in a couple of national open tournaments. It was a great experience for the young Walters, and when he returned to the States in 1974, he knew he was ready for the PGA Tour Qualifying School.

On July 21, 1974, a warm, sunny morning, just a few days before Q-school was scheduled to begin, Dennis was playing in a pro-member tournament at the Bonnie Brae Country Club in New Jersey. At the 18th hole, his approach shot was plugged in a greenside trap, but Dennis played a fine explosion shot to three feet and saved his par. Although that shot was played over 20 years ago and his score for the round was mediocre, Dennis remembers it as vividly as any shot he ever hit to win a championship. He can remember digging his feet into the soft sand and shifting them about to get just the right stance. He can remember making the swing and smoothly transferring his weight to the left side on the down swing. He remembers the flight of the ball, the smell of the grass, and the firmness of the green as he walked across it to tap in the short put. That shot would be the last competitive golf shot Dennis Walters would ever hit.

That afternoon he decided to play a few more holes at the Roxiticus Country Club with his friend Ralph Terry, a former New York Yankee who was the club's professional. When he reached the club, Terry was already on the course playing the 15th hole, so Dennis loaded his clubs on a cart and set out to join him. The 15th is a steep downhill par four, and as he drove down the path in pursuit of his friend, the old three-wheeled cart skidded on some loose gravel. Dennis struggled unsuccessfully to maintain control, and from that moment on, his memory of the accident is blurred. At some point, the vehicle swerved off the path and rolled into the trees. Dennis was thrown headlong from the cart. Although he didn't have a scratch on his body, was never unconscious, and felt no pain, he found as he lay where he had fallen that he was unable to move his legs. As he lay on the ground, people started to gather around him. His friend Ralph consoled him, saying he had once temporarily lost the feeling in his legs in a car accident. Walters was far more concerned with the condition of his prized driver. "I can remember clearly," he says. "I had an old MacGregor, Tony Penna driver. It was a special driver with a huge neck on it and a large face. I loved that driver, and I was laying there just hoping I hadn't scratched it up too badly. Ralph found it for me among the bushes, and then the ambulance came and took me to hospital."

At the hospital, tests revealed that Dennis had suffered severe damage to his spinal cord. That night he underwent surgery to remove a dislocated vertebrae. He spent the next six weeks attached to a rigid steel brace, strapped to his bed as if to some medieval torture rack. Since he couldn't move, the bed was rotated upside down every six hours to maintain his circulation. When he was moved to the Kessler Institute of Rehabilitation, Walters thought the time had come to bring his ailing body back to health. "After all" he said, "isn't that what rehabilitation is all about?" Instead, the people at the Institute taught him how to get himself in and out of a wheel chair. They taught him how to get dressed, a 45-minute ordeal, and they worked on the muscles in his upper body—the ones he could still use. After a month of rehabilitation, Dennis came to the stark realization that he was never going to walk again. For Dennis Walters, there would be no Hogan comeback—no Bobby Nichols story; his injuries were irreversible. All the determination, persistence, and courage in the world could do nothing to change the tragic facts. He was classified as a T-12 level paraplegic. In a few short seconds, the hopes and dreams of almost 20 years had vanished, along with the use of his legs. You can't be a professional golfer when you are paralyzed from the waist down, can you?

After five long, grueling months of rehabilitation, Dennis went home and immediately began searching for a way to play golf. He and his father visited the local community center, where there was a small golf course. He tried to hit the ball from his wheelchair, but kept sliding out onto the ground. That problem was solved by the addition of a seatbelt. After three weekends of practice, he could already produce shots of 170 yards. The following week the doctors finally confirmed Dennis' worst nightmare, that he would never regain the use of his legs. Says Walters, "When the doctor finally told me I would never walk again, it made me cry. Then he said I could never play golf again and that made me mad!"

The next day, Dennis was asked by Joe, his physical therapist, if he wanted to try something new. Game for anything that would increase his chances of playing golf, he readily agreed. Joe put splints on his legs and secured them with Ace bandages. After six months of laying on his back and sitting, Dennis was finally able to stand up again. He felt 10 feet tall. In fact, he remembers he felt as if he were floating, since he was standing straight, but only had feeling from the waist up. At first, Dennis moved with the aid of parallel bars, but he soon graduated to the agonizing task of moving his entire body on crutches. Of all the people in the hospital at that time with the same degree of paralysis, only Dennis made the transition to walking on crutches. His strength, patience, and determination to walk helped him endure the constant painful falls and the slow and humiliating struggle to return to an upright position. Finally, Dennis was fitted with a pair of metal leg braces, weighing over 30 pounds. Now, in addition to supporting his entire body weight with his arms, he had this extra load to carry. At home he had to deal with new problems. While he had mastered walking around the smooth hospital corridors, walking outside or on grass was a different story altogether. He recalls that, at one time, no part of his body did not bear the signs of a bruise or graze from his constant tumbles.

The World's Greatest Par

Dennis spent the winter of 1975 in Florida. He occupied his days at the Crystal Lake golf club, where his good friend Ralph was now the pro. Each day after breakfast, he made the short trip to the range and practiced, hour after hour, hitting balls while sitting in his wheelchair. While he was now becoming very proficient at striking the ball, he longed not just to hit balls, but to be out on the course playing.

One day, after hearing Dennis express this desire, his good friend Alex Turnyae pushed his wheelchair to the 1st tee and told him to try. Dennis split the fairway with a drive of 220 yards. His friend wheeled him to his ball and helped him get in position. Then Dennis smashed a long iron onto the green and two-putted from his chair for a world-class four—one of the greatest pars in the history of the game.

A New Beginning

Attempts to play while sitting in his wheelchair proved, however, to be impractical. He had trained himself to strike the ball pretty well from a sitting position, but he had great difficulty wheeling the chair on the course, and he couldn't go in the bunkers or on the greens. Then, one evening when he was sitting at the clubhouse bar between Alex and another friend, twisting slightly from side to side on his stool as he spoke with them, they came up with a possible solution. Why not mount a swivel seat on the side of a golf cart?

With the help of his father, Bucky, Dennis and his friends mounted a seat on a cart, complete with a seat belt to hold him in position. He had to modify his swing technique, but he focused on what he *could* do, rather than what he couldn't. As he progressed, Dennis practiced putting and hitting bunker shots one-handed, while supporting himself with the aid of a single crutch. Incredibly, he was soon able to break 80. Pretty good, but hardly good enough to make it on the PGA Tour. The question remained; how would he make a living? A career as a tour pro was clearly not an option.

Few people would have blamed Dennis if he had chosen the route of self-pity, and even he admits to bouts of depression. He has found that the best way to combat them when they arise is to head for the range and beat balls until the exhilaration of a perfectly executed shot drives away the sadness. None would have questioned him had he decided to give up golf. In fact, suggesting that he might still make his living playing the game caused many to speculate that he was suffering from advanced symptoms of self-delusion. But Dennis Walters never doubted his ability to succeed. Instead of giving up, he decided to keep fighting, with victory as his only acceptable goal.

During that winter of 1975, Dennis read books and watched films about Joe Kirkwood, the foremost trick-shot artist of the 1930s and 40s. Intrigued by the idea that he might follow this path as a career, he went to a clinic presented by famous trick-shot artist, Paul

Hahn, Jr. Watching Hahn's exhibition convinced Dennis that this indeed was something he could do, and he set about building a repertoire of what he called "shots from unusual lies." He designed and built a strange assortment of trick clubs and worked on adjustments to his swivel seat until he was ready to take his show on the road. All he needed now was an audience.

Dennis gave his initial public performance at the 1977 PGA Show for a fee of $150. It was a start. Word spread slowly that first year, and he did only five more shows, but he wasn't discouraged. He was once again doing what he loved. It wasn't competitive golf, but when he practiced his shots before a show, he felt as if he was indeed warming up for a tournament.

In 1978, Dennis was awarded the Ben Hogan Award, given annually to a golfer who has come back after sustaining major injuries. The following year he appeared on the television show *That's Incredible*, where he drove a ball from a tee held in host John Davidson's mouth. The publicity from this appearance gave his career a timely boost. At the same time, his determination and persistence on the practice tee were beginning to pay off. His repertoire of shots had increased, as had his showmanship. By now he was hitting shots with a huge array of clubs. There is the "slook shot," where he tees two balls side by side, slicing one ball and hooking the other one at the same time. Then there is his "3-iron," consisting of three clubheads welded together, end to end, with which he simultaneously hits a high shot, a low shot and one in between. He drives balls dead straight, well over 200 yards, with a collection of strange implements. His drivers are shafted with such unlikely things as a crutch, a radiator hose, a fishing rod, and a brass curtain rod, which he bends to produce or correct hooks and slices at will. One shaft features three hinges—count them, three! He hits balls from a three-foot tee, off a watch, and from beneath an egg without cracking it. After these and many other feats of pure golfing magic comes the grand finale. He concludes the Dennis Walters Golf Show with the "machine gun" shot, blasting five balls in rapid-fire succession as they roll across a piece of cardboard.

Dennis now appears at over 80 shows a year at PGA Tour, Senior PGA Tour, Nike Tour, and LPGA Tour events. He entertains corporate groups at their golf outings and performs at charity functions. Accompanied by his father Bucky, his sister Barbara, and his faithful dog Benjy Hogan, who is a delightful participant in the show, he travels thousands of miles each year with the special golf cart.

A Special Kind of Pro

Recently, the PGA elected Dennis to honorary lifetime membership. He is one of only five people ever to have received the honor. There is no question that he has, in his own way and by his own efforts, realized his ambition to become a PGA professional. His income last year would have placed him easily high enough on the official PGA money winner's list to have qualified him for exempt status on the your. Typically, he expects to do considerably better next year.

Dennis would much rather have collected winners' trophies at Hilton Head or Pebble Beach, but that wasn't to be. Instead, he has succeeded in his own way and by his own efforts. In 1994, he won the National Golf Foundation's Herb Graffis Award, presented to players who have made an outstanding contribution to the game. The heroes he once revered as a boy now praise his accomplishments. Jack Nicklaus declared his show to be, "One of the most entertaining hours I have ever spent." Gary Player said, "Dennis Walters is a great example of skill, courage, and determination for everyone to see." Arnold Palmer named him, "An inspiration to all of us." Against all the odds, Dennis Walters has made it. He is a golf professional and a true champion.

For Dennis, the thousands of hours spent on the practice tee perfecting his skills could hardly be categorized as work because of his consuming passion for the game of golf. Besides, he knew that with enough practice and persistence he would become a champion, and although his arena is not the one he originally envisioned, the end result is the same. People with all the traits of champions, like Dennis Walters, become champions no matter what "bad bounces" life throws at them.

It's a nice clean lie Sir, but you don't have a lot of green to play with. This one's going to run on you when it lands. Show me how good your touch is . . . That was a brave shot. Well played! Only three feet past the hole . . . Nice three!

How do you develop championship persistance? There are a number of ways of doing it, and several great champions had to find that out.

What is Persistence?

All champions suffer setbacks along the way—not tragedies, like the one that threatened to overwhelm Dennis, but setbacks nonetheless. Champions know that quitters never win and winners never quit. They learn that not giving up when they encounter minor difficulties leads to developing the ability to persist in the face of major adversity. Simply stated, not quitting on the little things leads to not quitting on the big things. They don't give up on a hole after a bad tee shot, and they don't stop trying their utmost in a tournament after having a bad opening round. The prospect of quitting is as unthinkable to them as the possibility of not becoming a champion!

The Turning Point for Some Famous "Quitters"

"No matter what happens, never give up on a hole. In tossing in your cards after a bad beginning, you undermine your whole game, because to quit between tee and green is more habit-forming than drinking a highball before breakfast."
Sam Snead

After an argument with local officials at the Pasadena Open who had changed his pairing, Sam Snead was hopping mad. So mad that he failed to break 40 on the front nine, an unheard of occurrence for Snead in those days. After knocking the ball out of bounds on the 12th hole, he tore up his card and walked off the course. The following week at Pinehurst, after another bad start, he quit a second time!

At the time, his actions seemed to him to be of little significance; he was playing like a 15 handicapper, and that's not what the fans had paid to see, so he quit. He quickly discovered that the other players, the fans, and the newspapers don't like a quitter. He was heavily criticized from coast to coast. When he realized just how strongly people felt about his behavior, he vowed never to do it again. He accepted that quitting is a loser's way out; wounded pride is no reason to give up. It was a turning point for Snead. From that point on, he played every shot to win, regardless of the conditions or the way he was playing.

When Arnold Palmer first came on tour in 1955, he also exited several events in their early stages. After shooting 78 in a tournament, he quit, and a few months later he did it again, withdrawing from the Motor City Open after an opening round 77. Then, a couple of years later, Palmer was near the lead in the late stages of a tournament when a wild drive and snap-hooked second shot left him in a terrible position. He was facing an almost impossible chip, over a steep bank then straight downhill to the flag. The slightest miscalculation would result in at least a bogey, and quite possibly a double-bogey. Either would move him out of contention. After studying the shot carefully, he hit a perfect bump and run shot into the bank that raced into the hole for a birdie three. In Sam Snead's opinion, pulling off that one shot seemed to have a monumental effect on young Palmer's attitude in difficult situations. Now he looked at every shot as an opportunity to make up for any previous error. Soon he would become famous for his "charges" *and* his recovery shots. The week after that life-changing chip shot, with his improved attitude firmly in place, he won the 1958 Masters, the first of four in which he would emerge victorious.

In his early years, Bobby Jones was renowned for his erratic temperament. During his first appearance on the hallowed links turf of St. Andrews, in the 1921 British Open, he lasted only until the third round. After a dismal 46 on the way out, playing into the teeth of a howling gale, he made double-bogey on the 10th, then left his ball in the famous bunker on the short 11th, and found himself looking triple-bogey right in the eye. He promptly marched off the course, throwing his scorecard in the Eden river as he went and appalling the traditionalist Scottish fans. He later confessed that, at 19, he did not have the maturity, patience, or experience to handle the course he later came to love above all others, with the possible exception of Augusta. Turn-of-the-century English professionals Harry Vardon and J.H. Taylor, who between them won 11 British Opens, gave this uncomplicated and timeless admonition to a young Bobby Jones: "No matter what happens, keep hitting the ball." Jones cherished that advice and never again quit during a tournament, proving that the traits of champions can be learned and acquired when one is blessed with abundant supplies of the raw material needed to become a champion.

The Final Key to Becoming a Champion

The trait of persistence is found in all champions, whether their special area of expertise is golf, tennis, or business. The champion realizes in advance that it is impossible to succeed without experiencing setbacks along the way. He understands that bad shots, bad tournaments, and even bad years are all part of the journey and must be endured on the road to the ultimate prize. He knows the sure cure for failure is to analyze, readjust if necessary, and continue with even more resolve than before.

Developing Persistence

Persistence is developed by accepting in advance that there are many bunkers and hazards along the fairway and there is no way to avoid them all the time. The important thing is to realize that finding yourself in one of them is not a career-ending disaster—it's part of the game.

After bogeying the opening hole of a tournament, Ben Hogan was offered polite consolation by his opponent, who said, "It sure was an unlucky break for you to make five there, Ben." Hogan replied, "That's why there are 18 holes." To a champion, that amounts to 17 more chances. If that isn't enough, he can comfort himself with the prospect of a fresh start on a completely new round of golf the following day. Next week there will be another tournament and then another. No player actually fails until he decides not to enter—not to even try, and the tour will go on with or without him. Winners will be rewarded and new champions will be crowned and acclaimed. Those champions will be the ones with persistence, the ones who hang in there and never give up, no matter what.

View Each Setback Positively

How you view problems, setbacks, and even complete failures plays a major role in how deep your reservoir of persistence is likely to be. Jack Nicklaus, the world's foremost golf champion, has won 20 major tournaments, a feat that may never be equaled. But that's only one way to look at his record. If you wanted to accentuate the negative, you could point out that he lost well over 100 majors when it was his stated goal to win. Does that make Nicklaus a loser? I certainly don't see it that way, and I'm sure Jack doesn't either!

Be Flexible

Being persistent doesn't mean doing the same thing over and over, hoping it'll work eventually. That's plain stubbornness. Championship persistence is the never-ending search for the right answers—for the combination of physical actions and mental strategies that makes everything fall into place. It's asking yourself and others positive questions when things go wrong, in order to make the necessary adjustments to your course of action. It's talking, and even more important, listening to others who've already been there, to find out how they did it. It's questioning them and yourself to make sure your approach is sound. Finally, it's a matter of holding firm to your general game plan, even when the going gets tough, but at the same time, being flexible enough to make small changes in order to grow.

Put Yourself in a Position to Win

To be successful, you have to endure temporary or intermittent failure and persist in regularly putting yourself in a position to win. Even if you choke three or four times as you come down the stretch with a chance to take it all, you gain the necessary experience to win next time out or the time after that.

Persistence Requires High Self-esteem

Champions never make the mistake of equating their self-worth with the way they play on any given day. Even the best can shoot an occasional 80; they know it isn't world-shattering, and their families and friends will still be there for them, as supportive and encouraging as ever. Of course, golf is important to a PGA Tour pro, but it isn't a life-and-death struggle.

Winners have confidence in themselves and in their ability to bounce back from adversity. They know that deep down inside them is a champion waiting to step forward and that it's only a matter of time until he makes his triumphant appearance. Self-doubt and self-pity are not for champions; they are crutches for losers.

Regroup and Move On

"I played so badly this year, I got a 'get well' card from the IRS!"
Johnny Miller

When problems of major proportions arise, a champion analyzes the situation and considers his options. Then he makes new plans and sets new goals based on a realistic assessment of the problem. It may mean starting from scratch and rebuilding his swing from the ground up, like Nick Faldo. It paid off for Nick. His resulting successes more than made up for a couple of lean years. It may require a total change of direction, as was the case with Ken Venturi, who moved smoothly into the commentator's booth after being afflicted by a disease that left very little feeling in his hands. The answer may be turning to golf course architecture, as did Tom Weiskopf when his game left him for a while. Men like Venturi and his counterpart on another network, Johnny Miller, have become champions in two associated but different careers. Whatever setbacks champions encounter, the same traits that made them champions in one field will ensure success for them in another. It takes determination, hard work, and persistence, and champions have plentiful reserves of these characteristics.

Swing Thoughts

- Champions have drive.

- Not quitting on little things leads to not quitting on big things.

- Champions are persistent.

- Champions regroup when faced with major obstacles.

Back in the Clubhouse

There are two ways to look at the world: the benevolent way and the malevolent way. People with a malevolent or negative worldview take a victim stance, seeing life as a continuous succession of problems and a process of unfairness and oppression. They don't expect a lot, and they don't get much. When things go wrong, they shrug their shoulders and passively accept that this is the way life is, and there isn't anything they can do to make it better.

On the other hand, people with a benevolent or positive worldview see the world around them as filled with opportunities and possibilities. They believe everything happens as part of a great process designed to make them successful and happy. They approach their lives, their work, and their relationships with optimism, cheerfulness, and a general attitude of positive expectation—they expect a lot, and they are seldom disappointed. Also, people with a benevolent worldview are able to deal constructively with mistakes and temporary setbacks.

When you develop the skill of learning from your mistakes, you are the kind of person who welcomes obstacles and setbacks as opportunities to flex your mental muscles and move yourself ahead. You look at problems as if they were rungs on the ladder of success that you grab onto as you pull your way higher and higher.

Two of the most common ways to handle mistakes are invariably fatal to high achievement. The first common, but misguided way to handle a mistake is to fail to accept it when it occurs.

According to statistics, 70 percent of all decisions we make will be wrong. That's an average. This means that some people will fail more than 70 percent of the time, and some people will fail less. It is hard to believe that most of the decisions we make could turn out to be wrong in some way. In fact, if this is the case, how can our society continue to function at all?

The fact is that our society, our families, our companies, and our relationships continue to survive and thrive because intelligent people tend to cut their losses and downplay their mistakes. Only when people refuse to accept that they have made a bad decision—and prolong the consequences by sticking to the bad decision—does the mistake become extremely expensive and hurtful.

In life, the quality of intellectual honesty is one of the most respected qualities possessed by individuals, especially leaders. When you are intellectually honest, you deal with your circumstances as facts and realities, rather than hoping, wishing, and praying that they could be different. And the minute you begin to deal straightforwardly with life, you become a far more positive, creative, and constructive person. You become far more effective in overcoming your obstacles and achieving your goals. You become far more admired and respected by other people and far more capable of achieving the critical results that are expected of you.

On the other hand, the unwillingness to face the fact that you are not perfect, that you have made and will continue to make mistakes, is a major source of stress. One of the great teachings of history is the principle of nonresistance. Nonresistance means that when the wind blows, you bend like a willow tree rather than snap like a pine tree. You remain flexible, fluid, and open to new ideas, new information, and new inputs. You accept that in a period of rapid change, nothing is written in stone.

The second common approach people take with regard to their mistakes—one that hurts innumerable lives and careers—is to fail to use their mistakes to better themselves and to improve the quality of their minds and their thinking.

Learning from your mistakes is an essential skill that enables you to develop the resilience to be a master of change rather than a victim of change. The person who recognizes that he or she has made a mistake and changes direction fast is the one who will win in an age of increasing information, technology, and competition. By remaining fast on your feet, you will be able to outplay and outposition your competition. You will become a creator of circumstances rather than a creature of circumstances.

Approach every mistake you make as a special learning experience, sent to teach you something valuable and necessary for your success in the future. Become an "inverse paranoid," a person who is convinced that there is a vast conspiracy in the world to make him or her successful. Play with the idea that there are a series of guardian angels out there who are acting on your behalf. Those angels are regularly planning learning experiences to enable you to grow as a person so you can reach the great heights that were meant for you.

Whenever something happens of an adverse nature, immediately counteract your natural tendency toward disappointment and frustration by saying, "That's good!" Then get busy looking into the situation to find out what is genuinely good about it. You must believe that difficulties come not to obstruct, but to instruct. If you analyze a problem situation you face, or a mistake you have made, you will find that it contains lessons and ideas that can be invaluable to you in the months and years ahead. In many cases, learning from mistakes with small costs and consequences will prepare you to avoid larger mistakes with huge costs and consequences.

Every day, sometimes all day long, you have problems in your work. In fact, if the problems did not exist, your job would not exist either. A powerful way to change your thinking is to realize that solving problems is what you are paid to do. Your job is to be a problem solver, no matter what your title might be. Every day you deal with problems and mistakes caused by you and others. The more of them you can spot and redirect before the consequences are felt, the more valuable you will become, and the more you will be paid.

Whenever my children make a mistake of any kind, I stop them, get their attention, and ask, "What have you learned?" I have asked them this question since they were two or three years old. Now, whenever they make a mistake of any kind, they know I am going to ask the question, so they are ready with the answer. I always tell my children that as long as they learn from a mistake and establish a rule or guideline for future action, they are growing and becoming smarter as they move through life.

In both your personal and professional life, there are seven steps you can take to deal with almost any mistake you make. The first step is to approach the mistake with a positive, constructive frame of mind, using techniques I mentioned earlier.

The second step is to define the mistake clearly. Exactly what happened? Write it down. Think on paper. The more clearly you can write about it, the more clearly you will understand the mistake, and the more easily you will see possible corrections.

The third step is to examine all the known causes of the mistake. How did it happen? Why did it happen? What critical variables triggered the mistake? Any attempt to pass over a mistake without identifying how it occurred in the first place will leave the roots of that mistake in the ground to grow up again in the future.

The fourth step is to identify all the possible ways of mitigating the mistake. What are all the different things you could do to minimize the cost of the mistake? The more ideas you have, the more likely you will be to come up with the approach that will prove most effective.

The fifth step is to make a clear, unequivocal decision about how to handle the mistake. Decisiveness is a characteristic of high-performing men and women. Almost any decision is better than no decision at all. Even the most effective leaders make mistakes, but then they quickly make decisions to offset the negative consequences.

The sixth step is to assign specific responsibility for taking the steps necessary to mitigate the mistake within a certain time frame. Who exactly is going to do what—and when, how, and to whom will they report? The failure to assign or accept responsibility to achieve results before a specific deadline will leave the situation open-ended, and it will often get worse as a result.

Finally, the seventh step in dealing with mistakes is to take action. Intense action orientation is a characteristic of the top 2 percent of the population.

The only guarantee in life is that most of the decisions you make and the conclusions you come to will eventually prove wrong. How you deal with those situations is a chief determinant of your success or failure.

Mistakes and problems are good. Without them, there would be no opportunities for greatness. When you accept a challenge life throws at you, when you see it as an inevitable part of the growing experience, you can turn it to your advantage.

Questions to Ponder

• Do you have a Plan B?

• What would you do if you were fired, or if your company failed?

• Do you maintain your friendships and relationships in good repair, so new opportunities regularly come your way?

This is it, Sir. The 18th. The most famous hole in golf . . . 540 yards . . . That's true! It looks a lot more frightening than it does on TV. Not a sight for the faint of heart, that's for sure. There are times when the wind's so strong off the ocean that you have to aim 30 or 40 yards out to sea just to keep your ball on the fairway. You can't bail out to the right; the out-of-bounds markers are just to the right of the traps you can see out there at about 220 yards. There's nothing for it but to start it down the rocks, trust your swing, and let it drift back toward the tree out there in the middle of the fairway. This is where you really have to put it all together . . . Great drive! That's the best of the day. It's drifting back toward the center of the fairway. That's a very fine shot, Sir! It rolled just past the tree.

Good thinking. Laying up with your 4-iron will leave you a full wedge to the green . . . You pulled it, Sir! Get down; get down! . . . It caught the sand again, but at least that saved it from going in the ocean . . . Just punch it out with the 9-iron, right at the center of the green . . . That's a little thin. It went over the back a few feet, but you shouldn't have any trouble from there. You've got about a 40-foot chip shot, and I know that's the strength of your game. . . . Hang in there! It isn't over until it's over. Let me make sure the flag's in the center of the cup. There we go. Chip it in, Sir. You can still make that 72 . . . Slow down, now. Hit the stick . . . Yes! Dead center! That's a working man's birdie if I ever saw one. Someday you'll be able to tell your grandchildren about that one.

PUTTING IT ALL TOGETHER

Studying the Stats

If you study the list of Masters winners over the last 40 years, you will discover a very interesting statistic. During the period from 1949 to 1986, seven great champions—Jack Nicklaus, Arnold Palmer, Ben Hogan, Sam Snead, Gary Player, Tom Watson, and Seve Ballesteros—finished first in more than half of the 38 Masters Tournaments—22 to be precise. This happened in an age of great players like Ken Venturi, Billy Casper, Tom Weiskopf, Ray Floyd, Johnny Miller, Tom Kite, and many others.

What about the British Open? During the same period, Nicklaus, Palmer, Player, Watson, and Ballesteros, joined by Bobby Locke, Peter Thomson, and Lee Trevino, accounted for no less than 27 of the victories. Ten men dominated 40 years of championship golf on both sides of the Atlantic Ocean.

Nicklaus was once asked how he was able to win so many major tournaments, especially bearing in mind that the "majors" are the hardest to win. Nicklaus replied, "You're wrong! Majors are the easiest tournaments to win. I just kind of hang in there and let the other players fall out of contention; then there are just a couple of guys to beat."

Now, where have I heard that before? Let me think. Oh yes. Bobby Jones said something very similar. Amazing how great champions think alike.

Why Do So Few People Become Champions?

That's the only question remaining to be answered. Why is it that so few rise to the very top in any field? After all, if the traits of champions are so well documented and relatively easy to emulate and develop, what's the problem?

The truth is, while many people possess *some* of the qualities of champions, no more than a handful in any walk of life ever put them all together. Many players work hard at their craft, but lack a solid strategy for making their hard work pay off. Others, with more natural talent or solid financial backing, may have most of what it takes, but lack the real desire and motivation to put in the extra effort that could propel them to greatness. Still others, with great reserves of talent and excellent work ethics, lack confidence or fear success—flaws that prevent them from ever achieving their true potential. In order to be the very best, *all* the traits of champions must be woven into the fabric of your life.

The Champion's Bottom Line

"You drive for show and putt for dough"
Anonymous

Champions start with big dreams. They build on those dreams to develop visions and specific goals. Their dreams fuel the desire that will carry them to those goals. They conquer fear of failure *and* fear of success by building up reserves of confidence. They focus on a single purpose and accomplish it before moving to another. They take personal responsibility for each and every action they take. They plan a detailed strategy for success and follow it, emphasizing their strengths and shoring up weaknesses. They have the self-discipline and total willingness to practice all the hours God gives in order to hone their skills to razor sharpness.

Out on the course, champions build a positive image by their appearance as well as their actions. Champions have class, not only in defeat, but in victory, too. Champions are motivated to practice, play, and stay on track as they move ever closer to the goals they have set for themselves. Champions don't let obstacles stand in their way.

When trouble looms, champions maintain the confident attitude that problems can be overcome. Champions are creative. When bad things happen or disaster strikes, champions have the persistence to come back and try again and again. When a comeback is clearly not possible on any terms, they adjust as necessary and find other ways to become champions.

In our round today we have discovered that becoming a champion is not a mystery; it's more like a giant jigsaw puzzle. As each new piece is added, the picture becomes clearer and the goal closer. We have discovered that champions are made, not born. Anyone, regardless of where he or she is now, can become a champion.

The Courage to Go for It

The final factor in the makeup of any champion is courage. The courage to dream big dreams and then bring them to fruition. The courage to endure hardship and make sacrifices when necessary. The courage to fight your fears under pressure. The courage to make a club selection and stick with it. The courage to trust your swing in the heat of battle. The courage to trust your intuition and hit a putt three feet wide of the hole to allow for the break. The courage to fight back from adversity. The courage to take chances and make the most of your God-given talents and the opportunities that present themselves to you.

All the practice and careful preparation in the world aren't worth a hill of beans until you get out there and play. Take each day as it comes, and play every course as if it were Pebble Beach. Whether you like it or not, it's the course you are playing that day. Make the most of the weather conditions; they are the same for everyone. Most important, play one shot at a time, and play to win.

Champions win the big ones consistently by always being in contention. Champions put *all* the pieces together, not just some of them.

Finally, always remember that champions in anything are the people who *decide* to be champions. It won't happen accidentally. You have to do it. The sooner you set out in pursuit of your dreams, the sooner they can come true.

Wonderful round, Sir . . . A dream, you say, shooting 72 at Pebble Beach? Well, remember what we said a few hours ago, just before you started your round. It all begins with great dreams . . . Your best round ever? I'm happy for you . . . It's nice of you to say so, and if I have helped you, that's just fine. But you hit the shots and stroked the putts, and you did it like a champion, if you don't mind my saying so.

I'll take care of your sticks for you . . . You'll be joining these gentlemen in the Tap Room? It's just through that door. You've *earned* a small celebration! I'll bring your car keys in a few minutes.

Back in the Clubhouse

Did you ever stop to think that everything you are or ever will be is completely up to you? You are where you are because of who you are. Everything that exists in your life exists because of you, because of your behavior, words, and actions. Because you have freedom of choice and because you have—consciously or unconsciously—chosen each and every circumstance of your life, you are completely responsible for all of your success and failure, your happiness and unhappiness, your present and future.

That thought is like a parachute jump: it's scary and exhilarating at the same time. It's one of the biggest and most important ideas that can ever occur to you or anyone else. The acceptance of personal responsibility is what separates the adult from the child. It's the great leap forward into maturity. Responsibility is the hallmark of the fully integrated, fully functioning human being. Responsibility goes hand in hand with success, achievement, motivation, happiness, and self-actualization. It's the absolute minimum requirement for the accomplishment of everything you could ever want in life.

Accepting that you're completely responsible for yourself and realizing that no one is coming to the rescue is the beginning of peak performance. There's very little you cannot do or have after you accept that "if it's to be, it's up to me!"

The opposite of accepting responsibility is making excuses and blaming people and things for what's going on in your life. And since everything we do is a matter of habit, if people get into the habit of making excuses, they get into the habit of evading responsibility at the same time. If they set a goal or objective for themselves, they immediately create an excuse that they hold in reserve just in case the accomplishment of the goal is too difficult or requires more self-discipline and persistence than they had thought. As soon as things start to go poorly, irresponsible people trot out their excuse and let themselves off the hook. But that won't get them anywhere in the long run.

A basic law of human life was first put forth by Socrates more than 400 years before Christ. It's the Law of Causality. I like to call it the Law of Cause and Effect. It states that for every effect in your life, there's a cause. If there's any effect you desire, or desire more of, you can trace it back to the cause, and by duplicating the cause, you can have the effect.

For example, everyone wants to be healthy. If you set a high level of physical health and energy as your goal, or the desired effect, you can have it simply by finding out the cause, by finding out what other healthy and energetic people do with regard to diet, exercise, and rest, and by doing the same thing. If you do, you're likely to get the same result. This is no miracle. It sounds simple, but in many cases, it's one of the hardest things in the world to do.

Unhappiness is an effect as well. If you wish to be happy, the first thing to do is to decide for yourself the kind of life situation in which you would feel wonderful. Think of the very best times of your life, and recall what you were doing, where you were doing it, and the people you were with at the time. Then write out, in complete detail, a description of your ideal lifestyle. Now you have defined the effect you desire.

Next, look at your current life and ask yourself, "What are all the things in my life that are inconsistent with the lifestyle that would make me happy?" In other words, look at the causes of the effects you don't like. Then make a decision to begin alleviating or removing those causes, one by one, until what you have left is the kind of life you want to live.

Your thoughts are very powerful. They have the power to raise and lower your blood pressure, your pulse rate, and your respiratory rate. They can affect your digestion. And if your thoughts are strong enough, they can even make you sick or healthy. Your thoughts tend to trigger images in your mind, and those images trigger feelings in your body that are consistent with them. If you think or read happy, healthy thoughts, you will have happy, healthy pictures and experience happy, healthy emotions. Every part of your mind is connected to every part of your body in a complex web of messages and impulses that affect everything you feel, say, and do.

Only you can think your thoughts; only you can decide what you'll dwell upon, what you'll read and listen to, with whom you'll associate, and the conversations you'll engage in. Therefore, you are totally responsible for all the consequences of all those behaviors. It's unavoidable.

Perhaps the most important part of self-responsibility involves your happiness and your peace of mind. There seems to be a direct relationship between responsibility and happiness on the one hand, and irresponsibility and unhappiness on the other. Let me explain.

First of all, the key to happiness is having a sense of control over what's going on in your life. The more you feel you're in control, the happier you'll be. Men and women who have risen to the top of their organizations tend to be far happier than people further down. This is because they feel far more in control of their destinies, far more capable of making decisions and taking action. The more responsibility you take in your company, the more power, authority, and respect you'll receive. People who want more money and more respect often think they can get it simply by asking for it or by politicking. The truth is that it will accrue to you rapidly as soon as you "step up to the plate" and undertake responsibility for results in your organization. The most respected people in any company are those who are the most capable of getting the most important jobs done on schedule.

The more responsibility you take, the more in control you are. And the freer you are, especially in your own mind, to make decisions and to do the things you want to do. So there's a direct relationship between responsibility, control, freedom, and happiness. The happiest people in the world are those who feel absolutely terrific about themselves, and this is the natural outgrowth of accepting total responsibility for every part of their lives.

At the other end of the spectrum, there is irresponsibility, or the failure to accept responsibility. Each person is somewhere in between, moving toward a greater level of responsibility or irresponsibility with every word and every decision. In fact, a good definition of insanity is "total irresponsibility," to the point of needing a straitjacket and a padded cell. Psychoanalyst Thomas S. Szasz wrote, "There is no such thing as insanity. There are only varying levels of irresponsibility."

A person who is completely irresponsible is subject to anger, hostility, fear, resentment, doubt—all sorts of negative emotions. This is because all negative emotions tend to be associated with blame. Fully 99 percent of all our problems exist only because we're able to blame someone or something for them. The instant we stop blaming, our negative emotions begin disappearing.

What's the antidote to blaming? It's simple. Since your mind can hold only one thought at a time, either positive or negative, you can override the tendency to blame and become angry simply by firmly saying, "I am responsible." You can't accept responsibility for a situation and be angry at the same time. You can't accept responsibility and be unhappy or upset. The acceptance of responsibility negates negative emotions and short-circuits any tendencies toward unhappiness.

The very act of accepting responsibility for a situation calms your mind and clarifies your vision. It soothes your emotions and enables you to think more positively and constructively. In fact, the acceptance of responsibility often gives you insight into what you should do to resolve the situation.

Here's an exercise: Consider the most common problems and difficulties people have in life. Apply this simple remedy of accepting responsibility to each one, and see what happens.

People have problems with other people—their spouses, their children, their friends, their coworkers, and their bosses. Someone once said that almost all of our problems in life have hair on top, come on two legs, and talk back. So think of the people in your life who cause you any stress or anxiety, and ask yourself who is responsible. Are they responsible for being in your life, or are you responsible for having them in your life?

You're a living magnet in that you invariably attract people into your life who harmonize with your dominant thoughts and emotions. The people in your life are there because you've attracted them by the person you are, by the thoughts you hold, by the emotions you experience. If you're not happy with the people surrounding you or the way they behave, you're responsible. You're attracting these people or this behavior, and you're keeping them there.

Let me give you an example. I have four beautiful children. For a long time, when my children were behaving in ways I felt were inappropriate, I had a tendency to blame or criticize them. However, the more I studied child raising and learned through experience, the more I found that children are almost totally reactive. Their behavior is almost always a response to what is going on around them and to their relationships with their parents. So I began asking the question, "What in me is causing my children to act this way?"

As soon as I turned the question around and looked to myself for the reason—in effect, accepting complete responsibility for my chil-

273

dren's behavior—I was able to see what I might be doing, or not doing, that my children were reacting to. Perhaps I wasn't spending enough one-on-one time with them. Perhaps I wasn't listening to them when they wanted to talk. Perhaps I was too quick to question their report cards.

I began to apply that simple principle to every other part of my life. I began asking, "What in me is causing this external situation?" Since the Law of Correspondence states that everything that is happening to you on the outside is due to something that is happening to you on the inside, the first place to look is within. As soon as you do that, you begin to see things you had completely missed when you were busy blaming others and making excuses. You begin to see that you're responsible in large measure for the things that are happening to you.

If you're in a bad relationship, who got you there? You likely weren't marched into the relationship and kept there at gunpoint. So it's largely a matter of free will and free choice on your part. As Henry Ford II once said, "Never complain, never explain." If you're not happy with the situation, do something about it. If you're not willing to do something about it, then don't complain.

There's a story about a construction worker who opens up his lunch box at the noon break and unwraps his sandwich to find that it contains sardines. He gets really upset and complains loudly to everyone around him about how much he hates sardines. The next day, the same thing happens: a sardine sandwich. Again, the construction worker shouts and complains about how much he hates sardines for lunch. The third day, it happens again. By this time, his fellow workers are getting fed up with his loud complaining. One of them leans over and says to him, "If you hate sardines so much, why don't you tell your wife to make you some other kind of sandwich?"

The construction worker turns to the fellow and says, "Oh, I'm not married. I make my own lunches."

Many of us get into the same situation as the construction worker's and complain about circumstances that are almost entirely of our own making. Ask where this might be true in your life.

Are you happy with your job? Are you happy with the amount of money you're earning? Are you happy with your level of authority and your activities each day? If you're not, you need to accept that you're completely responsible for every aspect of your job and your career. Why? Because you chose it freely. You took the job, and you accepted the wage. If you're not happy with your job situation, for any reason, then it's up to you to do something different.

You're earning today exactly what you're worth—not a penny more, not a penny less. In life, we tend to get exactly what we deserve. If you're not satisfied with the amount of money you're getting, look around you at people who are doing the kind of work you would like to do and earning the kind of money you would like to earn. Ask them what they're doing differently. What are the causes of the effects they're getting? Once you know what they are, accept complete responsibility for your situation, apply your wonderful mind and abilities, back them with willpower and self-discipline, and get busy making the changes you need to make to enjoy the life you want to enjoy.

Your great aim in life is to develop character. Character is composed of self-esteem, self-discipline, the ability to delay gratification, and the willingness to accept full responsibility for your life and everything in it. The more you say to yourself, "I am responsible," the stronger, better, and finer person you become. And every part of your life will improve at the same time.

I cleaned your clubs and put them in the trunk of your car, Sir. Here's the keys. Well, thank you for saying so. It was a pleasure carrying for you.

I know you're already doing well in life, but I hope you won't mind my saying that I sense there is greatness in you. You possess the traits of champions! I feel it in my bones, and as I told you before, these old bones never lie to me! I believe you have what it takes to get to the very top. Good luck to you, Sir, but I doubt you'll need it!

ABOUT THE AUTHORS

Andrew Wood

Entrepreneur, author, salesman, and marketing wizard, Andrew Wood is a classic American success story. Armed with a suitcase, golf clubs, $300, and big dream, Wood arrived in America from England at the age of 18. First with his own advertising agency and later with his own magazine, catalog company, and national franchise, Wood was a millionaire by the time he reached his early 30s.

It's this type of real-world success and the inevitable failures along the way that make Wood's programs so practical, inspirational, and most of all empowering. Add to this Wood's lifelong commitment to the research of what makes champions succeed and you gain unique insight into the very essence of success and achievement in business, sports, and life.

Wood is the author of several best-selling books and audio programs, including *Selling With Confidence, Building a Legendary Reputation, Making It Big, Legendary Leadership, Legendary Marketing*, and *Conquering Your Market With a One-Man Army*. His company, Personal Quest, provides training and consulting in sales, marketing, e-commerce, and personal performance. Wood is in high demand as an international speaker and consultant specializing in maximizing income through better sales and marketing strategies.

1651 W. Gulf to Lake Hwy.
Lecanto, FL 34461
Phone: 352-527-3553
Fax: 352-527-3570
Email: andrewwood@personal quest.com
Web site: www.PersonalQuest.com

277

Brian Tracy

Brian Tracy is one of America's leading authorities on human potential and personal effectiveness, and chairman of Brian Tracy International, a human resources company based in San Diego, California, with affiliates throughout North America and in 31 nations worldwide. He has had successful careers in sales and marketing, investments, real estate development, management consulting, and several other fields, and he has consulted at high levels with many billion-dollar plus corporations.

As an internationally renowned business consultant and motivational speaker, Brian addresses over half a million people each year on leadership, management, sales, strategic planning, and other topics. His exciting talks and seminars bring about immediate changes and long-term results.

Brian has produced and narrated many best-selling audio and video learning programs, including *The Psychology of Achievement, Fast Track to Business Success, The Psychology of Selling, Peak Performance Woman, The Psychology of Success*, and *24 Techniques for Closing the Sale*. He is also the author of several books, including *Maximum Achievement, Advanced Selling Strategies*, and *Success Is a Journey*.

Brian has traveled or worked in over 80 countries on five continents and speaks four languages. He enjoys a wide range of interests and has earned a bachelor's degree in commerce and a masters degree in business administration, as well as a black belt in Shotokan Karate. He lives near San Diego with his wife, Barbara, and their four children.

Brian is available to corporations, conventions, and public seminars. For rates and availability, please contact:

Brain Tracy International
462 Stevens Avenue, Suite 202
Solana Beach, CA 92075
phone: (619) 481-2977
fax: (619) 481-2445
email: briantracy@briantracy.com
Web site: www.briantracy.com

Since 1984, *Executive Excellence* has provided business leaders and managers with the best and latest thinking on leadership development, managerial effectiveness, and organizational productivity. Each issue is filled with insights and answers from top business executives, trainers, and consultants—information you won't find in any other publication.

"Excellent! This is one of the finest newsletters I've seen in the field."
—Tom Peters, co-author of *In Search of Excellence*

"Executive Excellence *is the* Harvard Business Review *in USA Today format."*
—Stephen R. Covey, author of *The 7 Habits of Highly Effective People*

"Executive Excellence *is the best executive advisory newsletter anywhere in the world—it's just a matter of time before a lot more people find that out."*
—Ken Blanchard, co-author of *The One-Minute Manager*

CONTRIBUTING EDITORS INCLUDE

Stephen R. Covey

Ken Blanchard

Charles Garfield

Peter Senge

Gifford Pinchot

Gary Hamel

Warren Bennis

Brian Tracy

For more information please call
Executive Excellence Publishing at:

1-800-304-9782

or visit our Web site: **www.eep.com**